Baptism and Eucharist

Ecumenical Convergence in Celebration

Baptism and Eucharist

Ecumenical Convergence in Celebration

Edited by Max Thurian
and Geoffrey Wainwright

World Council of Churches, Geneva
Wm. B. Eerdmans, Grand Rapids

Published by WCC Publications, Geneva,
in collaboration with Wm. B. Eerdmans Publishing Co.,
255 Jefferson Ave, S.E., Grand Rapids, Michigan 49503, USA
ISBN 2-8254-0783-6 (WCC)
ISBN 0-8028-0005-x (Eerdmans)

Faith and Order Paper No 117.

© 1983 World Council of Churches, 150 route de Ferney,
1211 Geneva 20, Switzerland
Photoset by Thomson Press (India) Limited, New Delhi
and printed in Switzerland
Reprinted, February 1986

TABLE OF CONTENTS

Preface ix

I. LITURGIES OF BAPTISM

Introduction   *Max Thurian* 3
1. The Ancient Church 5
   The Apostolic Tradition of Hippolytus 5
2. The Eastern Orthodox Tradition 9
   The Service of Holy Baptism 10
3. The Roman Catholic Tradition 20
   Rite of Baptism for One Child (1969) 20
   Simple Rite of Adult Initiation (1969) 25
4. The Anglican Tradition 31
   The Church in the Province of the West Indies 31
   The Church of England 35
5. The Lutheran Tradition 40
   Lutheran Church of Sweden (1963) 40
   Evangelical Lutheran Church of Germany 41
   Lutheran Churches in North America 47
6. The Reformed Tradition 51
   The Reformed Church in America 51
   Evangelical Reformed Church of the Canton of Zurich 54
   Church of Scotland 55
   The Waldensian Church 58
7. The Methodist Tradition 61
   British Methodist Conference 61
   United Methodist Church 64
8. The Baptist Tradition 66
   The Baptism of Believers (1960) 66
   Christian Initiation (1980) 69
   Infant Dedication and Thanksgiving (1980) 71
   A Baptist Service of Thanksgiving on the Birth of a Child (1980) 73
9. United Churches 75
   The Church of South India 75
   United Church of Christ in the Philippines 79
10. The Brethren ("Kirche der Böhmischen Brüder") 81
    Church of the Czech Brethren 81
11. The Church of Christ in Thailand 83

The Sacrament of Baptism or Receiving the Covenant (1981) (for Adults or Children) 83
12. The Church of the Lord (Aladura Church, Nigeria) 86
13. The Caribbean Conference of Churches 89
14. Example of an Ecumenical Baptismal Liturgy (1983) 94

II. LITURGIES OF THE EUCHARIST

Introduction   *Geoffrey Wainwright* 99
Historical Sketch 100
  1. Common Sources Rediscovered 100
  2. Old Controversies Re-examined 103
  3. Eucharistic Life Renewed 108
Liturgical Texts 111
  1. Justin Martyr 111
  2. Hippolytus: "The Apostolic Tradition" 113
  3. Roman Missal (1970): Eucharistic Prayer II 115
  4. Eastern Orthodox Liturgy of St John Chrysostom 117
  5. Roman Missal (1970): Eucharistic Prayer IV 119
  6. "A Common Eucharistic Prayer" (USA) 121
  7. Syrian Orthodox Church of the East 123
  8. The Roman Canon (Eucharistic Prayer I) 129
  9. Texts from Luther 132
    A. Formula of Mass and Communion for the Church at Wittenberg 133
    B. The German Mass 1526 135
10. Modern Lutheran Texts 136
    A. Germany (1955/77) 136
    B. Sweden (1975) 140
    C. USA (1978) 142
11. Reformed Texts from the Sixteenth Century 144
    A. Zwingli 144
    B. Calvin, Form of Church Prayers 147
12. Modern Texts from the Reformed Churches 149
    A. The Reformed Church of France 149
    B. United Church of Christ, USA: Service of Word and Sacrament I (1969) 154
    C. The Church of Scotland: Book of Common Order (1979) 156
13. Anglican Texts from the Reformation Period 158
    A. The Book of Common Prayer (1549) 159
    B. The Book of Common Prayer (1662) 161
14. Modern Anglican Prayers 162
    A. Church of England: Alternative Service Book (1980) 162
    B. The Episcopal Church in the USA: Book of Common Prayer (1979) 165
15. Methodist Eucharistic Prayers 169
    A. The British "Methodist Service Book" (1975): "The Sunday Service" 169
    B. The United Methodist Church, USA (1980) 171

16. Baptists 172
17. Disciples of Christ 174
18. The Old Catholic Church 176
19. Some Ecumenical Texts 178
    A. The Church of South India 178
    B. The Taizé Community 180
    C. The British Joint Liturgical Group 182
    D. Consultation on Church Union (USA) 184
20. Texts in New Contexts 186
    A. New Orders of the Mass for India 186
    B. The Church of Christ in Thailand 196
    C. Eucharistic Prayer for Australian Aboriginals (1973) 198
    D. From the Philippines 201
    E. The Zaïre Rite for the Mass 205

III. PASTORAL SETTING

1. Witness from the Orthodox Churches 213
   The Liturgy after the Liturgy   *Ion Bria* 213
   Confessing Christ Through the Liturgical Life 218
2. The Mass in Latin America 222
3. The Past and Future of the Eucharist Viewed from Sri Lanka 225
4. The Lord's Supper in an African Independent Church 231
5. Proposals from a West German Kirchentag 235
6. The Worship of the Congregation 238
7. The Eucharistic Liturgy of Lima 241

Select List of Books on the Eucharist and its Theology 256

PREFACE

This book is intended to help theologians and church leaders both to assess the current understanding and practice of Baptism and the Lord's Supper within the confessions and among them, and also to agree on what still remains necessary to attain complete consensus.

It is also hoped that the book will prove useful for teaching purposes in seminaries and parishes, for it is by now possible to learn and grow ecumenically in this matter.

The WCC Commission on Faith and Order hopes that the book will assist in the reception of the long-matured text on *Baptism, Eucharist and Ministry*. Attention is called to other aids, such as the volume of theological essays entitled *Ecumenical Perspectives on Baptism, Eucharist and Ministry* (Geneva, WCC, 1983), which address the texts on *Baptism, Eucharist and Ministry* very directly and in some technical detail, and the more popular discussion guide entitled *Growing Together in Baptism, Eucharist and Ministry* (Geneva, WCC, 1982).

MAX THURIAN   GEOFFREY WAINWRIGHT

I
LITURGIES OF BAPTISM

INTRODUCTION

In its liturgy the Church has always employed symbols to convey the meaning of the different stages of Christian initiation. It has made use of *water-symbols* from the Old Testament, the event of Jesus's baptism in the Jordan and the different ways of bringing out the significance of baptism in the New Testament: the paschal mystery in the case of St Paul, the forgiving of sins in the synoptic Gospels, rebirth through the Spirit in the Johannine theology.

Participation in the death and resurrection of Christ

Water is firstly the symbol of a medium—negative yet at the same time fertile—in which the creation (Gen. 1:2) and the re-creation at the time of the Flood (Gen. 6:8) were to take place, and through which God's people would pass (the Red Sea) in order to be delivered from bondage and gathered together for the journey towards the Promised Land (Ex. 14).

Jesus went down into the river Jordan where the people had gathered to wash away their sins and was baptized for justice's sake jointly with the sinners; and this baptism is continued when he took the way of the Suffering Servant leading through his passion, death and resurrection (Mark 10: 38–40).

At their baptism Christians are baptized into the liberating death of Christ in which their sins are washed away. The old self is crucified with him so that the sinful body may be destroyed, and that they may no longer be enslaved to sin. Being united with Christ in a death like his, they are united with him in a resurrection like his in order to walk in newness of life (Rom. 6:3–4). This sharing in the death and resurrection of Christ is the central meaning of baptism.

Conversion, pardon and purification

Water is also the symbol of an act of purification. The rites of washing in the Old Testament mean that, in order to approach the Holy One and to live in fellowship with God, it is necessary to be cleansed from all uncleannesses and purified from sin. Ezechiel's prophecy is interpreted as announcing baptism: "I will sprinkle clean water upon you, and you shall be clean from all your uncleannesses, and from all your idols I will cleanse you (purification). A new heart I will give you, and a new spirit I will put within you; I will take out of your flesh the heart of stone and give you a heart of flesh (conversion). And I will put my spirit within you (gift of the Holy Spirit) and cause you to walk in my statutes and be careful to observe my ordinances (life in faith). You shall dwell in the land which I gave to your fathers, and you shall be my people, and I will be your God" (becoming part of the Church) (Ez. 36:25–28).

John's baptism was already a baptism of repentance for the forgiveness of sins

(Mark 1:4). The New Testament emphasizes the cleansing aspect of baptism which washes the body with pure water, which washes away our sins, and by which we are sanctified and justified in the name of the Lord Jesus Christ and in the Spirit of our God. (Heb. 10-22, Acts 22:16, 1 Cor. 6:11; cf. Rev. 7:14 and 22:14, John 13:10).

For Christians, baptism—as a sharing in the paschal mystery—implies a confession of sins and a change of heart; the recipients of baptism are pardoned, cleansed, justified and sanctified by Christ, in the power of the Holy Spirit, to the glory of the Father who adopts them as his children.

Gift of the Spirit and reception into the Body of Christ

Again, water is the symbol of God's blessing in times of drought. As God pours water upon him that is thirsty and floods upon the dry ground, he pours the Spirit on his people that salvation may sprout forth and cause righteousness to spring up also (Isa. 44:3, 45:8).

At the moment when he came up out of the water, Jesus saw the heavens opened and the Spirit descending upon him like a dove; and a voice came from heaven: "Thou art my beloved Son; with thee I am well pleased" (Mark 1:11). The theophany of Jesus' baptism shows the Holy Spirit as consecrating the Messiah and the voice of the Father as revealing the Son.

By being adopted as children of the Father at baptism, Christians receive the gift of the Holy Spirit. They are born to the new life and made members of the Body of Christ which is the Church. The Spirit restores the recipient of baptism to a place in the Covenant with God. In the hearts of those baptized the Spirit starts the operation of faith, and effects the transfiguration of the human being to lead him or her towards likeness with the Son of God. God gives those receiving baptism the anointment of the Holy Spirit, puts his seal upon them and gives them his Spirit in their hearts as a guarantee of their inheritance until they acquire possession of it, to the praise of his glory (2 Cor. 1:21-22, Eph. 1:13-14).

The texts of the liturgies given below—some ancient and others modern—illustrate both the diversity and convergence in the celebration of what is one and the same baptism. The churches are sometimes closer to each other in their faith as expressed in their liturgical celebration than they consider themselves to be when making statements on doctrine.

I would like to express my gratitude to Dr Andreas Stolz for his assistance in the research on baptismal liturgies.

MAX THURIAN

1. THE ANCIENT CHURCH

THE APOSTOLIC TRADITION OF HIPPOLYTUS

This text[1] dates from approximately A.D. 215. It professes to be an account of the liturgical and pastoral practices which were then current and customary in Rome. It is one of the earliest available documents of the Western church's baptismal tradition and has been formative in later development.

XVI

1. Those who come forward for the first time to hear the word shall first be brought to the teachers at the house before all the people [of God] come in.

2. And let them be examined as to the reason why they have come forward to the faith. And those who bring them shall bear witness for them whether they are able to hear.

3. Let their life and manner of living be enquired into, whether he is a slave or free.

[Sections 4–24 consist of regulations determining the conditions under which men or women might be admitted to instruction, according to the manner of their past lives and their readiness to forsake evil ways and forbidden occupations.]

XVII

1. Let a catechumen be instructed for three years.

2. But if a man be earnest and persevere well in the matter, let him be received, because it is not the time that is judged, but the conduct.

XVIII

1. Each time the teacher finishes his instruction let the catechumens pray by themselves apart from the faithful.

---

[1] E.C. Whitaker's *Documents of the Baptismal Liturgy,* London, 2nd edition, 1970, reprinted with kind permission of SPCK. No text of this liturgy exists today. This one printed here is based on Dom Gregory Dix's attempt to discern the original from later works (still existing) that contain Hippolytus' tradition but with additions, alterations and excisions (Dom Gregory Dix, *The Apostolic Tradition,* SPCK, revised by H. Chadwick, 1968). The Roman figures represent also Dix's presentation signifying *the chapters* in the original he reconstructed.

2. But after the prayer is finished the catechumens shall not give the kiss of peace, for their kiss is not yet pure.

XIX

1. After the prayer let the teacher lay hands upon them and dismiss them. Whether the teacher be an ecclesiastic or a layman let him do the same.

2. If anyone being a catechumen should be apprehended for the Name, let him not be anxious about undergoing martyrdom. For if he suffer violence and be put to death before baptism, he shall be justified having been baptized in his own blood.

XX

1. And when they are chosen who are set apart to receive baptism let their life be examined, whether they lived piously while catachumens, whether they "honoured the widows", whether they visited the sick, whether they have fulfilled every good work.

2. If those who bring them bear witness to them that they have done thus, then let them hear the gospel.

3. Moreover, from the day they are chosen, let a hand be laid on them and let them be exorcized daily. And when the day draws near on which they are to be baptized, let the bishop himself exorcize each one of them, that he may be certain that he is purified.

4. But if there is one who is not purified let him be put on one side because he did not hear the word of instruction with faith. For the strange spirit remained with him.

5. And let those who are to be baptized be instructed to wash and cleanse themselves on the fifth day of the week [i.e., Thursday].

6. And if any woman be menstruous she shall be put aside and baptized another day.

7. Those who are to receive baptism shall fast on the Preparation [Friday] and on the Sabbath [Saturday]. And on the Sabbath the bishop shall assemble those who are to be baptized in one place, and shall bid them all to pray and bow the knee.

8. And laying his hand on them he shall exorcise every evil spirit to flee away from them and never to return to them henceforward. And when he has finished exorcizing, let him breathe on their faces and seal their foreheads and ears and noses and then let him raise them up.

9. And they shall spend all the night in vigil, reading the scriptures to them and instructing them.

10. Moreover those who are to be baptized shall not bring any other vessel, save that which each will bring with him for the eucharist. For it is right for every one to bring his oblation then.

XXI

1. And at the hour when the cock crows they shall first [of all] pray over the water.

2. When they come to the water, let the water be pure and flowing.
3. And they shall put off their clothes.
4. And they shall baptize the little children first. And if they can answer for themselves, let them answer. But if they cannot, let their parents answer or someone from their family.
5. And next they shall baptize the grown men; and last the women, who shall have loosed their hair and laid aside their gold ornaments. Let no one go down to the water having any alien object with them.
6. And at the time determined for baptizing, the bishop shall give thanks over the oil and put it into a vessel and it is called the Oil of Thanksgiving.
7. And he shall take other oil and exorcise over it, and it is called the Oil of Exorcism.
8. And let a deacon carry the Oil of Exorcism and stand on the left hand. And another deacon shall take the Oil of Thanksgiving and stand on the right hand.
9. And when the presbyter takes hold of each one of those who are to be baptized, let him bid him renounce saying:

I renounce thee, Satan, and all thy service and all thy works.

10. And when he has said this let him anoint with the Oil of Exorcism, saying:

Let all evil spirits depart far from thee.

11. Then after these things let him give over to the presbyter who stands at the water. And let them stand in the water naked. And let a deacon likewise go down with him into the water.
12. And he goes down to the water, let him who baptizes lay hand on him saying thus:

Dost thou believe in God the Father Almighty?

13. And he who is being baptized shall say:

I believe.

14. Let him forthwith baptize [baptizet: *probably,* let him dip. *So also 16 and 18*] him once, having his hand laid upon his head.
15. And after [this] let him say:

Dost thou believe in Christ Jesus, the Son of God,
Who was born of Holy Spirit and the Virgin Mary,
Who was crucified in the days of Pontius Pilate,
And died,
And rose the third day living from the dead
And ascended into the heavens,
And sat down at the right hand of the Father,
And will come to judge the living and the dead?

16. And when he says: I believe, let him baptize him the second time.
17. And again let him say:

Dost thou believe in the Holy Spirit in the Holy Church,
And the resurrection of the flesh?

18. And he who is being baptized shall say: I believe. And so let him baptize him the third time.

19. And afterwards when he comes up he shall be anointed with the Oil of Thanksgiving saying:

I anoint thee with holy oil in the Name of Jesus Christ.

20. And so each one drying himself they shall now put on their clothes, and after this let them be together in the assembly.

XXII

1. And the bishop shall lay his hand upon them invoking and saying:

O Lord God, who didst count these worthy of deserving the forgiveness of sins by the laver of regeneration, make them worthy to be filled with thy Holy Spirit and send upon them thy grace, that they may serve thee according to thy will; to thee is the glory, to the Father and to the Son with the Holy Ghost in the holy Church, both now and ever and world without end. Amen.

2. After this pouring the consecrated oil and laying his hand on his head, he shall say:

I anoint thee with holy oil in God the Father Almighty and Christ Jesus and the Holy Ghost.

3. And sealing him on the forehead, he shall give him the kiss of peace and say:

The Lord be with you.

And he who has been sealed shall say:

And with thy spirit.

4. And so shall he do to each one severally.

5. Thenceforward they shall pray together with all the people. But they shall not previously pray with the faithful before they have undergone these things.

6. And after the prayers, let them give the kiss of peace.

XXIII

[This section describes the Eucharist which followed baptism. A mixture of milk and honey, and a chalice of water were offered, as well as the bread and wine. The bread was administered first, followed by the water, the milk and honey, and the Eucharistic Cup, in that order. It has been suggested that the compound of milk and honey referred to here and elsewhere is a last trace of the meal in which the Eucharist originated and from which it was soon detached.]

2. THE EASTERN ORTHODOX TRADITION

In the Orthodox churches the sacrament of baptism is as a rule administered to infants.[2] It is rarely that adults present themselves to be baptized, partly because the Orthodox churches have only limited organized "mission" among people who are not Christians. The Office of Holy Baptism is based, however, on adult baptism and is in actual fact addressed to adults. This is shown quite clearly in the baptismal rite which implies that an infant to be baptized is not treated in any way other than as an adult. The same liturgy is used in both cases. Baptism is immediately followed by confirmation.

Looking at the Orthodox liturgies[3] we first find prayers related to child-birth and delivery which are not part of the liturgy proper. They are offered at different stages and must be considered separately. There are first the "prayers on the first day after a woman hath given birth to a child". Then follow the prayers "at the naming of a child when he receiveth his name, on the eighth day after his birth". This time the child is brought to the church by the midwife. The priest makes the sign of the cross upon the forehead, lips and breast of the child and says a prayer of intercession. Later, there are the prayers "for a woman on the fortieth day after child-birth". This time, the mother brings the child to the church in order that he be "churched", i.e., introduced into the Church. The priest offers again a prayer of intercession and, if the child has already been baptized, performs the "churching": he carries the child to the doors of the sanctuary, saying, "The Servant of God is churched...."

The Office of Holy Baptism begins with the *reception of the candidate as a catechumen*. The priest removes the person's clothes except for one garment. He places him with his face towards the east, breathes three times in his face, makes the sign of the cross upon him three times, lays his hand upon his head and prays for him. He says the three exorcisms, ordering the Devil to leave this person: "The Lord layeth thee under ban, O Devil: He who came into the world and made his abode among men... Begone, and depart from this creature, with all thy powers and thy angels." After further prayers for delivery from evil the priest breathes upon his mouth, his brow and his breast, saying, "Expel from him every evil and impure spirit, which hideth and maketh its lair in his heart. The spirit of error, the spirit of guile, the spirit of

---

[2] This introduction is taken from Lukas Vischer, *Ye Are Baptized*, Geneva, WCC, 1961, pp. 15–17.
[3] Our text is based on *An Orthodox Prayer Book*, ed. Fr. N.M. Vaporis, trans. by Fr. John von Holzhausen and Fr. Michael Gelsinger, Brookline, Mass., 1977, pp. 55–73, which describes the liturgy in the Greek Orthodox Church. Variations in other Orthodox churches are few.

idolatry and of every concupiscence; the spirit of deceit and of every uncleanliness... And make him a reason-endowed sheep in the holy flock of thy Christ..."

Then follows the renunciation of the Devil. The priest turns the person to the west and asks three times, "Dost thou renounce Satan, and all his Angels, and all his works, and all his service, and all his pride?" And each time the catechumen answers, "I do." If the person to be baptized comes from a different tradition, or is an infant, his godparent ("sponsor") answers in his place. The priest questions him three times, "Hast thou renounced Satan?" And the catechumen, or his sponsor, responds each time, "I have." He is then requested to spit upon Satan, and the priest turns him again to the east, asking him three times, "Dost thou unite thyself unto Christ?", and then, also three times, "Hast thou united thyself unto Christ?" When the catechumen has answered these questions, he recites the Nicene Creed, the Holy Symbol of the Faith. This is also said three times, whereupon the question, "Hast thou united thyself unto Christ?" is repeated three times again. When the catechumen has affirmed, for the third time, "I have," the priest orders him, "Bow down also before Him!", and he answers, "I bow down before the Father, and the Son and the Holy Spirit, the Trinity, one in Essence and undivided." A short prayer of intercession concludes this part of the liturgy.

THE SERVICE OF HOLY BAPTISM

The Priest enters the Altar and arrays himself in white vestments. While the candles are being lit, he takes up the Censer, goes to the Font, and censes round about. And giving up the Censer, he makes a Reverence.

Priest: Blessed is the Kingdom of the Father, and of the Son, and of the Holy Spirit, both now and ever, and to the ages of ages. Amen.

In peace let us pray to the Lord. Lord have mercy.

After each petition: Lord have mercy.

For the peace from above; for the salvation of our souls; let us pray to the Lord.

For the peace of the whole world; for the stability of the holy Churches of God, and for the union of all; let us pray to the Lord.

For this holy House, and for them that with faith, reverence, and the fear of God enter therein; let us pray to the Lord.

For our Most Reverend Archbishop (*Name*), for the venerable Priesthood, the Diaconate in Christ; for all the Clergy, and for all the people; let us pray to the Lord.

That this water may be hallowed by the might, and operation, and descent of the Holy Spirit; let us pray to the Lord.

That there may be sent down upon it the Grace of Redemption, the blessing of the Jordan; let us pray to the Lord.

That there may come down upon this water the cleansing operation of the Supersubstantial Trinity; let us pray to the Lord.

That we may be illumined with the Light of Knowledge and Piety through the descent of the Holy Spirit; let us pray to the Lord.

That this water may prove effectual for the averting of every plot of visible and invisible enemies; let us pray to the Lord.

That he (she) that is about to be baptized herein may become worthy of the incorruptible Kingdom; let us pray to the Lord.

That he (she) that now comes to holy Illumination, and for his (her) salvation; let us pray to the Lord.

That he (she) may prove to be a child of Light, and an inheritor of eternal blessings; let us pray to the Lord.

That he (she) may grow in, and become a partaker of the Death and Resurrection of Christ our God; let us pray to the Lord.

That he (she) may preserve the garment of Baptism, and the earnest of the Spirit undefiled and blameless in the terrible Day of Christ our God; let us pray to the Lord.

That this water may be for him (her) a laver of Regeneration unto the remission of sins, and a garment of incorruption; let us pray to the Lord.

That the Lord may listen to the voice of our prayer; let us pray to the Lord.

That He may deliver him (her) and us from tribulation, wrath, danger, and necessity; let us pray to the Lord.

Help us; save us; have mercy on us; and keep us, O God, by Your Grace.

Calling to remembrance our all-holy, pure, exceedingly blessed glorious Lady Theotokos and Ever-Virgin Mary, with all the Saints; let us commend ourselves and one another and all our life to Christ our God.

Priest (inaudibly): Let us pray to the Lord.

O compassionate and merciful God, Who tries the heart and reigns, and Who alone knows the secrets of men, for no deed is secret in Your sight, but all things are exposed and naked in Your eyesight: do You Yourself, Who perceives that which concerns me, neither turn away Your face from me, but overlook my offenses in this hour, O You that overlook the sins of men that they repent. Wash away the defilement of my body and the stain of my soul. Sanctify me wholly by Your all-effectual, invisible might, and by Your spiritual right hand, lest, by preaching liberty to others, and offering this in the perfect faith of Your unspeakable love for humankind, I may be condemned as a servant of sin. Nay, Sovereign Master that alone are good and loving, let me not be turned away humbled and shamed, but send forth to me power from on high, and strengthen me for the ministration of this Your present, great, and most heavenly Mystery. Form the Image of Your Christ in him (her) who is about to be born again through my humility. Build him (her) on the foundation of Your Apostles and Prophets. Cast him (her) not down, but plant him (her) as a plant of truth in Your Holy, Catholic, and Apostolic Church. Pluck him (her) not out, that, by his (her) advancing in piety, by the same may be glorified Your Most Holy Name, of Father, and of Son, and of Holy Spirit, both now and ever, and to the ages of ages. Amen.

The Priest reads aloud:

The Blessing of the Baptismal Waters

Great are You, O Lord, and wondrous are Your works, and no word will suffice to hymn Your wonders. For by Your Will have You out of nothingness brought all things into being and by Your power sustain all creation, and by Your Providence direct the world. You from the four elements have formed creation and have crowned the cycle of the year with the four seasons; all the spiritual powers tremble before You; the sun praises You; the moon glorifies You; the stars in their courses meet with You; the Light hearkens unto You; the depths shudder at Your presence; the springs of water serve You; You have stretched out the Heavens as a curtain; You have founded the earth upon the waters; You have bounded the sea with sand; You have poured forth the air for breathing; the angelic Powers minister unto You; the Choirs of Archangels worship before You; the many-eyed Cherubim and the six-winged Seraphim, as they stand and fly around You, veil themselves with fear of Your unapproachable Glory; for You, being boundless and beginningless and unutterable, did come down on earth, taking the form of a servant, being made in the likeness of men; for You, O Master, through the tenderness of Your Mercy, could not endure the race of men tormented by the devil, but You did come and save us. We confess Your Grace; we proclaim Your benificence; we do not hide Your Mercy; You have set at liberty the generations of our nature; You did hallow the virginal Womb by Your Birth; all creation praises You, Who did manifest Yourself, for You were seen upon the earth, and did sojourn with men. You hallowed the streams of Jordan, sending down from the Heavens Your Holy Spirit, and crushed the heads of dragons that lurked therein. DO YOU YOURSELF, O LOVING KING, BE PRESENT NOW ALSO THROUGH THE DESCENT OF YOUR HOLY SPIRIT AND HALLOW THIS WATER. And give to it the Grace of Redemption, the Blessing of Jordan. Make it a fountain of incorruption, a gift of sanctification, a loosing of sins, a healing of sicknesses, a destruction of demons, unapproachable by hostile powers, filled with angelic might; and let them that take counsel together against Your creature flee therefrom, for I have called upon Your Name, O Lord, which is wonderful, and glorious, and terrible unto adversaries.

And he signs the water thrice, dipping his fingers in it; and breathing upon it, he says:

LET ALL ADVERSE POWERS BE CRUSHED BENEATH THE SIGNING OF YOUR MOST PRECIOUS CROSS. We pray You, O Lord, let every airy and invisible spectre withdraw itself from us, and let not a demon of darkness conceal himself in this water; neither let an evil spirit, bringing obscurity of purpose and rebellious thoughts, descend into it with him (her) that is about to be baptized. But do You, O Master of All, declare this water to be water of redemption, water of sanctification, a cleansing of flesh and spirit, a loosing of bonds, a forgiveness of sins, an illumination of soul, a laver of regeneration, a renewal of the spirit, a gift of sonship, a garment of incorruption, a fountain of life. For You have said, O Lord: "Wash, and be clean; put away evil from your souls." You have bestowed upon us regeneration from on high by water and the spirit. Manifest Yourself, O Lord, in this water, and grant that he (she) that is to be baptized may be transformed therein to the putting away of the old man, which is corrupt according to the deceitful lusts, and to the putting on of the new, which is renewed according to the Image of Him that created him (her), That, being planted in the likeness of Your death through Baptism, he (she) may become a sharer of Your Resurrection; and, preserving the Gift of Your Holy Spirit and increasing the deposit of Grace, he (she) may attain unto prize of his (her) high calling and accounted among the number of the first-born whose names are written in Heaven, in You our God and Lord Jesus Christ, to Whom be all Glory and Might, together with Your Eternal Father and with Your All-Holy, Good, and Life-creating Spirit, both now and ever, and to the ages of ages.

Choir: Amen.

Priest: Peace be to all (+).

Choir: And to your spirit.

Priest: Let us bow our heads before the Lord.

Choir: To You, O Lord.

The Priest breathes thrice upon the Oil and signs it thrice, while it is held by the Godparent.

Priest: Let us pray to the Lord. Lord have mercy.

The Blessing of the Oil

Sovereign Lord and Master, God of our Fathers, Who did send to them in the Ark of Noah a dove bearing a twig of olive in its beak as a sign of reconciliation and salvation from the Flood, and through these things prefigured the Mystery of Grace; and thereby have filled them that were under the Law with the Holy Spirit, and perfected them that are under Grace: do You Yourself bless this Oil by the power (+) and operation (+) and descent of the Holy Spirit (+) that it may become an anointing of incorruption, a shield of righteousness, a renewal of soul and body, and averting of every operation of the devil, to the removal of all evils from them that are anointed with it in faith, or that are partakers of it.

To Your Glory, and to that of Your Only-Begotten Son, and of Your All-Holy, Good, and Life-creating Spirit, both now and ever, and to the ages of ages.

Choir: Amen.

Priest: Let us attend.

The Priest, singing Alleluia thrice with the people, makes three Crosses with the Oil upon the water.

Alleluia, alleluia, alleluia.

Blessed is God that enlightens and sanctifies every man that comes into the world, both now and ever, and to the ages of ages.

Choir: Amen.

The Priest pours some Oil into the hands of the Godparent. He then takes Oil and makes the Sign of the Cross on the child's forehead, breast, and between his (her) shoulders, saying:

The servant of God (*Name*) is anointed with the Oil of Gladness, in the Name of the Father, and of the Son, and of the Holy Spirit, both now and ever, and to the ages of ages. Amen.

And he signs his (her) breast and between his (her) shoulders, saying: For healing of soul and body.

And on the ears, saying: For the hearing of Faith.

And on the feet, saying: That he (she) may walk in the paths of Your commandments.

And on the hands, saying: Your hands have made me, and fashioned me.

The Baptizing

When he has anointed the whole body, the Priest baptizes him (her), holding him (her) erect, and looking towards the East, says:

The servant of God (*Name*) is baptized in the Name of the Father, Amen. And of the Son, Amen. And of the Holy Spirit, Amen.

At each invocation the Priest immerses him (her) and raises him (her) up again.

After the baptizing, the Priest places the child in a linen sheet held by the Godparent.

The Choir sings Psalm 31

Blessed are they whose iniquities are forgiven, and whose sins are covered. Blessed is the man whom the Lord imputes not sin, and in whose mouth there is no guile. Because I have kept silence, my bones waxed old through my crying all the day long. For day and night Your hand was heavy on me. I was turned into lowliness while the thorn was fastened in me. My sin I have acknowledged, and my iniquity I have not hid. I said, "I will confess against myself my sin unto the Lord." And You forgave the ungodliness of my heart. For this shall everyone who is holy pray to You in a seasonable time; moreover in a flood of many waters shall the billows not come nigh to him. For You are my refuge from the tribulation which surrounds me. O my rejoicing, deliver me from them that have encircled me. The Lord says: "I will give you understanding, and will teach you in this My way which you shall go; I will fix My eyes on you. Be not as the horse, or as the mule, which have no understanding. With bit and bridle would you bind their jaws; lest they come near to you." Many are the scourges of the sinner, but with mercy shall I encircle them that hope on the Lord. Be glad in the Lord, and rejoice, you righteous; and shout for joy, all you that are upright of heart.

The Priest says the Prayer of Confirmation.

Let us pray to the Lord.

Choir: Lord have mercy.

The Prayer of Confirmation

Blessed are You, Lord God Almighy, Fountain of Blessings, Sun of Righteousness, Who made to shine forth for those in darkness a light of salvation through the manifestation of Your Only-Begotten Son and our God, granting unto us, though we are unworthy, blessed cleansing in Holy Water, and divine sanctification in the Life-effecting Anointing; Who now also has been well-pleased to regenerate this Your servant newly illuminated through Water and Spirit, giving him (her) forgiveness of his (her) voluntary and involuntary sins: do You Yourself, Sovereign Master, Compassionate King of All, bestow upon him (her) also the Seal of Your omnipotent and adorable Holy Spirit, and the Communion of the Holy Body and Most Precious Blood of Your Christ; keep him (her) in Your sanctification; confirm him (her) in the Orthodox Faith; deliver him (her) from the Evil One and all his devices; preserve his (her) soul, through Your saving fear, in purity and righteousness, that in every work and word, being acceptable before You, he (she) may become a child and heir of Your heavenly Kingdom.

For You are our God, the God of Mercy and Salvation, and to You do we send up Glory, to the Father, and to the Son, and to the Holy Spirit, both now and ever, and to the ages of ages.

Choir: Amen.

And after the Prayer of Confirmation, the Priest chrismates the baptized and he makes on the person the Sign of the Cross with the Holy Chrism (Holy Myron), on the forehead, the eyes, the nostrils, the mouth, the ears, the breast, the hands, and the feet. At each anointing and sealing, he says:

SEAL OF THE GIFT OF THE HOLY SPIRIT, AMEN.

The Priest invests the baptized in a new clean robe, saying:

Clothed is the servant of God *(Name)* with the garment of righteousness, in the Name of the Father, and of the Son, and of the Holy Spirit. Amen.

The Troparion, in Tone 8

A robe of divine light bestow upon me, O You that for vesture array Yourself with Light; and bestow many mercies, O Christ our God, who are plenteous in mercy.

Then the Priest makes, together with the Godparent and the child, a circumambulation around the Font, three times; and for each of the three rounds the Choir sings:

As many of you as have been baptized into Christ, have put on Christ. Alleluia.

Glory...Both now...

As many...Alleluia.

Priest: Louder.

Choir: As many of you as have been baptized into Christ, have put on Christ. Alleluia.

Priest: Let us attend.

The Prokeimenon in Tone 3

The Lord is my light and my salvation; of whom then shall I fear? The Lord is the Protector of my life; of whom then shall I be afraid?

Priest: Wisdom!

The Reader: The Reading from the Epistle of the Holy Apostle Paul to the Romans. (Rom. 6:3–11)

Priest: Let us attend.

The Reader: Brethren, do you not know that all of us who have been baptized into Christ Jesus were baptized into his death? We were buried therefore with him by baptism into death, so that as Christ was raised from the dead by the glory of the Father, we too might walk in newness of life. For if we have been united with him in a death like his, we shall certainly be united with him in a resurrection like his. We know that our old self was crucified with him so that the sinful body might be destroyed, and we might no longer be enslaved to sin. For he who has died is freed from sin. But if we have died with Christ, we believe that we shall also live with him. For we know that Christ being raised from the dead will never die again; death no longer has dominion over him. The death he died he died to sin, once for all, but the life he lives he lives to God. So you also must consider yourselves dead to sin and alive to God in Christ Jesus.

Priest: Peace be to you that read. And to your spirit.

Choir: Alleluia, alleluia, alleluia.

Priest: Wisdom! Let us attend! Let us hear the Holy Gospel. Peace be to all (+).

Choir: And with your spirit.

Priest: The Reading from the Holy Gospel according to St Matthew. Let us attend. (Matt. 28:16–20)

Choir: Glory to You, O Lord; Glory to You.

Priest: At that time, the eleven disciples went to Galilee, to the mountain to which Jesus had directed them. And when they saw him, they worshipped him; but some doubted. And Jesus came and said to them, "All authority in heaven and on earth has been given to me. Go therefore and make disciples of all nations, baptizing them in the name of the Father and of the Son and of the Holy Spirit, teaching them to observe all that I have commanded to you; and lo, I am with you always, to the close of the age. Amen."

Choir: Glory to You, O Lord; Glory to You.

The ablution

Priest: Peace be to all (+).

Choir: And with your spirit.

Priest: Let us bow our heads before the Lord.

Choir: To You, O Lord.

Priest: Let us pray to the Lord.

Choir: Lord have mercy.

Priest says the Prayer: You that through Holy Baptism have granted forgiveness of sins to this Your servant, bestowing on him (her) a life of regeneration: do You Yourself, Sovereign Master and Lord, be pleased that the Light of Your countenance evermore shine in his (her) heart; maintain the shield of his (her) faith against the plotting of enemies; preserve in him (her) the garment of incorruption, which he (she) has put on undefiled and unstained; preserve in him (her) the Seal of Your Grace, being gracious unto us, and unto him (her) according to the multitude of Your compassions, for

glorified and blessed is Your all-honorable and majestic Name: of Father, and of Son, and of Holy Spirit, both now and ever, and to the ages of ages.
Choir: Amen.
Priest: Let us pray to the Lord.
Choir: Lord have mercy.
Priest: Sovereign Master and Lord our God, Who through the baptismal Font bestows heavenly Illumination to them that are baptized; Who has regenerated this Your servant, bestowing upon him (her) forgiveness of his (her) voluntary and involuntary sins; do You lay upon him (her) Your mighty hand, and guard him (her) in the power of Your goodness. Preserve unspotted his (her) pledge of Faith in You. Account him (her) worthy of Life everlasting and Your good favor. For You are our sanctification, and to You do we send up all Glory; to the Father, and to the Son, and to the Holy Spirit, both now and ever, and to the ages of ages. Amen.
Peace be to all (+).
Choir: And to your spirit.
Priest: Let us bow our heads before the Lord.
Choir: To You, O Lord.
Priest: Let us pray to the Lord.
Choir: Lord have mercy.
Priest: He (she) that has put on You, O Christ, with us bows his (her) head unto You; ever protect him (her) a warrior invincible against them who vainly raise up enmity against him (her), or, as might be, against us; and by Your Crown of Incorruption at the last declare us all to be the victorious ones.
For Yours it is to have mercy and to save, and unto You, as to Your Eternal Father and Your All-Holy, Good, and Life-creating Spirit, do we send up all Glory, both now and ever, and to the ages of ages.
Choir: Amen.
The Priest loosens the child's girdle and garment, and, joining the ends of these, he soaks them with clean water and sprinkles the child, saying aloud:
You are justified; you are illumined.
And taking a new sponge dipped in water, the Priest wipes his (her) head, the breast, and the rest, saying:
You are baptized; you are illuminated; you are anointed with the Holy Myrrh; you are hallowed; you are washed clean, in the Name of Father, and of Son, and of Holy Spirit. Amen.

The tonsure

Priest: Let us pray to the Lord.
Choir: Lord have mercy.
Priest: Sovereign Master and Lord our God, Who honored man with Your own Image, providing him with reason-endowed soul and comely body, that the body might serve the reason-endowed soul; for You did set his head on high, and therein planted the greater number of the senses, which impede not one another, covering the head that it might not be injured by the changes of

the weather, and did fit all the members serviceably thereunto, that by all it might render thanks unto You, the excellent Artist; do You Yourself, O Sovereign Master, Who by the Vessel of Your Election, Paul the Apostle, to do all things unto Your Glory, bless (+) this Your servant (*Name*), who is come now to make offering the firstlings of hair shorn from his (her) head; and bless his (her) Sponsor (+); granting them in all things to be diligent followers of Your Law, and to do all those things that are well pleasing unto You, for a merciful and loving God are You, and to You do we send up all Glory, to the Father, and to the Son, and to the Holy Spirit, both now and ever, and to the ages of ages.

Choir: Amen.

Priest: Peace be to all (+).

Choir: And to your spirit.

Priest: Let us bow our heads before the Lord.

Choir: To You, O Lord.

Priest: Let us pray to the Lord.

Choir: Lord have mercy.

The Priest lays his right hand upon the head of the child and prays: O Lord Our God, Who through the fulfillment of the baptismal Font have, by Your Goodness, sanctified them that believe in You: (+) do You bless this child here present, and may your blessings come down upon his (her) head; as You did bless the head of Your servant David the King through the Prophet Samuel, (+) so also bless the head of this servant (*Name*), through the hand of me, the unworthy Priest, visiting him (her) with Your Holy Spirit, that as he (she) goes forward to the prime of his (her) years, and the grey hairs of old age, he (she) may send up Glory to You, beholding the good things of Jerusalem all the days of his (her) life.

For to You are due all glory, honor and worship, to the Father, and to the Son, and to the Holy Spirit, both now and ever, and to the ages of ages.

Choir: Amen.

The Priest shears him (her) in the form of a Cross, snipping off four locks of hair, front, back, and over each ear, cross-fashion, saying:

The servant of God (*Name*) is shorn in the Name of the Father, and of the Son, and of the Holy Spirit.

Choir: Amen.

Priest: Have mercy on us, O God, according to Your great mercy. We beseech You, listen, and have mercy.

Choir: Lord have mercy.

Priest: Again let us pray for mercy, life, peace, health, and salvation for the servants of God, the newly illumined (*Name*), the Godparents, and all those who have come here together for this holy Sacrament.

For You are a merciful and loving God, and to You do we send up all Glory, to the Father, and to the Son, and to the Holy Spirit, both now and ever, and to the ages of ages.

Choir: Amen.

The Apolysis

Priest: Glory to You, O Christ our God and our hope; glory to You.

Priest: Glory to the Father, and to the Son, and to the Holy Spirit, both now and ever, and to the ages of ages. Amen. Lord have mercy; Lord have mercy; Lord have mercy. Master, bid the blessing.

He Who deigned to be baptized in the Jordan by John for our salvation, Christ our true God—through the intercessions of His all-pure Mother, of the holy and glorious prophet, Forerunner and Baptist John, of the holy, glorious all-praiseworthy Apostles, *(Name of Saint whose name the child has received),* and of all the Saints; have mercy and save us as our good and loving Lord.

Through the prayers of our holy Fathers...

Choir: Amen.

3. THE ROMAN CATHOLIC TRADITION

These two rites are in use since their authorization after the Second Vatican Council[4] (1969). The emphasis of the rite of infant baptism lies clearly with the involvement of parents and godparents whereas in the adult rite we find some stress laid on the immediate full reception of the candidate into the church by confirmation directly following baptism.

RITE OF BAPTISM FOR ONE CHILD (1969)

Reception of the child

First the celebrant questions the parents:
Celebrant: What name do you give your child? (or: have you given?)
Parents: N.
Celebrant: What do you ask of God's Church for N.?
Parents: Baptism.

The celebrant speaks to the parents in these or similar words:
You have asked to have your child baptized. In doing so you are accepting the responsibility of training him (her) in the practice of the faith. It will be your duty to bring him (her) up to keep God's commandments as Christ taught us, by loving God and our neighbor. Do you clearly understand what you are undertaking?
Parents: We do.

Then the celebrant turns to the godparents and addresses them in these or similar words: Are you ready to help the parents of this child in their duty as Christian parents?
Godparents: We are.

The celebrant continues: N., the Christian community welcomes you with great joy. In its name I claim you for Christ our Savior by the sign of his cross.

---

[4] The texts are from: *Rite of Christian Initiation of Adults,* approved for use in the dioceses of England and Wales, London, 1976, pp. 76–87, and *The New Rite of Baptism for Children,* 1969, by the International Committee on English in the Liturgy, pp. 29–41.

I now trace the cross on your forehead, and invite your parents (and godparents) to do the same.
He signs the child on the forehead, in silence. Then he invites the parents and (if it seems appropriate) the godparents to do the same.
All: Lord, hear our prayer.
Leader: Through baptism and confirmation, make him (her) your faithful follower and a witness to your gospel.
All: Lord, hear our prayer.
Leader: Lead him (her) by a holy life to the joys of God's kingdom.
All: Lord, hear our prayer.
Leader: Make the lives of his (her) parents and godparents examples of faith to inspire this child.
All: Lord, hear our prayer.
Leader: Keep his (her) family always in your love.
All: Lord, hear our prayer.
Leader: Renew the grace of our baptism in each one of us.
All: Lord, hear our prayer.
The celebrant next invites all present to invoke the saints.

Holy Mary, Mother of God	pray for us
Saint John the Baptist	pray for us
Saint Joseph	pray for us
Saint Peter and Saint Paul	pray for us
All you saints of God	pray for us

The names of other saints may be added, especially the patrons of the child to be baptized, and of the church or locality. The litany concludes:

Prayer of exorcism and anointing before baptism

After the invocation, the celebrant says: Almighty and ever-living God, you sent your only Son into the world to cast out the power of Satan, spirit of evil, to rescue man from the kingdom of darkness, and bring him into the splendor of your kingdom of light. We pray for this child: set him (her) free from original sin, make him (her) a temple of your glory, and send your Holy Spirit to dwell with him (her). (We ask this) through Christ our Lord.
All: Amen.

The celebrant continues: We anoint you with the oil of salvation in the name of Christ our Savior; may he strengthen you with his power, who lives and reigns for ever and ever.
All: Amen.

He anoints the child on the breast with the oil of catechumens.

The celebrant says: May you have strength in the power of Christ our Savior, who lives and reigns for ever and ever.
All: Amen.

And immediately he lays his hand on the child in silence.

Celebration of the sacrament

My dear brothers and sisters, we now ask God to give this child new life in abundance through water and the Holy Spirit.

Or:

My dear brothers and sisters, God uses the sacrament of water to give his divine life to those who believe in him. Let us turn to him, and ask him to pour his gift of life from this font on this child he has chosen.

Blessing and Invocation of God over Baptismal Water

Then, turning to the font, he says the following blessing (outside the Easter season): Father, you give us grace through sacramental signs, which tell us of the wonders of your unseen power.

In baptism we use your gift of water, which you have made a rich symbol of the grace you give us in this sacrament.

At the very dawn of creation your Spirit breathed on the waters, making them the wellspring of all holiness.

The waters of the great flood you made a sign of the waters of baptism, that make an end of sin and a new beginning of goodness.

Through the waters of the Red Sea you led Israel out of slavery, to be an image of God's holy people, set free from sin by baptism.

In the waters of the Jordan your Son was baptized by John and anointed with the Spirit.

Your Son willed that water and blood should flow from his side as he hung upon the cross.

After his resurrection he told his disciples: "Go out and teach all nations, baptizing them in the name of the Father, and of the Son, and of the Holy Spirit."

Father, look now with love upon your Church, and unseal for her the fountain of baptism.

By the power of the Spirit give to the water of this font the grace of your Son.

You created man in your own likeness: cleanse him from sin in a new birth to innocence by water and the Spirit.

The celebrant touches the water with his right hand and continues: We ask you, Father, with your Son to send the Holy Spirit upon the water of this font. May all who are buried with Chirst in the death of baptism rise also with him to newness of life. (We ask this) through Christ our Lord.

All: Amen.

Renunciation of Sin and Profession of Faith

The celebrant speaks to the parents and godparents in these words: Dear parents and godparents: You have come here to present this child for baptism. By water and the Holy Spirit he (she) is to receive the gift of new life from God, who is love.

On your part, you must make it your constant care to bring him (her) up in the practice of the faith. See that the divine life which God gives him (her) is kept safe from the poison of sin, to grow always stronger in his (her) heart.

If your faith makes you ready to accept this responsibility, renew now the

vows of your own baptism. Reject sin; profess your faith in Christ Jesus. This is the faith of the Church. This is the faith in which this child is about to be baptized.
The celebrant questions the parents and godparents.
Celebrant: Do you reject Satan?
Parents and godparents: I do.
Celebrant: And all his works?
Parents and godparents: I do.
Celebrant: And all his empty promises?
Parents and godparents: I do.

OR

Celebrant: Do you reject sin, so as to live in the freedom of God's children?
Parents and godparents: I do.
Celebrant: Do you reject the glamor of evil, and refuse to be mastered by sin?
Parents and godparents: I do.
Celebrant: Do you reject Satan, father of sin and prince of darkness?
Parents and godparents: I do.
Celebrant: Do you believe in God, the Father almighty, creator of heaven and earth?
Parents and godparents: I do.
Celebrant: Do you believe in Jesus Christ, his only Son, our Lord, who was born of the Virgin Mary, was crucified, died, and was buried, rose from the dead, and is now seated at the right hand of the Father?
Parents and godparents: I do.
Celebrant: Do you believe in the Holy Spirit, the holy catholic Church, the communion of saints, the forgiveness of sins, the resurrection of the body, and life everlasting?
Parents and godparents: I do.
The celebrant and the congregation give their assent to this profession of faith.
Celebrant: This is our faith. This is the faith of the Church. We are proud to profess it, in Christ Jesus our Lord.
All: Amen.

Baptism
Celebrant: Is it your will that N. should be baptized in the faith of the Church, which we have all professed with you?
Parents and godparents: It is.
He baptizes the child, saying:
N., I baptize you in the name of the Father,
He immerses the child or pours water upon it.
and of the Son,
He immerses the child or pours water upon it a second time.

and of the Holy Spirit.
He immerses the child or pours water upon it a third time.
Anointing with chrism
Then the celebrant says: God the Father of our Lord Jesus Christ has freed you from sin, given you a new birth by water and the Holy Spirit, and welcomed you into his holy people. He now anoints you with the chrism of salvation. As Christ was anointed Priest, Prophet, and King, so may you live always as a member of his body, sharing everlasting life.

I touch your ears to receive his word, and your mouth to proclaim his faith, to the praise and glory of God the Father.

All: Amen.

Conclusion of the rite
Next there is a procession to the altar, unless the baptism was performed in the sanctuary. The lighted candle is carried for the child.
A baptismal song is appropriate at this time, e.g.:
You have put on Christ,
in him you have been baptized.
Alleluia, alleluia.

Lord's Prayer
The celebrant stands in front of the altar and addresses the parents, godparents, and the whole assembly in these or similiar words: Dearly beloved, this child has been reborn in baptism. He (she) is now called the child of God, for so indeed he (she) is. In confirmation he (she) will receive the fullness of God's Spirit. In holy communion he (she) will share the banquet of Christ's sacrifice, calling God his (her) Father in the midst of the Church. In the name of this child, in the Spirit of our common sonship, let us pray together in the words our Lord has given us:

All present join the celebrant in singing or saying:
Our Father in heaven,
 holy be your Name,
 your kingdom come,
 your will be done,
 on earth as in heaven.
Give us today our daily bread.
Forgive us our sins
 as we forgive those who sin against us.
Do not bring us to the test
 but deliver us from evil.

Celebrant: God the Father, through his Son, the Virgin Mary's child, has brought joy to all Christian mothers, as they see the hope of eternal life shine on their children. May he bless the mother of this child. She now thanks God for the gift of her child. May she be one with him (her) in thanking him for ever in heaven, in Christ Jesus our Lord.

All: Amen.

Celebrant: God is the giver of a life, human and divine. May he bless the father of this child. He and his wife will be the first teachers of their child in the ways of faith. May they be also the best of teachers, bearing witness to the faith by what they say and do, in Christ Jesus our Lord.

All: Amen.

Celebrant: By God's gift, through water and the Holy Spirit, we are reborn to everlasting life. In his goodness, may he continue to pour out his blessings upon these sons and daughters of his. May he make them always, wherever they may be, faithful members of his holy people. May he send his peace upon all who are gathered here, in Christ Jesus our Lord.

All: Amen.

SIMPLE RITE OF ADULT INITIATION (1969)

Facing the candidate, the celebrant asks him:
N., what do you ask of God's Church?

Candidate: Faith.

Celebrant: What does faith offer you?

Candidate: Eternal life.

Celebrant: This is eternal life: to know the true God and the one he sent, Jesus Christ. God raised him from the dead to be the Lord of life and of all things, seen and unseen. In asking for baptism today you ask for this life. You would not do so unless you had come to know Christ and wanted to be his disciple. Have you completed your preparation for becoming a Christian? Have you listened to Christ's word and made up your mind to keep his commandments? Have you shared in our way of life and in our prayer?

Candidate: I have.

The celebrant turns to the godparent and asks:
You are this candidate's godparent. Before God, do you consider him (her) a suitable person to be received today into full communion with the Church?

Godparent: I do.

Celebrant: You have spoken in this candidate's (or: N's) favor. Will you continue to help him (her) to serve Christ by your words and example?

Godparent: I will.

With hands joined the celebrant concludes:
Let us pray.
Father of love and mercy,
we thank you in the name of our brother (sister)
who has experienced your guiding presence in his (her) life.
Today, in the presence of your Church,
he (she) is answering your call to faith:
let him (her) find joy and fulfillment in his (her) new life.
We ask this through Christ our Lord.
R. Amen.

Entry into the Church
The celebrant invites the candidate in these or similar words: N., we welcome you into the Church to share with us at the table of God's word.

Liturgy of the word
Readings and homily
Prayer and penitential rite
Congregation: Let us pray for our brother (sister) who is asking for Christ's sacraments, and for ourselves, sinners that we are: may we all draw nearer to Christ in faith and repentance and walk without tiring in the new life he gives us.

Reader: That the Lord will kindle in all of us a spirit of true repentance, let us pray to the Lord:

R. Lord, hear our prayer.

Reader: That we, who have been saved by Christ and have died to sin through baptism, may witness to his grace by our manner of life, let us pray to the Lord:

R. Lord, hear our prayer.

Reader: That the Lord will give our brother (sister) sorrow for his (her) sins and trust in God's love as he (she) prepares to meet Christ, his (her) Savior, let us pray to the Lord:

R. Lord, hear our prayer.

Reader: That by following Christ who takes away the sin of the world our brother (sister) will be healed of the infection of sin and freed from its power, let us pray to the Lord:

R. Lord, hear our prayer.

Reader: That the Holy Spirit will wash him (her) clean from sin and lead him (her) in the way of holiness, let us pray to the Lord:

R. Lord, hear our prayer.

Reader: That through his burial with Christ in baptism he (she) will die to sin and live only for God, let us pray to the Lord:

R. Lord, hear our prayer.

Reader: That on the day of judgment he (she) will come before the Father bearing fruits of holiness and love, we pray to the Lord:

R. Lord, hear our prayer.

Reader: That the world for which the Father gave his beloved Son may believe in his love and turn to him, let us pray to the Lord:

R. Lord, hear our prayer.

Prayer of exorcism and anointing of the catechumen
Celebrant:
Almighty God,
you sent your only Son
to rescue us from the slavery of sin

and to give to us the freedom of your children.
We now pray for our brother (sister)
who comes before you, acknowledging his (her) sinfulness.
He (she) has faced temptation
and been tested by the evil one.
By the passion and resurrection of your Son,
bring him (her) out of the power of darkness.
With the grace of Christ, make him (her) strong
and guide him (her) through life.
We ask this through Christ our Lord:

R. Amen.

The celebrant continues:

We anoint you with the oil of salvation
in the name of Christ our Savior.
May he strengthen you with his power,
who lives and reigns for ever and ever.

R. Amen.

The candidate is anointed with the oil of catechumens on the breast or on both hands or even on other parts of the body, if this seems desirable.

This anointing may be omitted

Celebration of baptism

Celebrant's instruction

Dear friends: Let us ask God our Father to be merciful to our brother (sister) N. who is asking for baptism. He has called him (her) to this hour. May he grant him (her) the riches of his light and strength to follow Christ with a courageous heart and to profess the faith of the Church. May he give him (her) the new life of the Holy Spirit, the Spirit whom we are about to ask to come down upon this water.

Then the celebrant turns to the font and blesses the water:

Father,
you give us grace through sacramental signs
which tell us of the wonders of your unseen power.
In baptism we use your gift of water
which you have made a rich symbol of the grace
you give us in this sacrament.
At the very dawn of creation
your Spirit breathed on the waters,
making them the wellspring of all holiness.
The waters of the great flood
you made a sign of the waters of baptism
that make an end of sin
and a new beginning of goodness.
Through the waters of the Red Sea
you led Israel out of slavery
to be an image of God's holy people
set free from sin by baptism.

In the waters of the Jordan
your Son was baptized by John
and anointed with the Spirit.
Your Son willed that water and blood should flow from his side
as he hung upon the cross.
After his resurrection he told his disciples:
"Go out and teach all nations,
baptizing them in the name of the Father, and of the Son,
   and of the Holy Spirit."
Father, look now with love upon your Church
and unseal for it the fountain of baptism.
By the power of the Spirit
give to the water of this font
the grace of your Son.
You created man in your own likeness:
cleanse him from sin in a new birth to innocence
by water and the Spirit.

The celebrant touches the water with his right hand and continues:

We ask you, Father, with your Son
to send the Holy Spirit upon the water of this font.
May all who are buried with Christ in the death of baptism
rise also with him to newness of life.
We ask this through Christ our Lord.

R. Amen.

Renunciation

After the font is consecrated, the celebrant questions the candidate:

Formula A

Celebrant: Do you reject Satan and all his works and all his empty promises?
Candidate: I do.

Formula B

Celebrant: Do you reject Satan?
Candidate: I do.
Celebrant: And all his works?
Candidate: I do.
Celebrant: And all his empty promises?
Candidate: I do.

OR

Formula C

Celebrant: Do you reject sin so as to live in the freedom of God's children?
Candidate: I do.
Celebrant: Do you reject the glamor of evil and refuse to be mastered by sin?
Candidate: I do.
Celebrant: Do you reject Satan, father of sin and prince of darkness?
Candidate: I do.

Profession of faith

Then the celebrant asks the candidate: N., do you believe in God, the Father almighty, creator of heaven and earth?

Candidate: I do.

Celebrant: Do you believe in Jesus Christ, his only Son, our Lord, who was born of the Virgin Mary, was crucified, died, and was buried, rose from the dead, and is now seated at the right hand of the Father?

Candidate: I do.

Celebrant: Do you believe in the Holy Spirit, the holy catholic Church, the communion of saints, the forgiveness of sins, the resurrection of the body, and life everlasting?

Candidate: I do.

After his profession of faith, the candidate is baptized at once.

Rite of baptism

N., I baptize you in the name of the Father,
he immerses him the first time,
and of the Son,
he immerses him the second time,
and of the Holy Spirit.
he immerses him the third time,
Either or both godparents touch the candidate.

Clothing with the white garment

The celebrant says:
N., you have become a new creation
and have clothed yourself in Christ.
Take this white garment
and bring it unstained to the judgment seat of our Lord Jesus Christ
so that you may have everlasting life.

Newly baptized: Amen.

At the words: Take this white garment, the godparent places the white garment on the neophyte. Another color may be used if local conditions require this.

If so desired, this rite may be omitted.

Presentation of the lighted candle

The celebrant takes the Easter candle in his hands or touches it, saying:

Godparent, please come forward to give the newly baptized the light of Christ.

The godparent approaches, lights a candle from the Easter candle and hands it to the neophyte. Then the celebrant says:

You have been enlightened by Christ.
Walk always as a child of the light
and keep the flame of faith alive in your heart.

When the Lord comes, may you go out to meet him
with all the saints in the heavenly kingdom.
Newly baptized: Amen.

Celebration of confirmation

The neophyte stands in front of the celebrant, who speaks to him in these or similar words:

N., born again in Christ by baptism, you have become a member of Christ and of his priestly people. Now you are to share in the outpouring of the Holy Spirit among us, the Spirit sent by the Lord upon his apostles at Pentecost and given by them and their successors to the baptized.

The promised strength of the Holy Spirit which you are to receive will make you more like Christ and help you to be a witness to his suffering, death, and resurrection. It will strengthen you to be an active member of the Church and to build up the Body of Christ in faith and love.

Then the celebrant stands and faces the people and with hands joined says:
Let us pray, dear friends,
to God the all-powerful Father
that he will pour out the Holy Spirit
on the newly baptized,
to strengthen him (her) with his abundant gifts
and anoint him (her) to be more like Christ, his Son.

All pray in silence for a short time.

Then the celebrant lays hand upon the candidate and says:
All-powerful God, Father of our Lord Jesus Christ,
by water and the Holy Spirit
you freed your son (daughter) from sin
and gave him (her) new life.
Send your Holy Spirit upon him (her)
to be his (her) Helper and Guide.
Give him (her) the spirit of wisdom and understanding,
the spirit of right judgment and courage,
the spirit of knowledge and reverence.
Fill him (her) with the spirit of wonder and awe in your presence.
We ask this through Christ our Lord. Amen.

The celebrant dips his right thumb in the chrism and makes the sign of the cross on the forehead of the one to be confirmed as he says:

N., be sealed with the Gift of the Holy Spirit.
Newly confirmed: Amen.
The celebrant adds: Peace be with you.
Newly confirmed: And also with you.

Celebration of the Eucharist

It begins with the general intercessions, than the newly baptized brings the gifts to the altar.

4. THE ANGLICAN TRADITION

We present here two Anglican liturgies, one from the West Indies (1964[5]) which reflects largely the Church of England practice at that time (based on the Proposed Rites, 1928), and the other representing the newest Anglican revision, *The Alternative Service Book of the Church of England*, 1980[6]. Whereas an emphasis of the West Indian liturgy lies with the long exhortation of parents and godparents at the end, the 1980 revision stresses more the involvement of the congregation ("Welcome") while placing a shorter exhortation at the beginning and paying less attention to exorcisms.

THE CHURCH IN THE PROVINCE OF THE WEST INDIES

The order for the administration of Holy Baptism (1964)

The introduction

The Priest says: Beloved in Christ Jesus, it is the will of God that all men should be saved from the fault and corruption of the nature which they inherit and from the actual sins which they commit. Also, our Saviour Christ saith, None can enter the kingdom of God except he be born again of water and the Holy Ghost; Let us therefore beseech him of his great mercy to grant to *this person (child)* that which by nature *he* cannot have, that through holy Baptism *he* may be born again and received into Christ's Church, and be made *a* lively *member* of the same.

Then shall he say the following Prayer: Almighty and immortal God, the helper and defender of all who turn to thee for succour, the life and peace of those who believe: We call upon thee for *this person (child)* that *he* coming to thy holy Baptism may receive remission of sin and thine eternal grace by spiritual regeneration. Receive *him*, O Lord, as thou hast promised by thy well-beloved Son, saying, Ask, and ye shall have; seek, and ye shall find; knock, and it shall be opened unto you: So give now unto us who ask; let us who seek find; open the gate unto us who knock; that *this person (child)* may enjoy the everlasting benediction of thy heavenly washing, and may come to

---

[5]The Church in the Province of the West Indies, *The Order for Baptism and Confirmation*, London, 1964, pp. 5-17.
[6]SPCK, pp. 243-249.

the eternal kingdom which thou hast promised by him who is the Resurrection and the Life, Jesus Christ our Lord. *R:* Amen.

He may add: O Lord God of hosts, before the terrors of whose presence the armies of Hell are put to flight: Deliver *this* thy *servant* from the might of Satan; cast out from *him* every evil and unclean spirit that lurketh in the heart and make *him* ready to receive the Holy Spirit of grace; through Jesus Christ our Lord. *R:* Amen.

Then shall the Priest or one of the Ministers say:

V: The Lord be with you;

R: And with thy spirit.

Hear the words of the Gospel according to Saint John.

R: Glory be to thee, O Lord.

John 3:1–8

At the Baptism of Children the following Lesson may be read instead of the above.

V: The Lord be with you;

R: And with thy spirit.

Hear the words of the Gospel according to Saint Mark.

R: Glory be to thee, O Lord.

Mark 10:13–16

R: Praise be to thee, O Christ.

Then shall the Priest say: Beloved, let us now faithfully and devoutly give thanks unto God our heavenly Father and say together,

Almighty and everlasting God, heavenly Father, we give thee humble thanks that thou hast called us to the knowledge of thy grace and to faith in thee: Increase this knowledge and confirm this faith in us evermore. Give thy Holy Spirit to *this person (child)* that *he* may be born again and be made *an heir* of everlasting salvation; through Jesus Christ, thy Son, our Lord, Who liveth and reigneth with thee in the unity of the same Holy Spirit, now and ever. Amen.

Psalm 42:1–7 or 23

The Baptism

The Blessing of the Water

Then shall the Priest (or the Bishop, if he be present) bless the water, saying:

V: The Lord be with you;

R: And with thy spirit.

V: Lift up your hearts;

R: We lift them up unto the Lord.

V: Let us give thanks unto our Lord God;

R: It is meet and right so to do.

It is very meet, right, and our bounden duty, that we should at all times and in all places give thanks unto thee, O Lord, Holy Father, Almighty, Everlasting God.

But now are we chiefly bound to praise thee because thou hast appointed the water of Baptism for the regeneration of mankind through thy beloved Son; Upon whom, when he was baptized in the river Jordan, the Holy Spirit came down in the likeness of a dove; and who, for the forgiveness of our sins, did shed out of his most precious side both water and blood, and after his mighty Resurrection gave commandment to his Apostles to go and teach all nations, baptizing them in the name of the Father, and of the Son, and of the Holy Ghost:

Hear, we beseech thee, the prayers of thy Church; Sanctify this water, by the same Holy Spirit to the mystical washing away of sin, and grant that all who are to be baptized herein, being buried with Christ into his death, may be raised with him unto newness of life and, serving thee faithfully with all thy Saints, may attain to the kingdom of thy Glory;

Through the same Jesus Christ, thy Son, our Lord, to whom with thee and the same Holy Spirit, be all honour and glory, throughout all ages, world without end. *R:* Amen.

The Priest shall then make these supplications: O merciful God, grant that the old Adam in *this person (child)* may be so buried that the new man may be raised up in *him*. *R:* Amen.

Grant that *he* may have power and strength to have victory, and to triumph against the devil, the world, and the flesh. *R:* Amen.

Grant that *he* being steadfast in faith, joyful through hope, and rooted in charity, may at last come to thy heavenly kingdom through thy mercy, O blessed Lord God, who dost live and govern all things, world without end. *R:* Amen.

You, Godparents, who have brought *this child* to be baptized and stand in the presence of God and his people, must now make on *his* behalf the promises which *he* will renew in *his* own *person* when *he comes* in due time to be confirmed.

The Promises

Do you renounce the Devil and all his works, the covetous desires of the world, and all the sinful lusts of the flesh?

Answer: I renounce them all.

Do you believe in God the Father Almighty, maker of Heaven and Earth?

Answer: I believe.

Do you believe in Jesus Christ, his only Son our Lord? that he was conceived by the Holy Ghost, born of the Virgin Mary; that he suffered under Pontius Pilate, was crucified, dead, and buried; that he descended into hell, and the third day rose again from the dead; that he ascended into heaven, and sitteth at the right hand of God the Father Almighty; and from thence shall come to judge the quick and the dead?

Answer: I believe.

Do you believe in the Holy Ghost; the holy Catholic Church, the Communion of Saints, the Forgiveness of sins, the Resurrection of the body, and the Life everlasting?

Answer: I believe.

Do you desire to be baptized into this faith?
Answer: That is my desire.
Will you obediently keep God's holy will and commandments and walk in the way of Christ all the days of your life?
Answer: I will with the help of God.
Priest: Name this *person (child)*.

Then naming the person or child after them, he shall dip him into the water or pour water upon him, three times, once at the mention of each Person of the Trinity, saying, N., I baptize thee in the Name of the Father, and of the Son, and of the Holy Ghost. Amen.

The Priest shall make a cross upon the forehead of each person (child) baptized, saying: Seeing that this *person (child)* has now by Baptism been made a member of Christ's Church I sign *him* with the sign of the Cross in token that hereafter *he* shall not be ashamed to confess the faith of Christ crucified, and manfully to fight under his banner against sin, the world, and the devil, and to continue Christ's faithful soldier and servant unto *his* life's end. Amen.

He may give to each person, or for a child to one of the Godparents, a lighted candle, after which he shall say: Receive the Light of Christ and walk as a child of light, that when the Lord cometh you may appear before him in the company of the Saints.

At the Baptism of Adults the Priest shall say: Beloved, you have been born again through the power of the Holy Spirit and made God's own child. Wherefore I now bid you call upon God as Father in the prayer which Christ his only-begotten Son has taught us, saying

(and the newly baptized shall say the Lord's Prayer, the people saying it with him (them))

At the Baptism of Children the Priest shall say: Beloved, *this child has* been born again through the power of the Holy Spirit and made God's own *child*. Wherefore I bid you on *his* behalf to call upon God *his* Father in the prayer which Christ his only-begotten Son has taught us, saying,

(and the Godparents shall say together the Lord's Prayer, the people saying it with them)

Our Father (as above)

Then shall the Priest say: Almighty God we most heartily thank thee that it hath pleased thee to regenerate *this child* with thy Holy Spirit, to receive *him* as thine own *child* by adoption, and to make *him a member* of thy holy Church and *an inheritor* of thine everlasting kingdom; through Jesus Christ thy Son, our Lord, to whom with thee in the unity of the same Holy Spirit, be all honour and glory, world without end. R: Amen.

Almighty God, our heavenly Father, whose dearly beloved Son Jesus Christ shared with the Blessed Virgin Mary and Saint Joseph the life of an earthly home at Nazareth: Bless, we beseech thee, the *home* of *this child;* and give such grace and wisdom to all who have the care of *him*, that by their word and good example *he* may learn truly to know and love thee, and so come to thy eternal home in heaven; through the same thy Son Jesus Christ our Saviour. R: Amen.

The Priest shall say to the Godparents and Parents: You who have brought *this child* to be baptized into the family of Christ's Church must see that *he is* instructed in the Creed, the Lord's Prayer, and the Ten Commandments as set forth in the Church Catechism, and all other things which a Christian ought to know and believe to his soul's health.

See also that *he is* brought up to worship with the Church, to hear sermons, and to be regular in private prayer.

Help *him* by your prayers and example to walk worthily of *his* Christian calling, remembering always that by Baptism we are pledged to follow the example of our Saviour Christ and to be made like unto him.

See also that *this child is* brought to the Bishop to be confirmed so that, strengthened by the Holy Spirit, *he* may devoutly and regularly receive the Body and Blood of Christ in the Holy Communion, and may go forth into the world to serve God faithfully in the fellowship of his Church.

Will you do these duties faithfully?

Godparents and Parents: I will.

When Baptism is administered as a separate Service the Priest shall say: Depart in peace, and the Lord be with you

R: Amen.

THE CHURCH OF ENGLAND

The baptism of children (1980)
The duties of parents and godparents

The priest says: Children who are too young to profess the Christian faith are baptized on the understanding that they are brought up as Christians within the family of the Church.

As they grow up, they need the help and encouragement of that family, so that they learn to be faithful in public worship and private prayer, to live by trust in God, and come to confirmation.

Parents and godparents, the *children* whom you have brought for baptism depend chiefly on you for the help and encouragements *they need*. Are you willing to give it to *them* by your prayers, by your example, and by your teaching?

Parents and godparents: I am willing.

And if the child is old enough to understand, the priest speaks to him in these or similar words: N, when you are baptized, you become *a member* of a new family. God takes you for his own *child,* and all Christian people will be your brothers and sisters.

The ministry of the word

Priest: The Lord is loving to everyone;

All: and his mercy is over all his works.

Priest: God is the creator of all things, and by the birth of children he gives to parents a share in the work and joy of creation. But we who are born of earthly parents need to be born again. For in the Gospel Jesus tells us that unless a man has been born again, he cannot see the Kingdom of God. And so God gives us the way to a second birth, a new creation and life in union with him.

Baptism is the sign and seal of this new birth. In St Matthew's Gospel we read of the risen Christ commanding his followers to make disciples of all nations and to baptize men everywhere; and in the Acts of the Apostles we read of St Peter preaching in these words: "Repent and be baptized in the name of Jesus Christ for the forgiveness of sins; and you shall receive the gift of the Holy Spirit. For the promise is to you and your children and to all that are afar off, everyone whom the Lord calls to him."

In obedience to this same command we ourselves were baptized and now bring *these children* to baptism.

Priest: We thank God therefore for our baptism to life in Christ, and we pray for *these children (N)* and say together

All: Heavenly Father, in your love
you have called us to know you,
led us to trust you,
and bound our life with yours.
Surround *these children* with your love;
protect *them* from evil;
fill *them* with your Holy Spirit;
and receive *them* into the family of your Church;
that *they* may walk with us in the way of Christ
and grow in the knowledge of your love. Amen.

The decision

The parents and godparents stand, and the priest says to them: Those who bring children to be baptized must affirm their allegiance to Christ and their rejection of all that is evil.

It is your duty to bring up *these children* to fight against evil and to follow Christ.

Therefore I ask these questions which you must answer for yourselves and for *these* children.

Do you turn to Christ?

Answer: I turn to Christ.

Priest: Do you repent of your sins?

Answer: I repent of my sins.

Priest: Do you renounce evil?

Answer: I renounce evil.

Either here or after the baptism proper, the priest makes the sign of the cross on the forehead of each child, saying to each: I sign you with the cross, the sign of Christ.

After the signing of each or all, he says: Do not be ashamed to confess the faith of Christ crucified.

All: Fight valiantly under the banner of Christ against sin, the world, and the devil, and continue his faithful *soldiers* and *servants* to the end of your *lives*.

Priest: May almighty God deliver you from the powers of darkness, and lead you in the light and obedience of Christ. Amen.

A hymn or psalm may be sung.

The baptism

The priest stands before the water of baptism and says: Praise God who made heaven and earth,

All: who keeps his promise for ever.

Priest: Almighty God, whose Son Jesus Christ
   was baptized in the river Jordan;
we thank you for the gift of water
   to cleanse us and revive us;
we thank you that through the waters of the
   Red Sea, you led your people out of slavery
   to freedom in the promised land;
we thank you that through the deep waters
   of death you brought your Son, and raised him to live in triumph.
Bless this water, that your *servants* who *are*
   washed in it may be made one with Christ
   in his death and in his resurrection,
   to be cleansed and delivered from all sin.
Send your Holy Spirit upon *them* to bring
   them to new birth in the family of your
   Church, and raise *them* with Christ to full and eternal life.
For all might, majesty, authority, and power
   are yours, now and for ever. Amen.

The priest says to the parents and godparents:

You have brought *these children* to baptism. You must now declare before God and his Church the Christian faith into which *they are* to be baptized, and in which you will help *them* to grow. You must answer for yourselves and for *these children*.

Do you believe and trust in God the Father, who made the world?

Answer: I believe and trust in him.

Priest: Do you believe and trust in his Son Jesus Christ, who redeemed mankind?

Answer: I believe and trust in him.

Priest: Do you believe and trust in his Holy Spirit, who gives life to the people of God?

Answer: I believe and trust in him.

The priest turns to the congregation and says: This is the faith of the Church.

All: This is our faith. We believe and trust in one God, Father, Son, and Holy Spirit.

The parents and godparents being present with each child, the priest baptizes *him*. He dips *him* in the water or pours water on *him*, addressing *him* by name.

Priest: N, I baptize you in the name of the Father, and of the Son, and of the Holy Spirit.

And each one of his sponsors answers: Amen.

The priest or other person may give to a parent or godparent for each child a lighted candle, saying to each: Receive this light.

And when a candle has been given to each one, he says: This is to show that you have passed from darkness to light.

All: Shine as a light in the world to the glory of God the Father.

The welcome

The priest and the congregation, representing the whole Church, welcome the newly baptized.

Priest: God has received you by baptism into his Church.

All: We welcome you into the Lord's Family.
We are members together of the body of Christ;
we are children of the same heavenly Father;
we are inheritors together of the kingdom of God.
We welcome you.

The prayers

The prayers that follow are omitted when baptism is administered at Holy Communion; and may be omitted when baptism is administered at Morning or Evening Prayer.

Priest: Lord God our Father, maker of heaven and earth, we thank you that by your Holy Spirit *these children have* been born again into new life, adopted for your own, and received into the fellowship of your Church: grant that *they* may grow in the faith into which *they have* been baptized, that *they* may profess it for *themselves* when *they come* to be confirmed, and that all things belonging to the Spirit may live and grow in *them*. Amen.

Priest: Heavenly Father, we pray for the parents of *these children;* give them the spirit of wisdom and love, that their *homes* may reflect the joy of your eternal kingdom. Amen.

Priest: Almighty God, we thank you for our fellowship in the household of faith with all those who have been baptized in your name. Keep us faithful to our baptism, and so make us ready for that day when the whole creation shall be made perfect in your Son, our Saviour Jesus Christ. Amen.

Priest: Jesus taught us to call God our Father, and so in faith and trust we say:

All: Our Father in heaven,
hallowed be your name,
your kingdom come,
your will be done,
on earth as in heaven.
Give us today our daily bread.
Forgive us our sins

as we forgive those who sin against us.
Lead us not into temptation
but deliver us from evil.
For the kingdom, the power, and the glory are yours
now and for ever. Amen.

Priest: The grace of our Lord Jesus Christ, and the love of God, and the fellowship of the Holy Spirit be with us all evermore. Amen.

5. THE LUTHERAN TRADITION

For the Lutheran tradition, we present here four texts:
A Swedish liturgy of 1963[7], the German liturgy of infant baptism of 1964[8], a German Adult Baptism[9] and the most recent American revision of 1978[10].

Perhaps the most striking of these is the almost rudimentary Swedish one, which leaves out normally common Lutheran features, such as exhortation (which is particularly emphasized in the 1964 German Infant Baptism), interrogation regarding faith and renunciation of the devil. The fact, however, that it does not contain any exorcism, seems to reflect a wider Lutheran concern in the last two decades: the 1978 American liturgy has taken the same decision.

In this latter liturgy, attention should be given particularly to the large part the congregation is given in the whole ceremony.

LUTHERAN CHURCH OF SWEDEN (1963)

Baptism

In the name of God, of the Father, and of the Son, and of the Holy Ghost.

Thank the Lord because He is good. His mercy lasts from generation to generation. He wants all men to be saved and to arrive at the full knowledge of the truth. He seeks us in His love. Without Him we are drifting into sin and death. That is why He sent His Son, Jesus Christ, into the world to save sinners. Thus He also reveals through Baptism that He wants to endow this child (these children) with His mercy and His compassion for it (them) through its (their) faith to win salvation in Jesus Christ, communion with the Holy one and participation in the inheritance of the blessed ones in heaven.

Our Lord, Jesus Christ, himself instituted Holy Baptism. He said: Matt. 28:18–20

Let us also hear the word of the Gospel about Jesus Christ and the children: Mark 10:13–16

---

[7] Handbok till den kristna Forsamlinguisjänst Stockholm, 1963, pp. 42–46.
[8] Agende für die Evangelisch-Lutherischen Kirchen und Gemeinden, Berlin, 1964, pp. 18–29.
[9] Agende für Evangelish-Lutherische Kirchen und Gemeinden, Berlin, 1963, pp. 50–57.
[10] *The Lutheran Book of Worship,* Lutheran Church in America, American Lutheran Church, Evangelical Lutheran Church in Canada, Lutheran Church Missouri Synod, Minneapolis, 1978, pp. 121–124.

Let us pray:

Our Father which art in heaven, Hallowed be thy Name, Thy kingdom come, Thy will be done, in earth as it is in heaven. Give us this day our daily bread; And forgive us our trespasses, As we forgive them that trespass against us; And lead us not into temptation, But deliver us from evil.

For thine is the kingdom, the power and the glory for ever and ever. Amen.

Thereafter the Minister says: Let us confess our Christian faith.

The congregation stands.

In the name of the Triune God we are now going to baptize this child (these children).

The Minister says while pouring water upon the child's head: I baptize thee.... in the name of the Father, and of the Son, and of the Holy Ghost.

Then the priest places his hand on the child's head and says: May the Lord bless you N... and protect you. May the Lord lift up his countenance upon you and be merciful unto you. May the Lord turn His countenance on you and give you peace.

In the name of God, of the Father, and of the Son, and of the Holy Ghost. Amen.

The Minister says to those standing near by (and to the congregation): This child (these children) which has (have) now been baptized in the name of Christ, has (have) been entrusted to you by God. May He also endow you with mercy that you may always bear in mind your responsibility and calling by bringing up this child (these children) in the right manner.

Support it (them) with your love and prayers. Take care to set a good Christian example for it (them) and do not forget the word of the Lord: "Those who accept such a child in my name accept me".

As the servant of Christ I exhort the congregation always to include this child (these children) in your prayers and, together with the parents, to assume responsibility for this child's (these children's) Christian upbringing.

The congregation sits.

The Minister prays for the child and those standing near by.

The Minister then says: May the Almighty God, our Father, grant you, according to the riches of His glory to be strengthened with might through His Spirit in the inner man and that Christ may dwell in your hearts through faith. May the grace of the Lord Jesus Christ and the love of God and the fellowship of the Holy Spirit be with you all. Amen.

EVANGELICAL LUTHERAN CHURCH OF GERMANY

The baptism of a child (1964)

Officiating Minister: The peace of the Lord be with you all.

Congregation: Amen.

Minister: Our Lord Jesus Christ said: (reading of Matt. 28:18b—20). He also said: 'Whoever believes and is baptized will be saved, but whoever does not believe will be condemned' (Mark 16:16).

The minister goes to the child who is to be baptized and makes the sign of the cross on the child's forehead and breast, saying as he does this: Receive the sign of the holy cross on the +forehead and on the+breast.

Minister: Let us pray. (If this part of the service is conducted at the altar, the minister turns to the altar as he prays.)

O Lord, graciously hear our prayer, we beseech Thee, and protect this child always by the power of the cross of Jesus Christ with the sign of which he (she) has been blessed. And since Thou hast chosen this child to be Thine own, deliver him (her) from all the chains of evil, grant him (her) the new birth and help him (her) to walk in the way of salvation and in the end to inherit the heavenly kingdom. Though Jesus Christ our Lord.

Congregation: Amen.

Minister: Lord Jesus Christ,
(Never-failing comfort of all who call upon Thee,
Deliverer of all who cry to Thee,
and peace of all who pray to Thee,
Thou who art the life of believers and the resurrection of the dead)
We pray to Thee for this child for whom we seek the gift of Thy baptism,
that he (she) through regeneration by the Spirit may obtain everlasting grace.
Accept him (her), Lord,
and, as Thou hast said:
   'Ask and it shall be given you,
   Seek and you shall find,
   Knock and it shall be opened unto you'
So do Thou now give Thy blessing to him who asks and open the door to him who knocks,
that this child may obtain the eternal blessing of this sacrament and receive the promised gift of Thy kingdom.

Thou who livest and reignest with the Father and the Holy Spirit for ever and ever.

Congregation: Amen.

Minister: O Christ our Lord and our Redeemer, Thou who hast power over all the powers of evil, make room for Thyself in the heart of this child. And as Thou didst open the eyes of the man born blind and loosen the tongue of the dumb, so take from this child all blindness of heart and remove the fetters of the devil, so that he (she) may know Thee and with all Thy faithful people praise and glorify Thee now and for evermore.

Congregation: Amen.

Minister: May the Lord preserve thy going out and thy coming in from this time forth and for evermore (Ps. 121:8).

Congregation: Amen.

The minister then preaches the baptismal sermon or reads an exhortation.

The questions to the parents and sponsors:
The questions may be introduced as follows:

Minister: Baptism is the gift and work of God alone. If your child is in due course to know and rightly use this gift of grace of his (her) baptism, he (she) needs the help of his (her) parents and the service of his (her) sponsors.

The parents and sponsors stand.

Dear parents. When you were married you received God's command and promise for your marriage and home. It is right, therefore, that you should accept your child as the gift of God the Creator, give him (her) a Christian upbringing and help him (her) to remain a living member of the Church of Jesus Christ. If you are ready to do all this, will you please respond: 'I am, so help me God.'

Parents: I am, so help me God.

Minister: Dear sponsors. You have accepted the office of sponsor to this child. On behalf of the Christian Church you should accept him (her), help the parents with his (her) upbringing and see to it that he (she) learns the Ten Commandments, the Christian Creed and the Lord's Prayer. If you are prepared to do this, please respond: 'I am, so help me God.'

Sponsors: I am, so help me God.

In the case of unmarried parents, this section is as follows:

Minister: Dear parents. This child has been entrusted to you as a gift of God the Creator. It is His will that you should bring him (her) up in the Christian faith and that he (she) should remain a living member of the Church of Jesus Christ. If you are ready to do this, will you please respond: 'I am, so help me God.'

Parents: I am, so help me God.

etc. etc...

In the case of an unmarried mother, this section is as follows:

Minister: Dear mother. This child has been entrusted to you as a gift of God the Creator. It is His will that you should give him (her) a Christian upbringing and help him (her) to remain a living member of the Church of Jesus Christ. If you are ready to do this, will you please respond: 'I am, so help me God.'

Mother: I am, so help me God.

etc. etc...

Minister: May the God of all grace grant you the aid of His Spirit and bless your ministry to this child.

Let us pray. *(goes to the altar)*

Lord God, Heavenly Father, graciously uphold these parents (this mother) and sponsors, that they may perform their ministry in obedience to Thy will and by their words and deeds show this child the way to everlasting life. Through Jesus Christ our Lord.

Congregation: Amen.

Minister (to the congregation): Hear how Jesus Christ calls the children to himself in the 10th chapter of the Gospel of Mark: (reads Mark 10:13–16).

Minister (to the sponsors (and parents)): To obtain this blessing for this child too, let us (lay our hands on him (her) and) pray together. *The minister (with the sponsors) lays his hand on the child.*

Minister, (parents) and sponsors pray together: Our Father who art in heaven, etc. etc. including the doxology.

Congregation: Amen.

Minister: The Lord preserve thy coming in and thy going out, from this time forth and for evermore (Ps. 121:8).

Congregation: Amen.

From this point the service can proceed in different ways (A, B or C).

A

Minister addresses the parents and sponsors: Dear parents and sponsors. If it is your desire that this child should be baptized and, by this holy sacrament, be delivered from the power of evil and set beneath the rule of Jesus Christ, will you please respond: 'I do so desire'.

Parents and sponsors: I do so desire.

Minister: If you are willing to confess the faith on this infant's behalf, to renounce the devil and all his works and ways and make a pledge to God the Father, the Son and the Holy Spirit, will you say with me:

OR

Dear parents and sponsors. You have heard the words of our Saviour: 'Whosoever believes and is baptized will be saved'. Anyone who believes in Jesus Christ, the Son of God and our Lord, is in holy baptism delivered from the power of Satan and set beneath the lordship of Christ so as to become a member of the body of Christ and remain by the power of the Holy Spirit in the fellowship of the Christian family.

This infant is not yet able to profess and bear witness to the Christian faith. (But in the Gospel Christ also promises the kingdom of God to the children when we bring them to him and entrust them to him as Lord. It is in order to begin this process that you parents and sponsors are here today.)

Now therefore, lovingly and prayerfully, speak up for this child by confessing the Christian faith and saying together:

OR

Dear parents and sponsors. At the command and promise of our Lord Jesus Christ, you have brought this child for baptism. For he has promised the kingdom of God to the children we bring to him. Let us now therefore commit this child to the Triune God, confessing our faith together in the words of the Apostles' Creed:

Minister, parents and sponsors say together the Apostles' Creed.

B

Minister: Dear parents and sponsors. If you desire that this child be baptized and by the holy sacrament be delivered from the power of the devil and set beneath the lordship of Christ, will you please respond: 'I do.'

Parents and sponsors: I do.

Minister: Will you answer on the child's behalf the questions I put to him (her). Do you renounce Satan and all his works and ways? If so, please respond: 'I do.'

Parents and sponsors: I do.

Minister: Do you believe in one God, the Father Almighty, Maker of heaven and earth.... (continuing in the words of the Apostles' Creed)? If so, please respond: 'I do.'

Parents and sponsors: I do.

C

Minister: Dear sponsors. In Christian love you have accepted this infant and are willing to represent him (her) in holy baptism. Will you therefore answer on the child's behalf the questions I now put to him (her).

Do you renounce Satan and all his works and ways?

Sponsors: I do.

Minister: Do you believe in one God, the Father Almighty, Maker of heaven and earth...(continuing in the words of the Apostles' Creed)?

Sponsors: I do.

Minister: Is it your desire to be baptized?

Sponsors: It is.

Continuation following A, B, or C.

The minister then asks: What is the name of this child?

The father or a sponsor states the child's name. The minister pours water on the child's head in a manner visible to the parents and sponsors and as he does so says:

I baptize you (name of the child) in the name of the Father and of the Son and of the Holy Spirit.

The Minister lays his hand on the child and says: May the Almighty God and Father of our Lord Jesus Christ who has caused you to be born again of water and the Holy Spirit and forgiven you all your sins, strengthen you with His grace unto everlasting life.

Peace + be with you.

Congregation: Amen.

Where it is the custom to use the baptismal robe: In accordance with whatever is the local custom, the baptismal robe is handed over by the sacristan to the minister who then puts it on the child, saying as he does so:

> Receive this white robe as a symbol of the justice of Christ. 'All who have been baptized into Christ have put on Christ.' (Gal. 3:27)

Where the use of baptismal candles is customary: A lit candle is handed to the minister by the sacristan and given to one of the sponsors on behalf of the child. The minister says:

> Receive this burning light and keep thy baptism spotless. 'Let your loins be girded and your lamps burning and be like unto those that wait for their lord.' (Luke 12:35, 36a)

Minister: Let us pray.

Almighty and Merciful God and Father, we give Thee hearty thanks and praise for graciously upholding Thy Church and increasing it; Thou hast also given this child a new birth by holy baptism and made him (her) a member of the body of Thy dear Son Jesus Christ. We humbly beseech Thee to keep this child in the grace he (she) has received. Keep us, and all those who are brought to baptism, in the true faith and in the communion of Thy Church unto everlasting life. Through Jesus Christ our Lord.

Congregation: Amen.

The baptism of an adult (1964)

The Minister says: The peace of the Lord be with you all.

Congregation: Amen.

Minister: Our Lord Jesus Christ says, 'All authority has been given unto me ...'(reading from Matt. 28:18b—20)

The minister goes to the candidate for baptism, and makes the sign of the cross on his (her) forehead and breast, saying: Receive the sign of the cross on the forehead+ and on the breast+.

If there are several candidates for baptism, the sign of the cross and the accompanying words will be repeated for each candidate.

Minister: Let us pray.

(moves to the altar)

We beseech Thee, Lord, graciously to hear our prayer and evermore to defend this our brother (sister) through the power of the cross of Jesus Christ, with the sign of which he(she) has been blessed. And since Thou hast chosen him(her) for Thine own, deliver him(her) from all the shackles of evil, grant him(her) the new birth and help him(her) to walk in the way of salvation so that he(she) may inherit the heavenly kingdom. Through Jesus Christ our Lord.

Congregation: Amen.

If the baptismal service is a separate act of worship, the baptismal sermon is preached at this point.

Minister: Reading of John 3:5–8.

Minister (to the candidate): If you desire to be baptized, say together with me the Church's creed in which you have been instructed:

Minister and candidate say together the Apostles' Creed.

Minister (to the sponsors): Let us (lay hands on the candidate and) pray together:

The minister lays his hand on the candidate.

Minister and sponsors pray together the Lord's prayer, including the doxology.

Congregation: Amen.

Minister (addressing the candidate): May the Lord preserve thy coming in and thy going out from this time forth and for evermore (Ps. 121:8). Dear brother (dear sister), If you are willing to renounce the devil and all his works and ways, please respond: 'I am.'

Candidate: I am.

Minister: If you believe in God the Father, Creator of all things, in Jesus Christ, the Son of God and our Lord, and in the Holy Spirit, who is the Lord and Giver of Life, will you respond: 'I do.'

Candidate: I do.

Minister: Do you desire to be baptized?

Candidate: I do.

Minister: I baptize thee *(naming the candidate)* in the name of the Father and of the Son and of the Holy Spirit.

The minister lays his hand on the candidate and says:

May the Almighty God and Father of our Lord Jesus Christ who has begotten you again through water and the Holy Spirit and forgiven you all your sins, strengthen you with his grace to eternal life. Peace+ be with thee. (3 John 15a)

Candidate: Amen.

Minister: Let us pray

(at the altar)

Almighty and Everlasting God, who hast graciously begotten this our brother (sister) of water and the Holy Spirit and granted him(her) the forgiveness of sins, bless him(her) with Thy Spirit, the Spirit of wisdom and understanding, the Spirit of counsel and of might, the Spirit of the knowledge and fear of the Lord, that he(she) may be filled with the light of Thy glory. Through Jesus Christ our Lord.

Congregation: Amen.

Minister: Go in +peace. The Lord be with you. (Mark 5:34b)

LUTHERAN CHURCHES IN NORTH AMERICA

Holy baptism (1978)

P: In Holy Baptism our gracious heavenly Father liberates us from sin and death by joining us to the death and resurrection of our Lord Jesus Christ. We are born children of a fallen humanity; in the waters of Baptism we are reborn children of God and inheritors of eternal life. By water and the Holy Spirit we are made members of the Church which is the body of Christ. As we live with him and with his people, we grow in faith, love, and obedience to the will of God.

A sponsor for each candidate, in turn, presents the candidate with these or similar words:
I present _____name_____ to receive the Sacrament of Holy Baptism.

*The minister addresses those candidates who are able to answer for themselves:*_____name_____ do you desire to be baptized?

R: I do.

The minister addresses the sponsors and parents.

When only young children are baptized, the minister says: In Christian love you have presented *these children* for Holy Baptism. You should, therefore, faithfully bring *them* to the services of God's house, and teach *them* the Lord's Prayer, the Creed, and the Ten Commandments. As *they grow* in years, you should place in *their* hands the Holy Scriptures and provide for *their* instruction in the Christian faith, that, living in the covenant of *their* Baptism and in communion with the Church, *they* may lead *godly lives* until the day of Jesus Christ.

Do you promise to fulfill these obligations?

R: I do.

When older children and adults are baptized also, the minister says:

P: In Christian love you have presented *these people* for Holy Baptism. You should, therefore, faithfully care for *them* and help *them* in every way as God gives you opportunity, that *they* may bear witness to the faith we profess, and that, living in the covenant of *their* Baptism and in communion with the Church, *they* may lead *godly lives* until the day of Jesus Christ.

Do you promise to fulfill these obligations?

R: I do.

Stand

When baptisms are celebrated within the Holy Communion, the Prayers may be said at this time, with special reference to those baptized.

After each portion of the prayers:

A: Lord, in your mercy,

C: hear our prayer.

The minister begins the thanksgiving.

P: The Lord be with you.

C: And also with you.

P: Let us give thanks to the Lord our God.

C: It is right to give him thanks and praise.

P: Holy God, mighty Lord, gracious Father: We give you thanks, for in the beginning your Spirit moved over the waters and you created heaven and earth. By the gift of water you nourish and sustain us and all living things.

By the waters of the flood you condemned the wicked and saved those whom you had chosen, Noah and his family. You led Israel by the pillar of cloud and fire through the sea, out of slavery into the freedom of the promised land. In the waters of the Jordan your Son was baptized by John and anointed with the Spirit. By the baptism of his own death and resurrection your beloved Son has set us free from the bondage to sin and death, and has opened the way to the joy and freedom of everlasting life. He made water a sign of the kingdom and of cleansing and rebirth. In obedience to his command, we make disciples of all nations, baptizing them in the name of the Father, and of the Son, and of the Holy Spirit.

Pour out your Holy Spirit, so that *those* who *are* here baptized may be given new life. Wash away the sin of *all those* who *are* cleansed by this water and bring *them* forth as *inheritors* of your glorious kingdom.

To you be given praise and honor and worship through your Son, Jesus Christ our Lord, in the unity of the Holy Spirit, now and forever.

C: Amen.

P: I ask you to profess your faith in Christ Jesus, reject sin, and confess the faith of the Church, the faith in which we baptize.

P: Do you renounce all the forces of evil, the devil, and all his empty promises?

C: I do.

P: Do you believe in God the Father?

C: I believe in God, the Father almighty, creator of heaven and earth.

P: Do you believe in Jesus Christ, the Son of God?

C: I believe in Jesus Christ, his only Son, our Lord. He was conceived by the power of the Holy Spirit and born of the virgin Mary. He suffered under Pontius Pilate, was crucified, died, and was buried. He descended into hell. On the third day he rose again. He ascended into heaven, and is seated at the right hand of the Father. He will come again to judge the living and the dead.

P: Do you believe in God the Holy Spirit?

C: I believe in the Holy Spirit, the holy catholic Church, the communion of saints, the forgiveness of sins, the resurrection of the body, and the life everlasting. Amen

The minister baptizes each candidate.

P: ____name_____, I baptize you

OR

P: ____name_____ is baptized

in the name of the Father,

The minister pours water on the candidate's head.

P: and of the Son,

The minister pours water on the candidate's head a second time.

P: and of the Holy Spirit. Amen.

The minister pours water on the candidate's head a third time.

A psalm or hymn may be sung as the minister and the baptismal group go before the altar.

P: The Lord be with you.

C: And also with you.

Those who have been baptized kneel. Sponsors or parents holding young children stand. The minister lays both hands on the head of each of the baptized and prays for the Holy Spirit:

P: **God, the Father of our Lord Jesus Christ, we give you thanks for freeing your sons and daughters from the power of sin and for raising them up to a new life through this holy sacrament. Pour your Holy Spirit upon** __name___:

the spirit of wisdom and understanding, the spirit of counsel and might, the spirit of knowledge and the fear of the Lord, the spirit of joy in your presence.

C: Amen.

The minister marks the sign of the cross on the forehead of each of the baptized. Oil prepared for this purpose may be used. As the sign of the cross is made, the minister says:

P: ___name_____, child of God, you have been sealed by the Holy Spirit and marked with the cross of Christ forever.

The sponsor or the baptized responds: "Amen."

After all have received the sign of the cross, they stand.

A lighted candle may be given to each of the baptized (to the sponsor of a young child) by a representative of the congregation who says:

Let your light so shine before others that they may see your good works and glorify your Father in heaven.

When small children are baptized, this prayer may be said.

P: O God, the giver of all life, look with kindness upon the *fathers* and *mothers* of *these children*. Let them ever rejoice in the gift you have given them. Make them teachers and examples of righteousness for their *children*. Strengthen them in their own Baptism so they may share eternally with their *children* the salvation you have given them, through Jesus Christ our Lord.

C: Amen.

Stand

The ministers and the baptismal group turn toward the congregation; a representative of the congregation says:

Through Baptism God has made *these* new *sisters and brothers members* of the priesthood we all share in Christ Jesus, that we may proclaim the praise of God and bear his creative and redeeming Word to all the world.

C: We welcome you into the Lord's family. We receive you as fellow members of the body of Christ, children of the same heavenly Father, and workers with us in the kingdom of God.

The ministers may exchange the peace with the baptized, with their sponsors and parents, and with the congregation:

Peace be with you.

R: Peace be with you.

6. THE REFORMED TRADITION

The four texts presented here show a remarkably unanimous expression of the Reformed tradition within recent liturgical developments.

The liturgy of the Reformed Church in America (1968)[11], the Swiss Reformed liturgy of 1969[12], the Scottish Presbyterian text of 1979[13], and the Waldensian text of 1934[14], all strongly emphasize God's covenant of grace that receives the children into the Church, nevertheless stressing the importance of the parents providing a Christian education, with the congregation's support (exhortation), thus showing little or no interest in interrogation, exorcism and renunciation of the devil. (Interrogation, of course, takes place in occasional adult baptisms.) Special attention has been given, moreover, by all of these to the participation of the congregation in the ceremony.

THE REFORMED CHURCH IN AMERICA

The order for the sacrament of infant baptism (1968)

Institution

Beloved in the Lord, attend to the words of the institution of the sacrament of holy Baptism, as they were delivered by our Lord Jesus Christ to his disciples after his resurrection: Matt. 28:18–20.

In fulfillment of our Lord's institution and command, the Church, acknowledging God's gracious covenant with his people, recognizes the Sacrament of Baptism as a sign and seal of membership in the body of Christ both to believing adults and to children of the faithful.

Scripture

One or more of these passages shall be read.
Gen: 17:7 and/or Acts 2:39 and/or Gal. 3:6–8, 29 and/or Eph. 4:4–6 and/or Mark 10:14–16

---

[11] *Liturgy and Psalms,* Reformed Church in America, New York, 1968, pp. 26–32.
[12] Kirchenbuch, Evangelisch Reformierte Landeskirche des Kantons Zürich, Zurich, 1969, pp. 252–255.
[13] *The Book of Common Order,* Church of Scotland, Edinburgh, 1979, pp. 46—54.
[14] *Liturgia,* Chiesa Evangelica Valdese, Torre Pelice, 1934, pp. 5—17.

Meaning of the sacrament

In the celebration of Christian Baptism we confess that we with our children are sinful by nature and under the judgment of God. We cannot enter into God's kingdom unless we are born again and seek our cleansing and salvation in him alone.

Baptism is a sign and seal of our ingrafting into the body of Christ. We are baptized in the name of the Triune God, who thereby assures us of the forgiveness of our sins, through the blood of Christ; of our adoption into the household of faith; of our daily renewing and cleansing by his Spirit; and of our resurrection to eternal life.

By this assurance we are called to new obedience: to hold fast to this one God, Father, Son, and Holy Spirit; to trust and love him with all our heart and soul and mind and strength; and to forsake the world, crucify our old nature, and walk in a new and holy life. And if we sometimes, through weakness, fall into sin, we must not therefore despair of God's mercy, nor continue in sin, since Baptism is the sign and seal of God's eternal covenant of grace with us.

That this Sacrament may be celebrated to God's glory, to the strengthening of our faith, and to the upbuilding of his Church, let us call on his name.

Prayer

Let us pray.

Almighty God, our Father in heaven, we thank thee for Jesus Christ, who by his cross and resurrection has redeemed us from sin and death, into which by our disobedience we have fallen, and has given us hope of eternal life. We bless thee, O God, that by him thou hast entered into a covenant of grace with thy people and appointed the holy Sacrament of Baptism to be its sign and seal.

Look on us in mercy, we pray, and sanctify with thy Word and Spirit this Sacrament to the use for which thou hast ordained it; and grant that *this child* now to be baptized may through the power of thy Holy Spirit be made *a* true *member* of Christ's body, the Church; and being kept in thy love, finally obtain *his* inheritance in thine eternal kingdom.

And remembering that we are not our own but belong to our faithful Savior, we offer thee ourselves as servants in the fulfillment of thy promise to be our God and the God of our children; through Jesus Christ our Lord. Amen.

Confession of faith

Dearly Beloved, since Baptism is in the name of the Triune God, let us arise and confess with the Church through the ages our Christian Faith in the words of the Apostles' Creed.

Vows

Minister to the parents: Since you, the parents of *this child,* desire holy Baptism for *him* you are sincerely to give answer to these questions before God and his Church:

Do you accept the Gospel of God's grace in Jesus Christ revealed in the holy

Scriptures of the Old and New Testaments, which we have now confessed in the Articles of the Christian Faith as the only way to eternal life?

Do you acknowledge that *this child* with us *is* sinful by nature and under the judgment of God, but *is* received by grace, sanctified in Christ, and numbered among his people, of which Baptism is the sign and seal?

Do you promise to instruct *this child* in the truth of God's Word and in the way of salvation through Jesus Christ; to pray for *him* and to teach *him* to pray; and to train *him* by your precept and example, as God may give you grace, in all holy living, and in the nurture and worship of the Church? What is your response?

The parents shall respond: I do.

Minister: The Lord bless you and your child, and give you grace faithfully to perform these promises.

Minister to the congregation: Do you, the members of this congregation, renew your vows under this covenant of grace, and promise to sustain the fellowship of faith and life within the Church of Christ, in which our children are made partakers of him and all his benefits? What is your response?

The congregation shall respond: We do.

Administration of the sacrament

When the minister and parents have come to the font, and the congregation is seated, the minister shall say: N ..., I baptize you in the name of the Father and of the Son and of the Holy Spirit. Amen.

Then the following declaration may be made: In the name of the Lord Jesus Christ, the only King and Head of his Church, I declare that *this child is* now received into the visible membership of the Holy Catholic Church, and *is* engaged to confess the faith of Christ crucified, and to be his faithful servant unto *his* life's end.

Prayer

Let us pray.

Almighty God, our heavenly Father, we thank thee that we may bring our children to thee, and baptize them in thy most holy name. Bless *this child* whom we have brought to thee, and guard, we pray thee, *his* life and health, and fulfill to *him* thy gracious promises. Incline *him* by thy Holy Spirit to take *his* place in the Church of thy Son Jesus Christ; enable *him* to overcome the temptations of the world; and, finally, to obtain an inheritance among thy saints in light.

Bless thy servants, *his* parents, that they may faithfully perform the duties laid upon them, training their *child* in the truth of thy Gospel, and walking before *him* and with *him* in the beauty of holiness.

Guide us, thy people, by Word and Spirit, in the fulfillment of our vow to sustain the fellowship and life within thy Church for the nurture of *this child*, that *he* may grow up into all the fullness of Christ.

Bless, we pray thee, all the children of thy Church, and prepare them hereafter to carry on the work now committed to us; through Jesus Christ our Lord.

General prayers concluding with the Lord's Prayer
Hymn
Benediction

EVANGELICAL REFORMED CHURCH OF THE CANTON OF ZÜRICH

Second order of baptism (1969)

Reading of Mark 10:13-16

Minister: Dear parents and godparents: In these words Jesus Christ called the children to himself and promised them the kingdom of God. When we now bring these children to him and welcome them into his Church by baptism, it is in accordance with his mind that we are acting.

We baptize with water as a sign that Christ accepts them as clean and calls them to live as children of God.

We may confidently pray the heavenly Father to guide them with His Holy Spirit.

Your chief concern, dear parents, will be to help your child to learn really to know and love God as Father so that trust in Him may become their firm foundation for life.

You yourselves must constantly renew your own trust in God. By doing so you will become for your child an example of supportive love and patience.

Give your child courage to do what is right.

Dear godparents, you have consented to support the parents in the upbringing of their child and to accompany the child with love and care as it grows up.

This you will be doing as representatives of the congregation which the child should regard as its home.

And we, too, the congregation, also share this responsibility for the children growing up in our midst.

Let us make sure that none of them are harmed in body or soul through our fault.

Let us help them, rather, to know the strength of Christian fellowship.

Invitation: And now bring your children forward.

The parents and sponsors now approach the font.

Baptismal question

Minister: Dear parents and godparents, you have been instructed as to the meaning of baptism and now desire that your child, too, should be baptized.

If you are ready to fulfill diligently the duty which you accept for this child by baptism, will you please respond: 'Yes, I am.'
Parents and godparents respond: Yes, I am.

Act of baptism
N. I baptize thee in the name of the Father, the Son and the Holy Spirit. Amen.

Baptismal blessing
The Lord bless thee and keep thee, the Lord preserve thy going out and thy coming in, from this time forth and for evermore.

Prayer: Merciful Father, in hope and confidence we commit to Thee these children. Protect them we beseech Thee so that nothing may separate them from Thee. Grant that they may one day enter joyfully into the discipleship of Christ. Grant wisdom and love to these parents and sponsors that they may be enabled to fulfill their responsibilities to their child.

And help us all to cooperate in bringing these children to Thee by our words and our example. Grant that Thy kingdom may grow in this congregation and among all humankind, until the day when all shall worship and serve Thee.

Baptismal hymn

Silent adoration

CHURCH OF SCOTLAND
(provisional text)

Order for the administration of holy baptism (to infants)

During the singing of a suitable Hymn, the infants shall be brought into the church, and the minister, standing at the font, shall say:

Beloved in the Lord, the Gospel tells us that our Lord Jesus Christ was himself baptized for our sake in the river Jordan and the Spirit came upon him.

More than that, the Gospel transmits to us the command of the risen Christ:

All authority in heaven and on earth has been given to me. Go therefore and make disciples of all nations, baptizing them in the name of the Father and of the Son and of the Holy Spirit, teaching them to observe all that I have commanded you; and lo, I am with you always, to the close of the age.

The Church remembers also the words of the apostle Peter on the day of Pentecost:

Repent, and be baptized every one of you in the name of Jesus Christ, for the forgiveness of your sins; and you shall receive the gift of the Holy Spirit. For the promise is to you and to your children and to all that are far off, every one whom the Lord our God calls to him.

The sacrament of baptism is the appointed way of entrance into Christ's Church.

It assures us of the washing away of sin, the start of a new life in Christ, and the gift of the Holy Spirit.

This promise is for believers, and also for their children, whose christian upbringing is committed to their parents and to the congregation.

Consider also these words from the Gospels:

They were bringing children to Jesus, that he might touch them; and the disciples rebuked them. But when Jesus saw it he was indignant, and said to them, "Let the children come to me, do not hinder them; for to such belongs the kingdom of God. Truly, I say to you, whoever does not receive the kingdom of God like a child shall not enter it." And he took them in his arms and blessed them, laying his hands upon them.

It is the duty of those who present their children for baptism to confess the faith wherein they are to be baptized, and to promise to bring them up in that faith, and in the way of Christ and his Church.

Then, the parents or other sponsors standing, the minister shall say to them:
Do you present *this child* to be baptized, earnestly desiring that *he* may be grafted into Christ as a member of his body the Church?
Answer: I do.

Do you believe in one God, Father, Son, and Holy Spirit; and do you confess Jesus Christ as your Saviour and Lord?
Answer: I do.

Do you promise, depending on the grace of God, to teach *this child* the truths and duties of the christian faith; and by prayer and example to bring *him* up in the life and worship of the Church?
Answer: I do.

Then the minister shall say: The Lord bless you and your *child* and enable you faithfully to keep these promises.

Then, addressing the congregation, he shall say:
This sacrament lays solemn obligations upon you the people of God. Will you be faithful to your calling as members of the Church of Christ, so that *this child,* and all other children in your midst, may grow up in the knowledge and love of Christ? In acceptance of this responsibility, let all stand.

The minister shall then say:
Let us confess the faith. (The Apostles' Creed)

Then the minister shall call the people to prayer, saying: Lift up your hearts.
We lift them up unto the Lord.
Blessed art thou, O God the Father, Creator of all things.
Blessed art thou, O Lord Jesus Christ, Son of God, baptized in Jordan, crucified at Calvary, risen and glorified.
Blessed art thou, O Holy Spirit of God, Lord and Giver of Life.

Send forth thy Holy Spirit, O God, to sanctify us all and to bless this water that *this child* may be born anew of water and the Holy Spirit. Grant that *he* may rise with Christ into newness of life and remain for ever in the number of thy chosen people; through Jesus Christ our Lord. Amen.

Then the parent, or other sponsor, presenting the child at the font (the congregation standing) shall give the child's name to the minister: and the minister, who may then take the child into his arms, shall call him *by* his *christian name or names and shall pour or sprinkle water on* his *head, saying:*

N.... I baptize you in the name of the Father, and of the Son, and of the Holy Spirit. Amen.

The blessing of God Almighty, Father, Son, and Holy Spirit, descend upon you, and dwell in your heart for ever. Amen.

This formula and blessing shall be repeated for each child.

Then may be said or sung: The Lord bless you and keep you; the Lord make his face to shine upon you, and be gracious unto you; the Lord lift up his countenance upon you, and give you peace. Amen.

Thereafter the minister, using the Christian name(s) and surname of each child baptized, shall say: According to Christ's commandment N.... M.... *is* now received into the membership of the one, holy, catholic and apostolic Church, and *is* engaged to confess the faith of Christ crucified, and to be his faithful soldier and servant unto *his* life's end.
(Here may be read: Matthew 18:5,6 and 10).

After which the minister shall say: Let us pray.

O God our heavenly Father, whose Son Jesus Christ took little ones into his arms and blessed them: we give thee thanks that thou hast received *this child* into thy Church and sealed *him* as thine own. Grant that *he,* being grafted into Christ, the true vine, may abide in him for ever, growing in wisdom as in stature, and in favour with God and man. Lead *him* through the perils of this earthly life, and bring *him* in due time to thy holy table to receive the communion of the body and blood of Christ, that by grace *he* may witness a good confession, and persevere therein to the end; through Jesus Christ our Lord. Amen.

Almighty God, we thank thee for thy love and mercy to *this mother* whom thou hast delivered to rejoice over *her* little *one.* Hallow the *home* enriched by the birth of *this child.* Grant thy help to the parents that in gratitude and faith they may order their family life in the way of thy commandments, serving one another in love; through Jesus Christ our Lord. Amen.

Most merciful God, in whose Church there is but one Lord, one faith, and one baptism, grant us grace ever to acknowledge the lordship of thy Son Jesus Christ, to confess with our whole lives the one true faith, and to dwell in love and unity with all who have been baptized into his name; through the same Jesus Christ thy Son our Lord, who taught his Church ever to pray and say:
Our Father...

Then may be sung a hymn or doxology.
Benediction.

THE WALDENSIAN CHURCH

The baptism of children (1934)

As the parents stand with the child in the place assigned to them by the usage of the particular church, the minister says: Brother N.N. (or the husband and wife N.N. or Sister N.N.) present their son (or daughter) for baptism as commanded by our Lord Jesus Christ. Let us welcome them with Christian joy and let us encompass him(her) with our prayers that the Lord be pleased to accept this little lamb into his flock.

You, who present your child, must understand the full meaning of baptism, as instituted by our Lord when he said to his disciples: "Go therefore, and make disciples of all nations, baptizing them in the name of the Father, and of the Son, and of the Holy Spirit" (Matt. 28:19).

Baptism is the token of entry into the Christian Church.

For the eternal salvation of your child, you must not place your confidence in the external aspects of a ceremony, but rather in the grace of God which this sacrament represents.

You must know that it is only baptism with the Spirit of God which gives new birth and salvation and, as water cleanses the body, cleanses our souls of sin and gives them a new life. Therefore, in asking today that your child be baptized, you affirm that neither for him(her) nor for you, is there any salvation except in Jesus Christ; that you entrust him/her to the mercy of the Heavenly Father who has summoned us to eternal life; that you dedicate him/her to the Saviour who, taking the little children into his arms and blessing them, promised that our children, together with us, would be kept by the love of God and under the guidance of his Spirit: finally, that you solemnly promise to give him/her a Christian education, until the day comes for him/her to confirm his/her baptism by public confession of his/her own personal faith.

Brothers and Sisters, it is for all of us, who belong to the family of God, to strive toward the unimpeded development of this work of grace in the little children, surrounding them with good example, sound instruction and earnest prayers. These sacred duties, however, are the special responsibilities of you, who present this child for Holy Baptism. Do you therefore, promise to pray for him/her unceasingly, to ensure that he/she is instructed in the Christian truth embodied in the Holy Scriptures, and to guide him/her by your example into a life of faith and obedience to the Commandments of God?

Answer: Yes.

Minister: May God help you to keep your promise.

Let us pray: O God our Heavenly Father: Whereas in your infinite goodness you have promised to be our Lord and the Lord of our children, we beseech you to fulfill this promise for the child we present to you today. We dedicate him/her to you, O Lord, Father, Son and Holy Spirit. Take him/her under your protection and receive him/her into your holy company. We baptize him/her with water. Baptize him/her, we pray, with the Holy Spirit, so that he/she may be cleansed of sin and become a new being in your image.

Reveal yourself to him/her as our Father and Saviour in Christ, that he/she may, by your grace, live in this world as one of your children and one day take his/her place in the kingdom of heaven.

Bless us, O Lord, together with those who present this child for Holy Baptism and all the members of his/her family, so that they may faithfully discharge their duty toward the creature you have entrusted to their care. Give to all of us the grace of belonging to you, now and for ever more. Grant this to us in the name of Jesus. Amen.

The Minister approaches the one to be baptized and having asked the father (or the one acting in his place) for the name, sprinkles water on the child's head and says: N.N., I baptize you in the name of the Father, of the Son and of the Holy Spirit.

The Minister adds: Lord bless this child and let him/her grow in wisdom, in stature and in grace, before God and man.

The Minister returns to his place to proceed with the service and the parents withdraw with the child.

The baptism of adults (1934)

As the candidate (or candidates) for baptism stand in the assigned place, the Minister says: The brother N.N. (or the brothers N.N....), having been examined by the Church Council as to his (their) faith, presents himself (themselves) to be baptized, as commanded by our Lord Jesus Christ and to be received into our communion. Let us welcome him(them) with Christian affection, and let us pray that it may be the pleasure of the Lord to accept him(them) into his Church.

Our Lord Jesus Christ, before ascending into heaven, told his disciples, "Go therefore, and make disciples of all nations, baptizing them in the name of the Father, and of the Son and of the Holy Spirit, teaching them to observe all that I have commanded you." Thus it is the will of God that those who have learned and accepted the gospel with faith shall receive baptism, which is a sign of their regeneration and the mark of God's grace.

This holy rite is a reminder to us that all human beings are stained by sin from the moment of birth and that our souls can be purified and regenerated only by the grace of God, symbolized by water, grace which has its source in the love of the Father, assured to us by the death and resurrection of the Son and communicated to us through the Holy Spirit.

To all who repent and believe in the Lord Jesus Christ, baptism, in addition to being a symbol, is also a token and a mark of the grace of God. Through it, the believing soul gains the certainty of pardon for one's own sins and joins the company of those whom the Lord Jesus redeemed with his blood.

So it is that you who ask to be baptized, declare before God and before his Church that you believe in God the Father, who has loved us, in his Son Jesus Christ who sacrificed himself for our salvation and in the Holy Spirit who regenerates and sanctifies us. You assert your desire to renounce the world and renounce sin and to dedicate yourself to God by obeying his commandments to your life's end.

You also promise diligently to use the means of grace which God has granted you to nurture and strengthen the Christian lives of your children.

Are these not the things which you declare and promise?

Response: Yes.

Minister: May God hear you and help you to keep your promises faithfully for all time.

Let us pray: All powerful and most merciful God, we thank you for having led this brother to knowledge of you and to faith in your Son Jesus Christ. While, in obedience to your commandment, we baptize him with water that he may be dedicated to you, do you, O Lord, we pray baptize him with your Spirit and fill his soul with the joyful assurance that his sins are forgiven and that You have received him, through the action of Jesus Christ, as one of your children. Grant him the grace to grow every day in his knowledge of the truth, in faith, in sanctity and in love for you and for his fellow human beings. Give him the strength to conquer temptation and overcome his weaknesses, comfort him in his afflictions and persecutions, help him to persevere to the end of his days, so that after he has glorified you on earth he may be received and be near you in glory, through our eternally blessed Saviour Jesus Christ. Amen.

The Minister approaches the candidate, who kneels. The Minister sprinkles water on his head and says: N.N., I baptize you in the name of the Father, of the Son and of the Holy Spirit. Amen.

May the Lord bless and keep you. May the Lord be your light and your strength, now and forever. Amen.

We now extend the hand of fellowship to you, recognizing you as a member of this Church and recalling to you the exhortation of Jesus Christ: "Be faithful unto death and I will give you the crown of life" (Rev. 2:10).

7. THE METHODIST TRADITION

The following Methodist liturgy was authorized for use by the Methodist Conference in 1975 (*The Methodist Service Book,* Methodist Publishing House, 1975). The ceremony itself could be said to represent the common core of almost all we here present (note, however, the *congregation's* promises!)—but it should be kept in mind that often Methodist churches have established a "Reception to Full Membership" ("commonly called Confirmation") for those who have been baptized and given Christian education, so that only after such reception can one properly speak of "membership of the Church" in the full sense of the word.

In the USA the United Methodist Church, in its "alternate text" for *Baptism, Confirmation and Renewal* (1976), sees Confirmation as the first of a possible series of "reaffirmations" of baptism which may take place in the life of an individual or congregation, or when a person joins the Methodist Church from another denomination. We print below an extract from the explanatory "introduction", then the rite itself in its relation to baptism, and finally the provided "commentary". With varying details, the Lutheran *Book of Worship* (1978) and the Episcopal *Book of Common Prayer* (1979) also present "Confirmation" as a special case among a broader category of (re)affirmations of baptism.

BRITISH METHODIST CONFERENCE

The baptism of infants (1975)

The preparation

The Lord's Prayer, if it is not to be said later

Any part of the Preparation of the Sunday Service

The Collect of the Day, or some other prayer, or this Collect:

Heavenly Father, we thank you that in every generation you give new sons and daughters to your Church, and we pray that *this child,* now to be received by baptism, may know you better and love you more day by day, through Jesus Christ your Son our Lord. Amen.

The ministry of the word

An Old Testament Lesson or an Epistle may be read here.

A Sermon may be preached here.

These passages from the Gospels are read, or two of them may be read here and one later: Mark 1:9-11, Mark 10:13-16, Matt. 28:18-20

The Minister says: Thus the children of Christian parents are brought to be baptized with water as a sign of the new life in Christ, and to be made members of God's family the Church. We bring *this child* whom God has entrusted to us and claim for *him* all that Christ has won for us. Christ loves *him* and is ready to receive *him,* to embrace *him* with the arms of his mercy and to give *him* the blessing of eternal life.

The baptismal prayer

The Minister at the Font and the people, all standing, say: Father, we thank you that you have created all things and made us in your own image;

That after we had fallen into sin you did not leave us in darkness, but sent your only Son Jesus Christ to be our Saviour;

That by his death and resurrection he broke the power of evil;

And that by sending the Holy Spirit you have made us a new creation.

The Minister says: Father, be present with us in the power of your Spirit.

We pray that *this child,* now to be baptized in this water, may die to sin and be raised to the new life in Christ. Amen.

We pray that *he* may learn to trust Jesus Christ as *his* Lord and Saviour. Amen.

We pray that by the power of the Holy Spirit *he* may have victory over evil. Amen.

From darkness lead *him* to light, from death lead *him* to eternal life, through Jesus Christ our Lord. Amen.

The promises and the profession of faith

The Minister says to the congregation: Members of the Body of Christ, who are now in his name to receive *this child,* will you so maintain the common life of worship and service that *he* and all the children among you may grow in grace and in the knowledge and love of God and of his Son Jesus Christ our Lord?

Answer: With God's help we will.

The Minister says to the parents or guardians of the child: You have brought *this child* to be baptized, and you will receive *him* again to be trained in the doctrines, privileges and duties of the Christian religion. I ask you therefore: Will you provide for *this your child* a Christian home of love and faithfulness?

Answer: With God's help we will.

Minister: Will you help *him* by your words, prayers and example to renounce all evil and to put *his* trust in Jesus Christ *his* Saviour?

Answer: With God's help we will.

Minister: Will you encourage *him* to enter into the full membership of the Church, and to serve Christ in the world?

Answer: With God's help we will.

If there are sponsors, the Minister says: Will you, who have come to support these parents, help them in the Christian upbringing of *this child?*

Answer: With God's help we will.

The Minister says: Let us confess the faith of the Church:

All say EITHER *the Apostles' Creed:*

OR

We believe in God the Father, who made the world; And in his Son, Jesus Christ, who redeemed mankind; And in the Holy Spirit, who sanctifies the People of God. Amen.

Then the Minister says to the parents of guardians: Do you then present *this your child* to be baptized?

Answer: We do.

The baptism

The Minister, taking each child into his arms, says to the parents or guardians: Name this child; *and, naming him accordingly, pours or sprinkles water upon him, or dips him in water, saying:* N., I baptize you in the Name of the Father, and of the Son, and of the Holy Spirit. Amen.

The Minister, making the sign of the cross on the forehead of the child, says: By baptism we receive this child into the congregation of Christ's flock, and pray that *he* may not be ashamed to hold fast the faith of Christ crucified, to fight against evil, and to persevere as Christ's faithful soldier and servant to *his* life's end. Amen.

All say or sing: The Lord bless you and keep you; the Lord make his face to shine upon you, and be gracious unto you; the Lord lift up his countenance upon you, and give you peace. Amen.

The Minister, or the Baptismal Roll Secretary, may give to the parents or guardians of the child a lighted candle, saying to the child: I give you this sign, for you now belong to Christ, the light of the world. Let your light so shine before men, that they may see your good works and give glory to your Father who is in heaven.

The final prayers

EITHER *the Minister says:* Let us pray.

Father, we thank you that you have received *this child* to be your own within your family the Church.

May *he* grow in the faith in which *he* has been baptized and come to profess that faith before men. Amen.

Bless the *home* of *this child* and give wisdom and affection to *his* parents that they may lead *him* in the way of perfect love. Amen.

Strengthen your Church in the Holy Spirit that, through our worship and ministry to the world, *this child* may learn to follow Christ. Amen.

OR *he* prays in *his* own words.

The Minister, whether proceeding with the service of public worship or dismissing the people, says: The grace of the Lord Jesus Christ, and the love of God, and the fellowship of the Holy Spirit, be with us all. Amen.

At the main service of public worship further lessons are read and the sermon is preached if they have not come earlier; and the service then proceeds as it usually does after the sermon. The intercessions may be shortened or omitted, and the Creed is not said again.

UNITED METHODIST CHURCH

Baptism, confirmation and renewal (1976)

Introduction [extract]

While the first act of renewal by those baptized in infancy is extremely important, its importance should not blind us to the need for reaffirmation at other times. For although God does not forget his promises to us, we do tend to forget them; and in times of stress we may doubt the truth of his promises even if we do not forget their existence. Furthermore, we frequently neglect the obligations placed upon us in the baptismal covenant. For these reasons it is appropriate for every Christian to renew the baptismal covenant from time to time.

For the sake of clarity and tradition, the term "confirmation" should be reserved for the first renewal of the baptismal faith made by those who received the sacrament during infancy or childhood. To this historic rite, however, two other categories should be added: special renewal (on the part of specific individuals) and general renewal (by the entire worshipping assembly of baptized persons).

The rite [extract]

Administration of water baptism and laying on of hands

As the water is administered, the minister says: (Name), I baptize you in the name of the Father and of the Son and of the Holy Spirit. *Amen.*

As hands are placed on the heads of those receiving baptism, the minister says: The power of the Holy Spirit work within you, that being born of water and the Spirit you may be a faithful witness of Jesus Christ. *Amen.*

When all candidates have been baptized, the minister says to them: Through baptism you are incorporated into Christ's New Creation by the power of the Holy Spirit and share in Christ's royal priesthood. With joy and thanksgiving we welcome you as *members* of the universal Body of Christ.

Confirmation and other renewal of the baptismal covenant

As the minister says the following words, water may be sprinkled towards all persons being confirmed or making other renewal of their baptismal faith: Remember your baptism and be thankful. *Amen.*

As hands are placed upon the head of each person separately, the minister says to each: (Name), the power of the Holy Spirit work within you, that having been born of water and the Spirit, you may continue to be a faithful witness of Jesus Christ. *Amen.*

Profession or renewal of full membership in the United Methodist Church

The minister asks those coming into full membership in this congregation of the United Methodist Church: As *members* of Christ's universal Church, will you be loyal to the United Methodist Church, participating in its mission by your prayers, your presence, your gifts, and your service; and as *members* of this congregation, will you do all in your power to effect fellowship and ministry in this community?

I will.

Commentary [extract]

Confirmation and other renewal of the baptismal covenant

The words "Remember your baptism and be thankful" are used whenever confirmation or other baptismal renewal is desired, whether on the part of individuals or of the entire congregation. Use of water is not mandatory; when water is used the quantity should be small, as this act is intended only as a reminder of baptism and ought not create the impression of being "rebaptism." For the same reason, the rubric indicates that water should "be sprinkled towards" those making renewal, not directly upon their heads as would be the case in baptism by sprinkling.

The placing of hands upon the head of each person separately, with the words *"(Name),* the power of the Holy Spirit work within you,..." is done only when there are individuals presenting themselves for confirmation or other renewal. These words are similar to those used after baptism, but the differences which do exist between the two indicate an important theological understanding: baptism is the beginning which cannot be repeated; in renewal God continues that which was begun in the sacrament itself.

Profession or renewal of full membership in the United Methodist Church

This is used with youths or adults just baptized or confirmed, or with those joining a congregation from another denomination. It may be used in other renewals as well.

8. THE BAPTIST TRADITION

The first text is from *Orders and Prayers for Church Worship: A Manual for Ministers,* compiled by Ernest A. Payne and Stephen F. Winward, 1960.

The second and the third are from *Praise God: a Collection of Material for Christian Worship* compiled by Alec Gilmore, Edward Smalley and Michael Walker, Baptist Union, London, 1980. The last text was provided by Principal Morris West of Bristol Baptist College.

THE BAPTISM OF BELIEVERS (1960)

Baptism should be administered in the presence of the Congregation during Public Worship.

Since we are baptized into the Church, it is desirable that Baptism should, if possible, be followed by the Lord's Supper, at which the reception of the new members should take place.

After the singing of a Baptismal Hymn, the Minister may read a selection from the following passages of Scripture.

Then Jesus came from Galilee to the Jordan to John, ... (Matt. 3:13–17, RSV)

(At this point the Service includes the following passages, the texts of which are given in full:)

Luke 3:21–2; John 3:5–8; Acts 2:38, 41–2; Acts 22:16; Romans 6:3–4; Romans 10:9–11; 1 Corinthians 12:12–13; Galatians 3:26–8; Colossians 2:12; 1 Timothy 6:12; 1 Peter 3:21–2.

(The following additional passages are also suitable, especially for the main New Testament Lesson during the service: Mark 1:1–13; Acts 8:26–40; Acts 9:1–19; Acts 10:34–48; Acts 16:11–15; Acts 16:16–34; Acts 19:1–7; Ephesians 4:1–6; Ephesians 5:21–33; Colossians 3:1–17; Titus 3:4–7; Hebrews 10:19–25; 1 John 5:6–12.)

The Minister may conclude the selected readings as follows: Jesus came and said to them, ... (Matt. 28:18–20, RSV)

The Minister may then say: Beloved brethren: You have just heard how our Lord Jesus Christ after his glorious resurrection and before his ascension into heaven, commanded his apostles to make disciples of all nations, baptizing them in the name of the Father, and of the Son, and of the Holy Spirit.

The Baptist Tradition

Let us now set forth the great benefits which we are to receive from the Lord, according to his word and promise, in this holy sacrament.

In baptism we are united with Christ through faith, dying with him unto sin and rising with him unto newness of life.

The washing of our bodies with water is the outward and visible sign of the cleansing of our souls from sin through the sacrifice of our Saviour.

The Holy Spirit, the Lord and giver of life, by whose unseen operation we have already been brought to repentance and faith, is given and sealed to us in this sacrament of grace.

By this same Holy Spirit, we are baptized into one body and made members of the holy catholic and apostolic Church, the blessed company of all Christ's faithful people.

These great benefits are promised and pledged to those who profess repentance toward God and faith in our Lord Jesus Christ. For all such believers, baptism is:

An act of obedience to the command of our Lord Jesus Christ:

A following of the example of our Lord Jesus Christ who was baptized in the river Jordan, that he might fulfill all righteousness:

A public confession of personal faith in Jesus Christ as Saviour and Lord:

A vow or pledge of allegiance to Jesus Christ, an engagement to be his for ever.

Addressing those who are to be baptized, the Minister shall say: Forasmuch as you now present yourselves for Baptism, it is necessary that you sincerely give answer, before God and his Church, to the questions which I now put to you.

Then shall he say to each person to be baptized: Do you make profession of repentance toward God and of faith in our Lord Jesus Christ?

Answer: I do.

Do you promise, in dependence on divine grace, to follow Christ and serve him for ever in the fellowship of his Church?

Answer: I do.

Then shall follow the Prayer: Almighty and everlasting God, we give thee humble and hearty thanks for our Saviour Jesus Christ, who died for our sins, was buried, and was raised on the third day. Graciously accept, we beseech thee, these thy servants, that they, coming to thee in baptism, may by faith be united with Christ in his Church, and receive according to thy promise the forgiveness of their sins, and the gift of the Holy Spirit. Grant that they, putting on the Lord Jesus Christ, may receive out of his fullness and evermore abide in him. Keep them strong in faith, steadfast in hope, abounding in love. Bestow upon them the manifold gifts of thy grace, that they may serve thee profitably in thy Church. Defend them in all trials and temptations, and grant that, persevering to the end, they may inherit eternal life; through Jesus Christ our Lord. Amen.

As each person to be baptized stands in the water, the Minister shall pronounce his or her names, and say: On thy profession of repentance toward God and faith in our Lord Jesus Christ, I baptize thee in the name of the Father and of the Son and of the Holy Spirit. Amen.

After each baptism the Minister may say: The Lord bless thee and keep thee: the Lord make his face to shine upon thee, and be gracious unto thee. The Lord lift up his countenance upon thee and give thee peace.

Alternatively, the Choir and Congregation may sing after each Baptism, or at the conclusion of the Baptisms, one of the Baptismal Sentences from the Hymn Book, or the verse of a hymn or the Doxology.

After the Baptisms, one of the following prayers may be offered: Eternal Father, keep, we beseech thee, thy servants from falling, and present them faultless before the presence of thy glory with exceeding joy: and unto thee, the only wise God our Saviour, be glory and majesty, dominion and power, both now and for ever. Amen.

Teach them, good Lord, to serve thee with loyal and steadfast hearts; to give and not to count the cost; to fight and not to heed the wounds; to strive and not to seek for rest; to labour and to ask for no reward, save that of knowing that they do thy will; through Jesus Christ our Lord. Amen.

Grant, O Lord, that as we are baptized into the death of thy Son our Saviour Jesus Christ, so by continual mortifying our corrupt affections we may be buried with him; and that through the grave, and gate of death, we may pass to our joyful resurrection; for his merits, who died, and was buried, and rose again for us, thy Son Jesus Christ our Lord. Amen.

O God of hope, fill them with all joy and peace in believing, so that by the power of the Holy Spirit they may abound in hope: through Jesus Christ our Lord. Amen.

O God of peace, who broughtest again from the dead our Lord Jesus, the great shepherd of the sheep, by the blood of the eternal covenant, equip them with everything good that they may do thy will, and work in them that which is pleasing in thy sight: through Jesus Christ, to whom be glory for ever and ever. Amen.

If desired, a Hymn may now follow, and the normal order of public worship be continued. If it be the end of the service, the Minister may say: Go forth into the world in peace; be of good courage; hold fast that which is good; render to no man evil for evil; strengthen the faint-hearted; support the weak; help the afflicted; honour all men; love and serve the Lord, rejoicing in the power of the Holy Spirit. Amen.

OR

May God Almighty, the Father of our Lord Jesus Christ, grant you to be strengthened with power through his Spirit in the inward man; that Christ may dwell in your hearts through faith, and that you may be filled unto all the fullness of God. Amen.

OR

The grace of the Lord Jesus Christ, and the love of God, and the fellowship of the Holy Spirit, be with you all. Amen.

CHRISTIAN INITIATION (1980)

Among Baptists of late there has been a growing tendency to bring closer together the act of baptism, reception into membership and admission to communion. In other branches of the church at the same time there has been a tendency to see the wholeness of Christian initiation in terms of strengthening the links between baptism, confession of faith (or confirmation) and communion.

One result of this theological discussion for Baptists is that the act of baptism as a confession of faith is increasingly seen as part of a larger act of initiation which often then finds expression in one service of baptism and communion.

The practice however is by no means universal, many ministers and churches preferring to separate baptism and reception into membership either by several hours on the same day or perhaps even by several weeks. Those who wish to do this should have no difficulty in taking what is outlined below and dividing it to suit their purposes.

In either case, however, we see five essential elements in the whole process of Christian initiation which should find expression in the worship whether it is in one service or in two. They are:

1. Reading of scripture (including the gospel) and our reasons for engaging in Christian initiation, including the fact that baptism bears witness to what God has done and continues to do, and that our act of baptism is our response to that love.

2. Profession of faith and commitment.

3. Prayers, including a prayer for God's action in the Spirit that those who are baptized may become children of God, entering into newness of life in Christ, becoming part of his body and sharing his Spirit.

4. Baptism in the name of the Trinity, possibly with the laying on of hands.

5. Reception into membership and admission to communion.

Order of service

The preparation

Call to Worship. Hymn. Prayer of confession and assurance of forgiveness. Responsive Reading

The Word

Reading of Scripture. Hymn. Sermon

The response

Statement of belief concerning Christian initiation including gospel reading. Baptismal hymn. Act of Baptism. Invitation to Baptism. Offering. Prayers of Intercession

The communion

Hymn

Reception into membership. Presentation of gifts, including bread and wine. Prayer of Thanksgiving. Words of institution (including the breaking of the bread and the raising of the cup). Sharing of bread and wine. Silence, followed by the Lord's Prayer. Hymn

Dismissal

Some ministers may prefer to celebrate baptism at the beginning of the service, using the sermon as an opportunity to give a charge to the newly-baptized.

Statement

Let us now recall what we understand concerning the benefits promised by our Lord to those who receive believers' baptism and become members of his Church.

In baptism we become one with Christ through faith, sharing with him in his death and resurrection, and the washing of our bodies with water is a sign of the cleansing of the whole of our life and personality.

In baptism we mark the receiving of the Holy Spirit who has brought us to the moment of commitment and who will strengthen us for future endeavour.

In sharing in this act we are obeying the commandments of our Lord, making confession of our personal faith in him, and becoming part of the one holy, catholic and apostolic church.

Minister (addressing each candidate in turn): Do you acknowledge Jesus Christ as your Saviour and Lord?

Candidate: I do.

Minister: Do you promise with the help of the Holy Spirit to serve him in the Church and in the world unto your life's end?

Candidate: I do.

Minister: A.B., upon a profession of your faith and at your own request I baptize you in the name of the Father, the Son and the Holy Spirit.

Since the act of baptism very often leads others to ask for baptism, once all the candidates are baptized the minister may then wish to invite those present who have not made this act of commitment either to come forward there and then (though not necessarily with a view to being baptized at that moment) or to meet him in the vestry afterwards.

Reception into membership

Where members are to be received in by the laying on of hands the minister may first address the congregation: The laying on of hands, as practised by the apostles, is an act of acceptance and commissioning. In accepting these candidates we pray for them, and we invite all of you to continue daily to pray for those who have accepted the claims of Jesus Christ on their lives. In commissioning them for service we both pray and believe that the Holy Spirit will strengthen them that they may fulfill their calling as servants of Jesus Christ.

As he lays hands on each candidate the minister may say: Bless, O Lord, this your servant. Strengthen *him* by the Holy Spirit, as we now in your name commission *him* for the service and ministry of Jesus Christ our Lord. Amen.

Ministers who do not wish to lay hands on candidates may use the same prayers and emphasis together with the right hand of fellowship.

When those being received have not been baptized as believers and have not otherwise made a public profession of faith, prior to offering the right hand of fellowship the minister may put to them the two questions normally put to candidates for baptism.

Candidates being received in by transfer from another Baptist church and those who are already full members of another branch of the church may be received in with the right hand of fellowship and the words: In the name of the Lord Jesus Christ, and on behalf of this congregation, I welcome you into membership of this church.

INFANT DEDICATION AND THANKSGIVING (1980)

Infant Dedication and Thanksgiving, more than most Christian ceremonies, admits of an infinite variety. In some cases it is a simple act of thanksgiving, in others it is an act of dedication on the part of the parents and in others it is thought of as an occasion of infant blessing.

To some the service is understood to relate only to children of Christian parents, to others it belongs to everybody. Some churches take it as an adjunct to the morning service and worshippers are asked to stay and share in it; others take it as the opening act of morning worship to emphasize the nature of the church as a family and the arrival of an infant as a family event.

In this book we do not try to reach conclusions on these major issues. Instead we seek to combine a variety of diverse elements, assuming that the user will select what expresses the emphasis he wishes to make. We do, however, suggest the following order of events:

    Reading of Scripture
    Statement about Infant Dedication
    Act of Dedication
    The Blessing
    Prayers of Thanksgiving and Hope
    The Lord's Prayer
    Hymn

Reading of Scripture

Ps. 8, Mark 10:13–16 or others

Statement about infant dedication

At this point the parents shall stand, holding the baby. Other children may stand around in token of welcome and may also hold lighted candles to signify the links between the child and the light of the world.

Here in scripture we see God's love and care for all human life and we read of God's will that all life shall belong to him. In the action of Jesus we see the readiness with which he receives children.

Therefore, following the will of God and the example of Jesus, we rejoice this morning to receive A.B. together with *his* parents into the fellowship of this church. We welcome them as Jesus welcomed the children and their mothers. We join with the parents in an act of thanksgiving for the new life which God has given them, and we bless him for a child born and brought into his house with thanksgiving.

We remember what God has already done for this child in Jesus Christ. We acknowledge his love and care for *him* from this day forward. And in faith we know that through the fellowship of the Church he is able to lead *him* to the fullness of life.

Thus, in receiving this child in this way we acknowledge *his* relationship with God expressed in fellowship with his church and our own responsibility to encourage and sustain this relationship until this child responds to his love in faith and baptism.

Act of dedication

Minister: Do you promise to be a good father and a loving mother to your child?

Parents: Yes, we do.

Minister: Do you also promise to bring up your child in the spirit of the gospel?

Parents: Yes, we do.

Minister: Do you also promise to remain faithful to your child, whatever the future may bring, and to respect *him,* wherever *he* may go, and to remember always that your child is born of God?

Parents: Yes, we do.

Minister: By what name do you wish your child to be called now and in eternal life?

Parents: A.B.

Minister: A.B. May this name be written for ever in the book of life, in the palm of God's hand.

The Minister shall ask those present to stand.

Minister: Do you also acknowledge that this child is born of God and do you promise that you will always stand by *him* in friendship?

All: Yes, we do.

The blessing

A.B., the Lord bless you and keep you, the Lord make his face to shine upon you and be gracious unto you; the Lord lift up his countenance upon you and give you peace.

The children may here lift up their candles and shout hurray.

Prayers of thanksgiving and hope, for example:
Lord God, our Father
you have given your Son, Jesus Christ, to us

as the good shepherd who knows us all by name.
We thank you for your grace and your faithfulness
for the new life that you have created
for this child who has been among us
and whom you have entrusted to us.
You have given *him* ears to hear with and eyes to see with.
Bless too this child's mouth
so that *he* may learn how to laugh
and to speak the language of men.
Bless also *his* hands and feet
and may *he* learn from *his* own experience
that everything you have made is good.
We ask you to shelter this child
and keep *him* safe in this rough world.
Keep everything that is bad and inhuman away from *him*,
protect *him* from evil influences
and never let *him* be perverted.
May *he* be secure with *his* parents
and may we who are mature and responsible
never give scandal to this child but lead *him* to the truth.
If, however, sin should ever have power over *him*
be merciful to *him*, Lord God—
you make good all human guilt and shortcomings
and are yourself, even before this child is able to sin,
the forgiveness of all sins through Jesus Christ, our Lord. Amen.

A BAPTIST SERVICE OF THANKSGIVING ON THE BIRTH OF A CHILD (1980)

This Service normally forms an integral part of morning Family Worship. It is always held when the whole church family is present in the worship.

The parents of the child, together with any other children of the family, sit at the front of the church together with a lay representative of the church membership.

The presiding minister welcomes the family and, as necessary, introduces them.

The minister reminds the congregation that the church is gathered together with the family to give thanks to God for the gift of the child, to take vows of responsibility towards the child and to ask for God's blessing on the child.

Verses of scripture are read, e.g. Deuteronomy 11:18-20 and Mark 10:13-16.

The parents then stand with the mother holding the child and the lay representative of the church stands alongside the family. The presiding minister then asks the following questions:

(In the questions the Christian name of the child is usually inserted, instead of the impersonal terms contained within the following questions.)

Q: Do you, the mother and father of this child, acknowledge with thanksgiving the goodness of God which has brought to you the gift of this son/daughter?

A: We do.

Q: Do you recognise the serious responsibility which comes to you with the gift, that it is your duty to teach him/her from his earliest years of Jesus Christ, that he she may be ready, when he/she reaches years of discretion, to offer his/her life in the service of that same Jesus Christ, who loves him/her and who gave his life for him/her?

A: We do.

Q: To this end, therefore, do you resolve, that guided by the Holy Spirit you will seek to fulfill this responsibility by so ordering your home, your words, your deeds, that this your child shall at all times be surrounded by holy living and Christlike example?

A: We do.

Q: To assist you in this high endeavour will you seek always and accept gladly the cooperation of this church and congregation both in your home and in the ongoing life of the Church?

A: We will.

The following questions are then addressed to the lay representative of the church:

Q: Do you, the representative of this church and congregation, pledge its support for the parents in their task?

A: I do.

Q: Does this church and congregation accept its share of the responsibility of bringing up this child to know Jesus Christ and to this end do the people here gathered undertake to pray for this home and to serve this child, in every way possible, for the sake of Jesus?

A: We do.

The congregation is then asked to stand whilst the minister takes the child in his arms and offers a prayer—usually the blessing from Numbers 6:24–26.

The minister returns the child to its parents (usually the father), the congregation is seated and further prayer is offered which is normally extemporary, but including always thanksgiving for the gift of the child, intercession for the parents, the home and any other children in the family, and asking God that the family and the church together may so fulfill the vows taken that the child may come ultimately to confession of faith in Christ in Believer's Baptism.

A suitable hymn is then sung.

9. UNITED CHURCHES

The following two examples of liturgies from united churches give an indication of different ways of solving the problem of a "united liturgy". The Church of South India Rites of 1962[15] in their emphasis on the promises to be given by parents, sponsors and congregation, recall the Reformed tradition, whereas the Methodist element is reflected in the "Service for the Reception of Baptized Persons into the Full Membership of the Church" which is to follow the baptism, and the *obsignatio crucis* reminds us of the Anglican tradition.

The 1962 liturgy of the United Church of Christ in the Philippines[16], on the other hand, may be regarded as something of a minimal liturgy, only containing the most essential elements in the constituent traditions[17].

THE CHURCH OF SOUTH INDIA

The baptism of infants (1962)

The declaration of the word

When the people are gathered at, or proceeding to, the place of baptism, a hymn may be sung, after which the minister says: Our help is in the name of the Lord:

R: Who hath made heaven and earth.

Let us pray.

Almighty God, thou Shepherd of Israel, who didst deliver thy chosen people from the bondage of Egypt, and didst establish with them a sure covenant: Have mercy, we beseech thee, on thy flock, and grant that *these children who are* by baptism to be received into thy heritage, may be delivered from the bondage of sin through thy covenant of grace, and attain the promise of eternal life which thou hast given us in thy Son our Saviour Jesus Christ; who

---

[15] *The Book of Common Worship,* London, 1963, authorized by the Synod in 1962 (reprint from P. Jagger, *Christian Initiation 1558–1969,* London, 1970, pp. 304–309).

[16] *The Book of Common Worship,* United Church of Christ in the Philippines, Quezon City, 1962, pp. 20–24.

[17] Presbyterian, Congregationalist, Disciples, Brethren, Methodist.

liveth and reigneth with thee and the Holy Spirit, ever one God, world without end. Amen.

The people may sit.

Dearly beloved, we are met together to administer holy baptism to *these children*, that, according to Christ's command, *they* may be sealed as *members* of Christ, *children* of God, and *heirs* of the kingdom of heaven.

Hear therefore the words of our Lord and Saviour Jesus Christ:

Go and make disciples of all nations, baptizing them in the name of the Father, and of the Son, and of the Holy Spirit. St Matthew 28:19

Truly, truly, I say to you, unless one is born of water and the Spirit, he cannot enter the kingdom of God. St John 3:5

Hear also what is written in the Gospel according to St Mark:

They were bringing children to him, ... St Mark 10:13–16

The minister expounds the teaching of Scripture concerning baptism in his own words.

Or he says: You hear in this Gospel the words of our Saviour Christ, when he commanded the children to be brought to him. You perceive how he took them in his arms and blessed them. Jesus Christ is the same yesterday and today and for ever. He loves *these children* and is ready to receive *them*, to embrace *them* with the arms of his mercy, and to give *them* the blessing of eternal life.

These little *children belong* with you to God. In Holy Baptism he establishes *them* in the family and household of faith, that *they* may grow up as *members* of Christ and *heirs* of the kingdom of heaven.

The profession of the faith

All stand. The minister says to the parents (and godparents): It is the duty of those who present *children* for baptism to make confession of the faith in which *they are* baptized and to promise to bring *them* up in the way of Christ.

Do you believe in one God, the Father, the Son, and the Holy Spirit?

The parents (and godparents) answer: I believe
Let us therefore profess our faith.

The Apostles' Creed is said or sung by all: I believe in God the Father almighty, ...

The promises

Will you, by God's help, provide a Christian home for this child and bring *him* up in the worship and teaching of the Church, that *he* may come to know Christ *his* saviour?

Answer: We will, God being our helper.

Will you so order your own lives that you do not cause this little one to stumble?

Answer: We will, God being our helper.

Will you encourage *him* later to be received into the full fellowship of the

Church by Confirmation; so that, established in faith by the Holy Spirit, *he* may partake of the Lord's Supper and go forth into the world to serve God faithfully in his Church?

Answer: We will, God being our helper.

The minister says to the congregation: Dearly beloved, will you be faithful to your calling as members of the Church of Christ, so that *these* and all other children in your midst may grow up in the knowledge and love of him?

The congregation answer: We will, God being our helper; and we welcome *them* into our fellowship.

The baptism

The minister says: Let us pray in silence for *the children* about to be baptized, that *they* may receive the fullness of God's grace.

The people may kneel.

Silence is kept for a space. Then the minister says: The Lord be with you:

R: And with thy spirit.

The minister prays in his own words.

Or the following litany is said or sung:

Blessed art thou, O Lord God, heavenly Father, who hast created all things and given us the element of water:

R: Blessed art thou, O Lord.

Blessed art thou, O Lord Jesus Christ, the only-begotten Son of God, who wast baptized in the Jordan and didst die and rise again:

R: Blessed art thou, O Lord.

Blessed art thou, O Lord, the Holy Spirit, who didst descend upon Jesus Christ and upon the Church:

R: Blessed art thou, O Lord.

Be present, O God, with us who call upon thy threefold name, and bless this water, that it may signify the washing away of sin, and that *those* baptized therein may be born again to eternal life:

R: Hear us, we beseech thee.

Grant *them* thy Holy Spirit, that *they* may be baptized into the one body, and ever remain in the number of thy faithful and elect people:

R: Hear us, we beseech thee.

Grant that, being united with Christ in his death and resurrection, *they* may die unto sin and live unto righteousness:

R: Hear us, we beseech thee.

Grant that *they* may put off the old man and become a new creation in Christ Jesus:

R: Hear us, we beseech thee.

From darkness lead *them* to light; from death lead *them* to everlasting life:

R: Hear us, we beseech thee.

All stand. The minister, having asked the Christian name, pours water upon each child, saying: N, I baptize thee in the name of the Father, and of the Son, and of the Holy Spirit. Amen.

The Minister says over each child baptized: We have received this child into the congregation of Christ's flock (+ and do sign *him* with the sign of the cross).

Then he says for all together: May *these children* never be ashamed to confess the faith of Christ crucified, but continue his faithful *servants* unto *their lives'* end. Amen.

Then may be said or sung: The Lord bless you and keep you: the Lord make his face to shine upon you, and be gracious to you: the Lord lift up his countenance upon you, and give you peace. Amen. Numbers 6:24-6

A hymn of praise is sung. A procession may be made from the place of baptism into the body of the church.

The light

The parents of the children baptized may be given lighted lamps or tapers. When they have received them, the minister says:

Let your light so shine before men, that they may see your good works:

R. And give glory to our Father who is in heaven. St Matthew 5:16

Or some other brief forms of words may be said.

The thanksgiving

The Minister says: Let us pray.

Our Father, who art in heaven,...

The minister says, or the minister and people say together: We yield thee hearty thanks, most merciful Father, that it has pleased thee to receive *these children* for thine own *children* by adoption and to incorporate *them* into thy holy Church. And we humbly beseech thee to grant that *they* may more and more show forth in *their lives* that which *they* now *are* by thy calling; so that, as *they are* made *partakers* of the death of thy Son, *they* may also be *partakers* of his resurrection, and finally, with all thy Church, inherit thine everlasting kingdom; through the same Jesus Christ our Lord. Amen.

The minister says: Almighty God our heavenly Father, whose blessed Son shared at Nazareth the life of an earthly home: Bless, we beseech thee, the *homes of these children,* and grant wisdom and understanding to all who have the care of *them,* that *they* may grow up in thy constant fear and love; through the same thy Son Jesus Christ our Lord. Amen.

A hymn may be sung, and the thank-offering is taken.

If baptism is administered otherwise than at the Lord's Supper or at Morning or Evening Worship, the minister dismisses those that are gathered together with this blessing: May God almighty, the Father of our Lord Jesus Christ, grant you to be strengthened with might through his Spirit in the inner man; that Christ may dwell in your hearts through faith, and that you may be filled with all the fullness of God. Amen.

UNITED CHURCH OF CHRIST IN THE PHILIPPINES

Sacrament of baptism for infants (1962)
The Pastor reads the Scripture

Deut. 6:4–7   Matt. 18:2–6
Ps. 103:17–18   Acts 2:39

Then the Pastor shall say: Dearly beloved, in performing this sacrament of baptism we give testimony to our faith that God our Father is also the Father of our children; that Jesus Christ who gave himself as a sacrifice for us also gave himself in love for our children. They belong, with us who believe, to the membership of the Church through the covenant made in Christ, and verified for us by God in this sacrament.... Our Lord Jesus said, "Let the children come to me, and do not hinder them, for to such belongs the kingdom of heaven. Who ever does not receive the kingdom of God as a little child, he shall not enter therein." And he took them up in his arms and put his hands upon them and blessed them.

Let us pray.

Most merciful God we thank thee for encouraging Christian parents to bring their children to thee with the faith that they receive the forgiveness of their sin and spiritual renewal through the gift of the Holy Spirit. We pray that this child be born again and that he (*these children*) become an heir (*heirs*) of everlasting salvation; through our Lord Jesus Christ, who liveth and reigneth with thee and the same Holy Spirit, now and forever. *Amen.*

Question: In bringing this child (*these children*) here to be baptized do you confess your faith in Jesus Christ as your Saviour and Lord?

Answer: I do.

Question: Do you accept for yourselves and for this child (*these children*) the covenant of God, being assured that the Heavenly Father loves this child (*these children*) and desires to deliver him (*them*) from sin and to live a life under the control of the Holy Spirit?

Answer: I do.

Question: Do you promise to provide for your child (*children*) instruction in prayer, in the teachings of the Bible, and in all other things which a Christian ought to know and believe for his soul's good?

Answer: I will, with God's help.

Question: Will you encourage him (*them*) when he is (*they are*) of proper age, to confirm in the house of God the faith you are now declaring?

Answer: I will so encourage him (*them*).

What is the Christian name of this child?

Then the pastor, taking the child in his arms, or leaving it in the arms of the parent, pronouncing the Christian name of the child, shall sprinkle or pour water upon the head of the child, saying:

_____, I baptize thee in the name of the Father, and of the Son, and of the Holy Spirit. Amen.

The blessing of God Almighty, Father, Son, and Holy Spirit, descend upon you and dwell in your heart forever. Amen.

Then the Pastor shall ask the Congregation to stand and shall say: This child is (*these children are*) now publicly received into the fellowship of Christ's flock; and you the people of this congregation in receiving this child (*these children*) promise with God's help also to be his (*her*) sponsor to the end that he (*she*) may confess Christ as his (*her*) Saviour and Lord and come at last to His eternal kingdom. Jesus said, "Whoever receives one such child in my name receives me."

Then the Pastor shall say: Let us pray.

Heavenly Father, grant this child (*these children*) as he grows (*they grow*) in years, may also grow in grace and knowledge of the Lord Jesus Christ, and grant that by the renewing influence of the Holy Spirit, he (*she*) may ever be a true child (*children*) of God, serving Thee faithfully all his (*her*) days, through Jesus Christ our Lord. Amen.

10. THE BRETHREN ("KIRCHE DER BÖHMISCHEN BRÜDER")

Another very concise, "basic" baptismal formula is that of the "Kirche der Böhmischen Brüder"[18]: note, however, the explicit mention of the presbyters' duties and the making of a promise on their part.

CHURCH OF THE CZECH BRETHREN

Order of baptism (1981)

Words of institution

Hear the words of the institution of baptism: Matthew 28:19f.

Brief declaration of the meaning of baptism

Baptismal confession of faith

Dear parents and sponsors, will you join with this congregation in confessing your faith in God, Father, Son and Holy Spirit, into which faith this child is to be baptized.

Let us confess our faith by saying together the Apostles' Creed which binds together Christians of all times and all churches:

The Apostles' Creed

Questions to the Parents and Sponsors: If it is your desire, dear parents and sponsors, that this child should be baptized, will you please respond: "It is."

Parents and sponsors respond: "It is."

If you are willing by your word and example in the life of the Church of Jesus Christ, to bring up this child in this faith and so to lead him(her) to his(her) Lord Jesus Christ, will you please respond: "The Holy Spirit helping me, I am."

Parents and sponsors respond: "The Holy Spirit helping me, I am."

Questions to the presbyters/church elders: By baptism this child will be incorporated into the fellowship of the Church of Jesus Christ for the whole of his(her) life. I now therefore put this question to the presbyters in the Church

---

[18] Typed copy sent to us by Prof. Smolik of Prague in August 1981.

of Christ in this congregation: Are you willing, as presbyters of this church, to welcome lovingly the child now to be baptized and, together with his(her) parents and sponsors, to shoulder the responsibility for his(her) Christian upbringing? If you are willing to do this, please respond: "The Holy Spirit helping us, we are."

The presbyters respond: "The Holy Spirit helping us, we are."

Prayer: O Lord Jesus Christ, risen from the dead and alive for evermore, receive this child as your own and grant that the sign of water may by the power of the Holy Spirit become the pledge of your love and faithfulness to this child.

Act of baptism

Post-baptismal prayer

Our Lord and Father in Jesus Christ: Thou art the Giver of life. We thank Thee that Thou dost once again remind us of this in the life of this child. In company with his(her) family we rejoice at his(her) birth and because Thou hast preserved his(her) mother in health. Grant, we beseech Thee, that the sign of baptism we have just witnessed may assure us anew of Thy faithfulness, we who have also been baptized. Renew our confidence that Thou art ever with us in this present life, and strengthen in us the hope of everlasting life. By Thy strong hand keep us in the convenant of holy baptism that we may continue always to confess joyfully and thankfully the name of Jesus Christ our Saviour and Risen Lord. Hear us as we pray together in the words which Thou hast taught us to pray: Our Father...

Blessing: Numbers 6:24–6

11. THE CHURCH OF CHRIST IN THAILAND

An emphasis similar to the Brethren's baptism is to be found in the following baptismal liturgy of the Church of Christ in Thailand[19], namely the promises made by parents, godparents and the whole congregation to take over responsibility in the candidate's Christian education, and to love and pray.

THE SACRAMENT OF BAPTISM OR RECEIVING THE COVENANT (1981) (FOR ADULTS OR CHILDREN)

(After the proclamation of God's Word in the sermon and the recital of the Apostles' Creed according to the tradition of the Church from the earliest times, *the Presider* shall say:)

Presider: Brothers and sisters, beloved in Jesus Christ, Jesus Christ commanded his apostles and after them the Church in all the world to preach the Gospel among all nations of the earth in order that they should be baptized, and to teach them to be obedient to his word. This ceremony is called a sacrament because it was commanded by Jesus Christ. For this reason we baptize those whom the Lord has called in this sacrament of baptism.

The sacrament of baptism has six meanings:

First, in baptism Jesus cleanses our hearts from sin, and gives us power to struggle and win the victory over the power of sin.

Second, in baptism we die with Jesus Christ and rise with him to receive life new and eternal.

Third, in baptism, the Holy Spirit enters our hearts to admonish, guide, and strengthen us for the service of God.

Fourth, in baptism we become parts of the people of God, members of the Body of Christ, the Church.

Fifth, in baptism we are anointed as servants of God in the world, and witnesses to God through our thoughts, words, and deeds.

Sixth, in baptism we proclaim and demonstrate our faith in the Lord and our trust in his promises to his people.

---

[19] Typed copy sent to us in August 1981, from the "Worship Book"—undated.

(The Presider shall put the following questions to the candidate for baptism, or to the parents who are presenting their child for baptism.)

Presider: Beloved, in the presence of the Lord and this congregation, you are to answer faithfully the following questions. Do you believe and trust in one Lord who has revealed himself as the Father, Creator of all things, as the Son born as the human being Jesus Christ, and as the Holy Spirit, the Giver of life?

Candidate (or parents): I do.

Presider: Do you desire to receive (or do you wish your child to receive) baptism in the name of Jesus Christ according to the meanings previously stated?

Candidate (or parents): I do.

(The congregation will stand to respond to the question addressed to them.)

Presider: I now address the officers and members of this congregation. Jesus Christ wills that his Church should teach everyone who is baptized in his name. Do you as members promise to teach these new disciples, and your children and grandchildren to understand God's word, to love and pray for them, and help them to be faithful followers of Jesus Christ unto the end.

Congregation: We do so promise.

Let us pray. Almighty God, we thank you for your steadfast love promised to us in this sacrament, and for our hope in you. As we baptize with water, be pleased to baptize with the Holy Spirit, so that what we do may be confirmed as your own work, and what we say as your word, to the end that we may all be united with Jesus Christ by faith, and live a life depending solely on his grace.

Congregation (continuing in prayer): O Lord, who has called us from death to new life, we commit our lives to you, and with the Church universal, praise you for the love by which you have given us this new life, in the name of Jesus Christ our Lord. Amen. (Water shall be used to anoint the head of the candidate.)

Presider: N——————————, I baptize you in the name of the Father, and the Son, and the Holy Spirit. You are now within the covenant of God. Amen.

(When all candidates have been baptized, the Presider shall say the following words, and the following or other prayer.)

Presider: This child of God is a member of the Holy Catholic Church. "See what love the Father has given us, that we should be called children of God; and so we are" (I John 3:1). Let us pray: God of grace, we beseech you on behalf of your child, to keep him/her, direct him/her in the course of life, and give him/her a strong faith that he/she may grow in spirit and the knowledge of Jesus Christ depending on his grace throughout the whole of life. Amen.

(In the baptism of a child the following prayer may be used) Lord, we beseech you on behalf of your servants N—————— and N——————————— who have given their child to you in baptism, that they may love their child with your love, teach him/her in your truth, and guide him/her in the way of our Lord. Amen.

Congregation (continuing in prayer): O Lord, help us to recall the promises we received in our own baptism, to renew our faith and trust in you. Give us, we pray, strength to obey you. Constrain us with your Word that we may serve you faithfully for the sake of your name. Amen.

12. THE CHURCH OF THE LORD (ALADURA CHURCH, NIGERIA)

1. Naming service

The naming service is unique. It contains some parts of the Anglican Infant Baptism (Book of Common Prayer, 1662): consecration, taking and naming the child, sprinkling, sign of the cross, prayer. Aladura Church rejects infant baptism but has an extensive interest in children, naming and blessing them in church[20].

Jehova's command
Praise and prayer
Psalms
Selection of three to pray for the child
Lesson, message
Water poured into basin
Consecration of water
"Name this child"
"We name it in the Name of the Father....", sprinkling water on head
Obsignatio crucis
Laying on of hands
Presentation of palm leaves
Songs
Hymn
Refreshments

2. Churching of mother and child

(close to the Anglican Book of Common Prayer, adding a blessing and dedication of the child)

---

[20] We reproduce here *African Independent Church:* The life and Faith of the Church of the Lord (Aladura) by H.W. Turner, Clarendon Press, Oxford, 1967, pp. 182–199.

3. Adult baptism
   (for those older than 18)

Name
Abrenuntiatio diaboli
Interrogatio
Promises of a holy life

Baptism in flowing water, three times immersion. Triune Formula. Prayer of intercession

What is your name?

R: My name is...

In thy confession, dost thou promise to renounce the devil and his works, adultery, fornication, and all the carnal desires of the flesh, and the vain pomp and glory of the world, pride, strife, quarrel, hatred, blasphemy, malice, anger, and all obscene word, trust in man, and belief in the use of juju, medicine of all kinds for thy need and cure?

R: I renounce them all.

Dost thou believe in God the Father Almighty, Maker of everything, Heaven and earth? and dost thou believe in Jesus Christ thy Saviour and thy Redeemer, and dost thou believe in the Holy Ghost which sanctifieth and abideth with us forever and ever?

R: All these I steadfastly believe.

Wilt thou walk uprightly and steadfastly in, and abide by the Rules and Regulations of the Church of the Lord, and wilt thou trust in the Lord alone? through prayer, in times of sickness and infirmity, in times of various temptations and tribulations, in times of need, and wilt thou remain steadfast and firm, through thy life, in use of the Holy Water (water of life) which was given to the Holy Oshitelu, unto everyone that turns unto Him; and dost thou believe that God has truly sent this His servant as His Harbinger, yea as the last Elijah, to prepare the way of the Lord?

R: Yea, all these I steadfastly believe, and promise to do, God helping me.

Priest: I baptize thee in the Name of the Father, and of the Son, and of the Holy Ghost. Amen. (Immersion in the water three times.)

The rite involves a threefold immersion in moving or "living" water, such as flowing river or the sea, although where these are not within reach any water deep enough, such as a reservoir, will serve; in the dry season there are many places where baptisms will not be held at all. This emphasis on immersion is another common aladura departure from the baptismal practices of the older churches, where sprinkling is the usual method; whether baptism be interpreted as a cleansing or as sharing in the dying and rising of Christ, the symbolism is more vivid and complete, and the ceremony is a more memorable event in the life of the worshipper.

Then the person being baptized shall be prayed for, for steadfastness, and free from the bondage of Satan, and that he may be overshadowed by the Holy Ghost to have a true rebirth into newness of life.

The baptismal service having been held some distance away from the church, a need has been felt for a service at the church itself where the practical business of entering the name of the new member in the church register, and receiving his first tithes, can be attended to. It seems that the "Process of Membership Enrolment" developed for this purpose is Adejobi's own contribution and is not in general use.

The following is an outline of the service:

1. Private preparation in fasting, prayer, and confession to God for three or seven days.

2. After ordinary service the candidate gathers with the minister and church officers on the mercy ground; there he rolls seven or twenty-one times, makes public confession of his sins, and receives prayers for forgiveness from the officers.

3. Water having been blessed with Psalm 24 the candidate is sprinkled by the minister for cleansing, given seven palm leaves for victory, and further prayers.

4. Some holy water is then drunk.

5. The new member is led into the church, where his name is added to the church register and he pays his church tithes or dues.

6. Further fasting during the next three to twenty-one days, with prayers morning and evening from the minister and church officers.

We note here the sprinkling and the giving of palm leaves found in several of the other rites of the Church, and a greater emphasis on confession and the associated cleansing than occurs in connection with baptism itself. To this extent the service supplements the sacrament. The drinking action was omitted from the form Adejobi inserted in the *Book of Rituals,* so that we cannot regard this as a new development of importance. In some ways this service might be looked upon as equivalent to the various forms of reception of new members after their baptism as adults that are found in some of the Reformed churches.

13. THE CARIBBEAN CONFERENCE OF CHURCHES

THE CELEBRATION OF HOLY BAPTISM

The Christian Council of Trinidad and Tobago after several years of study and discussion has finally agreed on the common rite of baptism and a common baptismal certificate.

When at all possible, this rite should be used as part of a community celebration of worship (for some traditions this would include the Eucharist). It is intended to witness to the oneness of Christians in baptism. The rite would be especially appropriate for use close to or during the Week of Prayer for Christian Unity or at other times when the Unity of the Church is highlighted. It incorporates options for both adult and infant baptism.

Presiding Minister: Baptism is the Sacrament by which God our Father adopts by grace new sons and daughters. In the waters of baptism we are incorporated into the death and resurrection of our Lord. Born again by water and the Spirit, we are made members of the Body of Christ. United in fellowship with Christ and his people, we grow in faith, love and obedience to the will of God.

Presentation of candidates

Infant candidates shall be presented by their parents individually or collectively.

Presiding Minister: What do you ask of God's church for *this child?*

Parents: We ask that (*name/these children*) be united in baptism with the Body of Christ.

Presiding Minister (addressing those candidates able to answer for themselves): What do you ask of God's Church?

Candidate: I/We ask to be united in baptism with the Body of Christ.

Presiding Minister: In asking for baptism, you are asking to follow Jesus Christ. You would not do so unless you had come to know him and wanted to be his disciple. Have you completed your preparation for becoming a Christian? Have you listened to God's word, understood the teachings and beliefs of the Church according to the scripture? Have you shared in our worship and our way of life?

Candidate: I/We have.

Presiding Minister (addressing parents): You have presented (*name/these children*) for baptism. I now ask you in the presence of God and *his people/this congregation,* do you promise faithfully to bring *him* up in the faith we share, preparing *him* to bear witness to our faith? Will you live your lives in such a way that *this child* will see in you what it means to follow Christ? Will you make sure that *this child* is given the opportunity to share in the worship of the Church and comes to know the basic teachings and beliefs of the Church according to the scripture?

Parents: We promise to help *him* to be a disciple of Jesus Christ.

Presiding Minister (addressing sponsors): Are you prepared to help these parents to carry out their duties as Christian mothers and fathers?

Sponsors: We are, with God's help.

Presiding Minister (addressing the congregation—infant or adult baptism): Are you prepared to foster a fellowship to enable *this person* to grow in Christian commitment to worship of God, spreading the Good News, and to service of others?

All: We are, with God's help.

Service of the word

Presiding Minister: Let us listen to the word of God.

Some of the following scripture passages shall be read at this point. (Passages are taken from the Good News Bible).

Ezekiel 36:24–28

Psalms may be sung or recited between readings. Appropriate psalms are: 8, 23 (22), 29(28), 34(33), 42(41), 43(42), 84(83), 93(92), 122(121).

1 Corinthians 12:12–13

Matthew 28:19–20

Mark 10:13–16 (infant baptism)

Alternative readings:
- Isaiah 44:1–3
- Galatians 3:26–28
- Romans 6:3–4
- Mark 1:9–11
- John 3:1–6
- John 4:5–14
- John 15:1–11

A homily shall be given after the readings.

It is recommended that the profession of faith be made immediately before the reception of baptism, below.

Intercessions

Presiding Minister or other Leader: Let us pray for those who are to be baptized, for their (parents and) sponsors, and for all the baptized everywhere. Grant that, as they share in our Lord's death and resurrection, they may grow into the fullness of His life and share in His glory.

All: Lord, hear our prayer.

Presiding Minister or other Leader: Fill them with your Holy Spirit so that they may lack no spiritual gift and always live in faith, hope and love. Enable us as a community of faith, and especially their (parents and) sponsors, by word and example, to help them grow strong as living members of the church and finally to enter the joy which is prepared for all the faithful.

All: Lord, hear our prayer.

Presiding Minister or other Leader: Bless the home(s) in which *this* newly baptized will live. Fill the home(s) with the spirit of your love and understanding. (Bless the parents of *this child,* making them aware of your Spirit at work in their lives as they bring up their *child* to love and serve you).

All: Lord, hear our prayer.

Presiding Minister or other Leader: Empower all who are baptized into the Body of Christ and the way of his cross, always and everywhere to witness to the Lord by word and life. Help us all to experience our oneness with each other as baptized people of God.

All: Lord, hear our prayer.

Additional bidding prayers and thanksgivings may be added.

Presiding Minister: Into your hands, O Lord, we commend all for whom we pray, trusting in your mercy, through your Son, Jesus Christ, our Lord.

All: Amen.

Rite of baptism

Baptism may be administered by immersion, pouring or sprinkling.

Presiding Minister: The Lord be with you.

All: And also with you.

Presiding Minister: Let us pray.

Gracious Father: we give you thanks, for in the beginning of time at the creation of the world, your Spirit moved over the waters and you created heaven and earth. We thank you that by the gift of water you nourish and sustain us and all living things.

We thank you that in the waters of the Jordan your Son was baptized by John and anointed with the Spirit. By the baptism of his own death and resurrection your beloved Son has set us free from bondage to sin and death. He has opened the way to everlasting life with him in heaven.

We thank you for water as a sign of cleansing, rebirth and entrance into your Kingdom. In obedience to your Son's command, we make disciples of all nations, baptizing them in the name of the Father, and of the Son, and of the Holy Spirit. Pour out your Holy Spirit, gracious Father, to make this water a means of new life and a sign of unity for us, your people. May all who are buried with Christ in the death of baptism rise also to newness of life with him who lives and reigns with you and the Holy Spirit, one God, forever.

All: Amen.

Presiding Minister (addressing the baptismal group and the entire congregation): Do you believe in God, the Father Almighty, Creator of heaven and earth?

All: We do believe.

Presiding Minister: Do you believe in Jesus Christ, his only Son, our Lord,

who was born of the Virgin Mary, was crucified, died, and was buried, rose from the dead, and is now seated at the right hand of the Father?
All: We do believe.
Presiding Minister: Do you believe in the Holy Spirit, the holy Catholic Church, the communion of saints, the forgiveness of sins, the resurrection of the body, and life everlasting?
All: We do believe.

OR

Presiding Minister: Let us profess our common Christian faith into which we were baptized using the words of the Apostles' Creed.
All: I believe in God...
Presiding Minister: (Name), I baptize you in the name of the Father, and of the Son, and of the Holy Spirit.

Here the signing of the cross on the candidate's forehead may take place with an appropriate blessing for those traditions desiring such a blessing.

Here also some traditions may wish to make use of a lighted candle for added symbolism to the baptismal event. The anointing with oil and clothing with a white garment may also take place. The ecumenical certificate may be presented here, or after the concluding prayers.

Celebration of confirmation

In adult baptism, confirmation may be administered here in accordance with one's tradition. The following prayer may be included.

Presiding Minister: God our Father, we ask you to send the gifts of your Holy Spirit on *this* newly baptized: the spirit of wisdom and understanding, the spirit of counsel and power, the spirit of knowledge and reverence. Fill *him* with the spirit of wonder and awe in your presence. May *he* always experience and know *his* oneness with you and *his* oneness with all your people baptized into the Body of Christ. Amen.

In administering confirmation, the following may be said.

Presiding Minister: (Name), be sealed with the Holy Spirit, the gift of the Father.
Candidate: Amen.
Presiding Minister: Peace be with you.
Candidate: And also with you.

Concluding prayers

Presiding Minister: God and Father of our Lord Jesus Christ, we give you thanks for bringing your sons and daughters into new life in baptism. In the spirit of our common sonship, we pray to you in the words our Saviour gave us.

All: Our Father in heaven, hallowed be your Name, your kingdom come, your will be done, on earth as in heaven. Give us today our daily bread. Forgive us our sins as we forgive those who sin against us, Save us from the time of trial and deliver us from evil. For the kingdom, the power, and the glory are yours now and forever.

(Or the Lord's Prayer in its traditional form)

Presiding Minister: (Prayer for parents—infant baptism): Almighty God, you are the giver of all life. We ask you to bless the mother(s) and father(s) of *this child*. They thank you for the gift of their *child*. Help them to teach *him,* by word and example, the truth of your love. Amen.

(Prayer for sponsors and all present—infant or adult baptism): Almighty God, you are our ever present help. We ask you to strengthen and support the sponsors and all here present. They are a people called by you. Keep them in your loving care. Amen.

Presiding Minister or other Leader (in adult baptism): God has given us *this* new *brother*. We receive *him* with love and assure *him* of our joy over *his* entrance into our fellowship and the fellowship of Christ's Body, the Church universal.

All: We welcome you into the Lord's family. We receive you as a *son* of the heavenly Father, *a* fellow *member* of the Body of Christ, and *an* heir with us of the Kingdom of God.

Presiding Minister: The peace of the Lord go with you always. Amen.

Appropriate hymns to sing before or after this ecumenical celebration of baptism could include "The Right Hand of God", "Lord Make us One" (from Sing a New Song No. 2, CCC Hymnal), and "They'll know we are Christians by our Love".

The text of the Apostles' Creed and the Lord's Prayer is that of the International Consultation on English Texts (ICET).

14. EXAMPLE OF AN ECUMENICAL BAPTISMAL LITURGY (1983)

Illustration of the Lima Document on Baptism, Eucharist and Ministry[21]

The baptismal liturgy takes place between the Liturgy of the Word and the Eucharist.

The welcome

N. (names of the parents, or of the adult seeking baptism) as a Christian community we welcome you with great joy to celebrate the baptism which you request [for N., child's name], a baptism of water and the Spirit, in which the covenant with God, Creator and Father, is renewed in forgiveness, in which Christ makes us pass through his death and resurrection to be born into new life, in which the Holy Spirit is given us, to bring us into the body of the Church.

The thanksgiving (offered near the water of baptism)

The Lord be with you.
—And also with you.
Lift up your hearts.
—We lift them up to the Lord.
Let us give thanks to the Lord our God.
—It is right to give him thanks and praise.
It is truly right and fitting to give you glory, to offer you our thanksgiving, loving Father, all-powerful Creator: who give us water,
water which gives life, cleanses and satisfies our thirst.
—Blessed be you, O Lord.
By your invisible power, O Lord, you perform wonders in your sacraments, and in the history of salvation you have used water, which you have created, to make known to us the grace of baptism.
—Blessed be you, O Lord.
At the beginning of the world your Spirit hovered over the waters, prepared your work of creation, and planted the seed of life.
—Blessed be you, O Lord.
By the waters of the Flood You declared the death of sin and the birth of a new life.
—Blessed be you, O Lord.

---

[21] Composed by Fr Max Thurian.

You brought the children of Abraham through the waters of the Red Sea, and the people, freed from slavery, journeyed towards the Promised Land.
—Blessed be you, O Lord.
Your beloved Son was baptized by John in the waters of Jordan, was anointed by the Spirit and appointed prophet, priest and king.
—Blessed be you, O Lord.
Lifted up from the earth on the cross, your Son was immersed in the baptism of suffering; he has cast fire upon the earth to set hearts aflame and draw all people to himself.
—Blessed be you, O Lord.
The risen Christ said to his disciples: "All authority in heaven and on earth has been given to me. Go therefore and make disciples of all nations, baptizing them in the name of the Father and of the Son and of the Holy Spirit, teaching them to observe all that I have commanded you; and lo, I am with you always, to the close of the age".
—Blessed be you, O Lord.
And now, O Lord, look in love upon your Church, and by your Holy Spirit let the spring of baptism well up among us: may your servant, made in your image, God our Father, be cleansed of all that disfigures that likeness; may he/she be buried with Christ into death and be raised with him to life; may he/she receive the Holy Spirit so as to witness to the Gospel in the Church for the world.
—Blessed be you, O Lord.

The exhortation

(for the baptism of a child)
Dear parents and sponsors, the child which you present for baptism is now to be baptized: in his love, God will give him/her a new life; he/she will be born again of water and the Spirit. Be careful to help him/her grow in faith, that this life of new birth may not grow weak through sin or indifference, but that it may grow stronger in him/her day by day. As a sign that you are prepared for this responsibility, I invite you to recall your own baptism and to declare your faith in Jesus Christ, the faith of the universal Church into which every Christian is baptized.

OR

(for the baptism of an adult)
N., you are now to be baptized: in his love, God will give you a new life; you will be born again of water and the Spirit. Be careful to grow in faith, that this life of new birth in you may not grow weak through sin or indifference, but that it may grow stronger in you day by day. As a sign that you are ready to commit yourself in faith to the service of Christ and his Church, I invite you to fight against the power of evil, and to declare your faith in Jesus Christ, the faith of the universal Church into which every Christian is baptized.

The renunciation

(may be used at the baptism of an adult) So as to live in the liberty of the sons and daughters of God, to be a faithful follower of Jesus Christ and to produce the fruits of the Holy Spirit, do you renounce being ruled by the desires of this

world, the snare of pride, the love of money, and the power of violence?
—I renounce them.

The declaration of faith

Do you believe in God, the Father almighty, creator of heaven and earth?
—I do so believe.
Do you believe in Jesus Christ, his only Son, our Lord; who was conceived by the power of the Holy Spirit, and born of the Virgin Mary; who suffered under Pontius Pilate, was crucified, died, and was buried, and descended to the dead; who rose again on the third day, ascended into heaven, and is seated at the right hand of the Father, and will come again to judge the living and the dead?
—I do so believe.
Do you believe in the Holy Spirit, the holy catholic Church, the communion of saints, the forgiveness of sins, the resurrection of the body, and the life everlasting?
—I do so believe.

OR

The Apostles' Creed.
At the baptism of a child, the parents and sponsors are asked: Do you wish N. to be baptized in the faith of the Church which we have just declared?
—We do.
At the baptism of an adult, the candidate is asked: Do you wish to be baptized in the faith of the Church which we have just declared?
—I do.

The baptism

N., I baptize you in the name of the Father and of the Son and of the Holy Spirit.

The laying on of hands or chrismation

Receive the seal of the gift of the Spirit: may it make you a faithful witness to Christ to the glory of God the Father. (silence)

Conclusion

For you, there is a new act of creation. You have put on Christ.
(The person baptized may receive a white garment.) You will be guided by the Spirit of light. (He/she may receive a candle lit from the pascal candle.) You are now part of the body of the Church. You are a member of the royal priesthood, the holy fellowship. (He/she may be given the sign of the cross in oil on the forehead.) You belong to the people chosen to proclaim the praise of him who has called you out of darkness into his marvellous light. Alleluia!

II
LITURGIES OF THE EUCHARIST

INTRODUCTION

Convergence in the understanding and practice of the Lord's Supper has been one of the most remarkable achievements of the churches in the area of faith and order in the twentieth century. If the churches are now able to approve the WCC Faith and Order text on the *Eucharist*, they will at once be marking the progress so far made and taking a further step towards full consensus in eucharistic doctrine and observance. For the churches to have come already so close together is, at the human level, a work of the biblical, liturgical and ecumenical movements, which have in some degree affected almost every church. Two guiding stars have been fixed on by the churches in their common search: they have attended carefully to the Church of the New Testament and the early centuries, and they have tried to reckon with the social and cultural circumstances of our time. The contemporary concern has corrected any tendency towards archeologism, while attention to origins has counteracted any pastoral drift towards the ephemeral. Christian authenticity requires that it be the *original gospel* which is celebrated *in today's world*.

The first part of this section tries to state very concisely (1) the manner in which the early centuries of eucharistic history are now viewed by liturgical scholars, (2) the ways in which biblical exegetes and sacramental theologians are facilitating the solution of confessional controversies concerning the Lord's Supper, and (3) the methods used in the twentieth century liturgical movement to deepen and renew the experience of the eucharist in the Christian communities. The central and weightiest part then reproduces texts from eucharistic rites ancient, intermediate and modern. The purpose here is to let readers see for themselves the common origins, the intervening divergences, and the newly developing congruences. The final part offers a few examples which locate contemporary eucharistic understanding and practice in their pastoral setting. These are meant as a stimulus to reflection and discussion by individuals and groups in their own social and cultural context.

GEOFFREY WAINWRIGHT

HISTORICAL SKETCH

1. COMMON SOURCES REDISCOVERED

According to one of the best loved stories in the Gospels, the risen Lord on the road to Emmaus expounded to the two disciples the scriptures concerning himself, and then became known to his companions in the breaking of the bread (Luke 24:13–35). By the middle of the second century, Justin Martyr outlined for us a complete service of word and sacrament. From his texts given on pp. 111–113 it appears that the regular Sunday assembly of the Christians took place in this order:

1. The reading of the scriptures
2. The exposition of the readings
3. The prayers of intercession
4. The bringing of the bread, wine and water to the president of the congregation (perhaps a mixed cup of wine and water)
5. The eucharistic prayer spoken by the president and sealed by the people's amen
6. The breaking of the bread (see later)
7. The sharing of the bread and wine over which thanks have been given.

That is the backbone of the celebration which came to be known in the Church as the eucharist, the sacred liturgy, the Lord's meal, the holy communion, the divine oblation.

The "service of the word", the first three items on Justin's list, is indebted to the synagogue, though of course "the Old Testament" is now read and interpreted in a Christian light, and the "records of the apostles" become our "New Testament" scriptures. The "service of the meal", the other four items on Justin's list, borrows from Jewish table customs, though of course the prayers are given Christian content, and the actions and words are related to what Jesus did and said at the Last Supper in the accounts given by the first three Gospels and by Saint Paul.

Although some of its details have since been modified, a brilliant thesis put forward in 1945 by the Anglican liturgical scholar, Gregory Dix, greatly illuminated our understanding of "The Shape of the Liturgy". From the New Testament accounts of the Last Supper Dix extracted seven significant actions of Jesus with the bread and the cup:

Bread
1. He took
2. He thanked God over it
3. He broke
4. He gave it to his disciples

Cup
5. He took
6. He thanked God over it
7. He gave it to his disciples

At the Last Supper, the actions with the bread and with the cup were separated by the rest of the meal; but when, for reasons we can only surmise, the bread and the cup were brought together in the Church's execution of the Lord's command to "do this", the seven actions could be "telescoped" into four:

1. The taking of the bread and wine
2. The thanking of God over them
3. The breaking of the bread
4. The giving of the bread and wine.

These give us the "four-action shape" of the service of the meal:

1. The bringing of the elements to the president of the assembly, who takes them (what Dix still calls "the offertory").
2. The eucharistic prayer (about which more will be said in a moment).
3. The breaking of the bread before eating (technically called "the fraction"; Justin does not mention the fraction, but since "the breaking of bread" could early serve as a name for the whole service and the action occurs in all ancient liturgies, we may take it that his service included it).
4. The distribution of the bread and wine and their consumption in communion.

On the Lutheran side, for instance, Dix's "shape" is well exploited by H.C. Schmidt-Lauber, *Die Eucharistie als Entfaltung der Verba Testamenti*[1]. On the Roman Catholic side, the clarification of the structures was carried out in an exemplary manner by J.A. Jungmann, *Missarum Sollemnia: Eine genetische Erklärung der römischen Messe*[2]. The principal nuance which more recent work has introduced is to underline the thanksgiving and the communion, with the presentation of the gifts and the breaking of the bread being seen as preparatory in each case to the main actions.

While Justin gives us the basic outline, the structure grew more elaborate in the course of the centuries, and some components were expanded while others atrophied. The work of the modern liturgical movement has been to clarify the basic structure as found in Justin, and to restore the proportion of its parts. Where that has taken place, it is possible for Christians of many denominations to assist at the Sunday service of others and to recognize its shape as the one with which they themselves are familiar, and which is nothing other than the one to which their predecessors of eighteen centuries ago were accustomed.

As the centuries went by, the service had in fact become impoverished by the omission of readings from the Old Testament and by the decline of the sermon. On the other hand, the sacrificial themes, which (as we shall see) had been associated from the start with the meal, were developed in a particular direction and led, in the western Church especially, to a magnification of "the offertory" and an apparently one-sided emphasis in the eucharistic prayer ("the canon"). In the sixteenth century, the Protestant Reformers considered this to be the outcrop of erroneous views on man, sin and salvation; and in their liturgical reforms, they docked many medieval excrescences. Unfortu-

---

[1] Kassel, Stauda, 1957.
[2] Vienna, Herder, 1948.

nately they were prevented by the polemical context and by the lack of scholarly resources from recapturing an earlier understanding and structure of the eucharist, so that the Protestant rites emerge as more or less drastic truncations in comparison with the Church of the Fathers. In the twentieth century, both Protestants and Roman Catholics, from their different starting points, have been able to return more closely to a eucharistic order and theology which had on the whole been better preserved in the East.

It is the eucharistic prayer, often called the anaphora, which gives most evident verbal expression in the rite itself to the way the celebrating church understands what is taking place. By it God is blessed and thanked for his goodness in creation and redemption, and he is asked to extend his benefits and bring his saving purpose to completion. This is how we proclaim the Lord's death and announce his resurrection until he come. By the Holy Spirit, in fidelity to Jesus' word of promise and in response to our prayer, God makes the bread we shall eat and the wine we shall drink the means of our communion with Christ and therefore the pledge and foretaste of our final salvation with all the saints in the divine kingdom. The scriptural text which has perhaps helped most towards this understanding of the eucharistic prayer is 1 Timothy 4:4f.:

> For everything created by God is good, and nothing is to be rejected if it is received with thanksgiving; for then it is consecrated by the word of God and prayer.

Based on W.J. Grisbrooke's analysis[3], the following scheme should aid the understanding of technical terms when the eucharistic prayers are being presented. The typical eucharistic prayer is composed thus:

(1) Introductory dialogue; (2) preface or (first part of the) thanksgiving; (3) Sanctus; a transition which may either (4) continue the thanksgiving or (5) take the form of a preliminary epiclesis, if not both; (6) narrative of the institution; (7) anamnesis-oblation; (8) epiclesis; (9) intercessions; (10) concluding doxology and amen.

Or in more detail:

(1) *Introductory dialogue* between president and people. This locates the prayer and sets its dominant theme. The most widespread form, allowing for minor variants, is:

> Lift up your hearts:
> *We lift them to the Lord.*
> Let us give thanks to the Lord our God:
> *It is right to give him thanks and praise.*

(2) *Preface* is not meant in the sense of mere preliminary or foreword, but of public proclamation. The keynote of the preface is praise, which easily shades into thanksgiving. God is praised for his very being and is thanked for creation and for his saving work in Christ. In the West, a special seasonal emphasis is often made; this is called a "proper preface". The preface leads into the

(3) *Sanctus*. With the "Holy, holy, holy" the earthly Church joins in the

---

[3] "Anaphora", in J.G. Davies, ed., *A Dictionary of Liturgy and Worship*, London, SCM, and Philadelphia, Westminster Press, 1972, pp. 10–17.

worship of heaven. To this may be added the *Benedictus:* "Blessed is he who comes in the name of the Lord."

(4) *Thanksgiving* is resumed, with a sharp focus on God's gift of Jesus Christ to us. This culminates in the recollection of the institution of the sacrament at the Last Supper, unless the institution narrative is also preceded by a

(5) *Preliminary epiclesis.* An epiclesis is simply an invocation or "calling-upon" of God, though it may more precisely mean a prayer for God to give the Holy Spirit. At this point it will be a prayer that God may, in whatever sense, sanctify the bread and wine for sacramental use.

(6) *Institution narrative.* To ensure that this is locked into the prayer-structure, a syntactical link is made, e.g. "*For* in the night in which he was betrayed" or "And when he had given thanks to you, Father".

(7) *Anamnesis-oblation.* "Anamnesis" means memorial, and more will be said about this below. The anamnesis here picks up from "Do this in remembrance of me" at the end of (6) and "recalls", before God and the world, the saving work of Christ. It concentrates on the death and resurrection but may stretch from Christ's conception to his ascension, and even (by anticipation) his final coming. The anamnesis usually takes participial form: "Recalling therefore his death and resurrection...", and the main clause is formulated "We offer..." (i.e. the oblation). This is one of the most delicate points in the whole eucharistic prayer, for it engages our understanding of the sacrificial aspect of the eucharist. We offer to God from his own gifts to us. A circumlocution usually stops short of saying "we offer Christ"; rather "we offer this bread of life and this cup of salvation", or "we offer this sacrifice of praise". Sometimes the self-oblation of the worshippers is expressed at this point.

(8) *Epiclesis.* If this has not already happened in (5), God may be asked to give the Holy Spirit to sanctify the elements. In any case, God will be asked to give salvation to all faithful communicants.

(9) *Intercessions.* The fuller form will have occurred in the service of the word. The intercessions at this point are therefore resumptive. A commemoration of the saints is often woven in here.

(10) A solemn concluding *doxology* is met by the people's *amen,* underlining the fact that the president has been voicing the prayer of the whole assembly.

That is how modern liturgical scholarship envisages a "classical" eucharistic prayer; and contemporary compositions in official liturgical revisions have approximated more or less closely to that structure.

2. OLD CONTROVERSIES RE-EXAMINED

Modern liturgical scholarship and sacramental theology have shed fresh light on several old controversies between the confessions, and the resolution of most of the conflicts is now in sight. The single most valuable contribution is probably one that depends on the work of scriptural exegetes concerning the notion of "memorial" in the Bible. The Hebrew root is ZKR, and the Greek word used in the New Testament accounts of the last Supper is *anamnesis*: "Do this for my memorial." While scholars give different nuances to their explanations, there exists a rather widespread agreement that a "memorial" can properly be understood as a human action undertaken at God's command in order to put the ecclesial community in touch with the saving action of God which is being commemorated before God. This process is neither magical nor mechanical: it neither compels God to do something he would otherwise be reluctant to do nor involves the use of a time-machine. It rests rather upon the constant purpose of the eternal God who has revealed himself for our salvation in Jesus Christ, the same yesterday, today and for ever, and who never ceases to work by the Holy Spirit for the completion of his kingdom. This provides an opportunity to settle old arguments between Catholics and Protestants, or among Protestants, concerning both "the eucharistic sacrifice" and the presence of Christ. It also helps in the controversies between East and West about the relation between the roles of Christ and of the Holy Spirit in the eucharist.

Since the scriptures interpret the death of Christ in sacrificial terms, it is inevitable that the eucharistic proclamation of his death will bear a sacrificial aspect. The link is already made in the New Testament accounts of the institution of the eucharist at the Last Supper: the sacrificial significance of "the body" and "the blood which will be shed" is unmistakable, and the idea is reinforced by the word "covenant" in the saying over the cup. The Lord's Supper was early called a "sacrifice of praise" (cf. Heb. 13:15) and was viewed as fulfilling the text of Malachi 1:11: "From the rising of the sun to its setting my name is great among the nations, and in every place incense is offered to my name and a pure offering" (cf. *Didachè* 14:3; Justin, *Dialogue with Trypho* 41:2, 117:1). There can be no question of *repeating* the once-and-for-all self-oblation of Christ (Heb. 7:27; 9:12, 10:10–14); rather Christ's death on the cross is gratefully *recalled* before God, in order that even now, at our great High Priest's intercession, we may find help in time of need (Heb. 4:14–16), may in the Spirit enjoy access through him to the Father (Eph. 2:18), and may offer ourselves, newly transformed in Christ, as a living sacrifice to God (Rom. 12:1f). Rather than our reaching up to heaven to bring the Saviour down, we find that in and through his appointed "memorial" the Lord comes in the Spirit to his people and joins them with himself at his own Table, in anticipation of the great feast when death will have been abolished and every tear wiped dry (Isa. 25:6–9).

Instead of continuing my own statement of a eucharistic theology in which old controversies may be overcome, let me reprint part of a report in which I survey a wide range of recent literature on the Lord's Supper. This will give a better indication of the horizons of agreement now open at the theological level.

"Recent thinking on the eucharist"*

The sacraments as signs
The most notable feature of sacramental theology as a whole, in the past fifteen years, has been the recovery of the character of the sacraments as *signs* or *symbols* (authors

---

*Reprinted from *The Expository Times* 88 (1977), pp. 132–35.

vary in their preference for the one or the other of these terms). The approach has been broadly phenomenological: theology has examined the rites as they have been experienced within the human reality and more particularly within the Christian tradition. In general anthropological terms, signs are means of self-expression, of personal communication: the body is the fundamental sign; language is the most supple sign; natural and cultural objects are drawn into the process. There is a 'logic of action' (J.R. Lucas' phrase, in *Thinking about the Eucharist: Papers by members of the Church of England Doctrine Commission,* S.C.M. [1972]); there is, says F.J. Leenhardt, 'un langage gestuel' (*Parole visible,* Delachaux & Niestlé [1971]). There is no opposition between 'symbol' and 'reality': J.P. de Jong has insisted that the eucharist, for instance, is a 'symbolic reality', with an equal stress on each term (*De eucharistie, symbolische werkelijkheid,* Gooi & Sticht [1966]). Within the Christian tradition, the sacraments are acted signs which allow and embody a meeting with God in Christ (E. Schillebeeckx, *Christ the Sacrament of Encounter with God,* Eng. tr. Sheed & Ward [1963]). This personalist understanding has largely replaced the tendency of theologians to deal with the sacraments as 'channels of grace' in a somewhat impersonal sense.

Transsignification
It is within this context of sacraments as signs that Roman Catholic theologians have been trying to reinterpret the Thomistic and Tridentine doctrine of eucharistic transubstantiation. Some have talked of transsignification and transfinalization: a change in meaning or purpose. The movement sprang from articles by J. de Baciocchi, S.M.—and (strangely perhaps) from the short essay of F.J. Leenhardt, *Ceci est mon corps* (Delachaux & Niestlé [1955], Eng. tr. in O. Cullmann and F.J. Leenhardt, *Essays on the Lord's Supper,* Lutterworth [1958]), in which the Genevan Reformed theologian sought to make 'transubstantiation' acceptable to Protestants. When Christ gives the bread with the words 'This is my body', said Leenhardt, the bread is no longer, in its deepest constitution, what the baker made it but what the Word has made it. In Germany, the line of transsignification was pursued by B. Welte in his contribution to M. Schmaus (ed.), *Aktuelle Fragen zur Eucharistie* [1960]: it was he who launched the example of the cloth-become-flag, the change in meaning being a real and objective change. In the Netherlands, P. Schoonenberg and L. Smits cast light on the eucharist from a phenomenology of personal presence: a person may make himself present to another in his gift (his 'present'!). The Dutch debate can be followed in the fourth chapter of J.M. Powers, *Eucharistic Theology* (Burns & Oates [1968]) and in E. Schillebeeckx, *The Eucharist* (Eng. tr. Sheed & Ward [1968]). The interpretation of the eucharist as transsignification exploits the insights of modern anthropology into man as meaning-giver. When these insights are set within a suitable theological and Christological framework (the eucharist as the gift of the Word-made-flesh, the God-Man...), the charge of 'extrinsicalism' which Schillebeeckx levelled already against Leenhardt seems unjustifiably harsh. Schillebeeckx himself is of the opinion that although transsignification has a limited value, it does not adequately safeguard the ontological change which the old transubstantiation expressed. The debate, however, continues, as may be seen from the fourth issue of the *Zeitschrift für katholische Theologie* for 1975 and the literature there reviewed.

Memorial and sacrifice
Work on the biblical notion of memorial has profited eucharistic theology among both Catholics and Protestants. An influential book here was M. Thurian's *Eucharistic Memorial* (Eng. tr. Lutterworth [1960-61]). Whereas since the 1920s O. Casel had been drawing inspiration largely from Hellenistic sources for his idea of the Christian sacraments as 'mystery-memorials', Thurian called attention (and his work has been broadly confirmed by O.T. specialists) to the dynamic value of 'memorial' in Hebrew thinking. Memory provokes action, and the cult serves to 'remind' God. Ritual

'memorial' may make present, if not a mighty deed of God from the past, then at least its saving benefits. This rich notion of memorial appears to be unlocking the controversial problem of the so-called eucharistic sacrifice.

As early as the 1920s and 1930s, a rapprochement between Protestants and Catholics had seemed to be on the way. It became fairly widely accepted that the vehement rejection by the Reformers of 'the eucharistic sacrifice' had been occasioned by the distorted Catholic teaching of the time. F. Clark, S.J., issued a radical challenge to this view in his *Eucharistic Sacrifice and the Reformation* (D.L.T. [1960]; 2nd ed. Blackwell [1967]). He produced ample evidence that the orthodox, 'Tridentine', Catholic doctrine of the mass had been clearly taught by the theologians of the late middle ages, and that the Reformers rejected this doctrine with open eyes. Clark's awkward book was virtually ignored in ecumenical circles. But the rather searching criticisms made of his thesis by his fellow Catholic N. Lash, in *His Presence in the World* (Sheed & Ward [1968]), show that the ecumenical embarrassment nevertheless need not have been so great: Clark had greatly underestimated the complexity of the relationship between verbal orthodoxy and the practical context (Lash, 126–37).

In recent years, the eucharistic concentration on the Cross has been broadened to include the other 'mighty acts' of God in Christ within the 'memorial'. The old Roman Catholic rite did not lack reference to the resurrection: and this was brought out by W.B. McGrory, *The Mass and the Resurrection* (Catholic Book Agency, Rome [1964]). The Council of Trent, however, stressed the representation of the sacrifice on the Cross. But Vatican II now spoke more readily of the paschal mystery of Christ's death and resurrection. A scholarly example of this tendency is J.M.R. Tillard, O.P., *L'Eucharistie, pâque de l'Église* (Cerf [1964]). Drawing on biblical, patristic, thomistic and liturgical resources, the Dominican author presents the eucharist as the Church's 'two-stage' sacramental participation in Christ's 'Passover': the eucharist embodies the Church's continuing passage from sin to newness of life.

Tillard gave welcome emphasis to the 'ethical' reality of which the eucharist is the sacramental expression. This tendency is taken even further in L. Dussaut, *L'Eucharistie, pâques de toute la vie* (Cerf [1972]). Here it is held that the Pauline emphasis on death and resurrection is too narrow: the eucharist is rather (in the perspective of the Fouth Gospel and of Hebrews) the memorial of the *whole* of Christ's life, with all that is thereby implied in the way of ethical example. Dussaut capitalizes on the bi-polar character of the Last Supper, where the action with the bread started the meal and the action with the wine took place 'after supper'. In the eucharist, the bread, sign of the body, signifies the incarnation, and the wine, sign of the blood, signifies the passion. The whole of Christ's life was a 'sacrificial meal': a sacrifice to God for men, a meal bringing men and God into fellowship. The eucharist allows men, in the time of the Church, to share the life and destiny of Christ in surrender to God: it provides a 'ritual' focus of the 'personal' sacrifice of Christ and of the Church. This kind of personalizing and ethicalizing of sacrifice which the Catholic author undertakes ought to attract Protestants who have readily allowed the sacrament to be a 'sacrifice of praise and thanksgiving' for the work of Christ and an offering of 'ourselves, our souls and bodies'. J.L. Houlden has shown that 'the eucharistic sacrifice' has served in sacramental theology as a portmanteau term to include many and varied themes (*Thinking about the Eucharist*, 81–98). The heart of the Christian faith, however, is grateful surrender to God in and through Christ; and of this the eucharist is a proper sacramental focus.

Related to the richer concept of memorial is the increased stress, rather new in the West (though not to Calvin!), on the pneumatological dimension of the eucharist. This is apparent in both Tillard and Dussaut and is pretty general in recent writing. The Holy Spirit is the 'remembrancer' of Christ. It is 'in the Spirit' that the glorified Christ holds sacramental fellowship with his Church.

The eschatological dimension

Talk of the paschal mystery and of the Holy Spirit already implies 'eschatology'. The understanding of the eucharist has benefited from the rediscovery of the eschatological character of the gospel in the twentieth century. Thus P. Lebeau, in *Le vin nouveau du royaume* (Desclée de Brouwer [1966]), devoted attention to a scriptural text which, though it had engaged the Church Fathers, had failed to interest more recent theologians of the eucharist: Mk 14^{25} = Mt 26^{29}. And F.X. Durrwell, in *L'Eucharistie, présence du Christ* (Editions Ouvrières [1971]), sought to understand the eucharistic Presence in the light of Christ's Parousia. My *Eucharist and Eschatology* (Epworth [1971]) showed also how, in turn, the lived reality of the eucharist could provide a hermeneutical key to 'eschatology', challenging or confirming different features of modern interpretations of the eschatological import of the gospel: the eucharist supplies a sign, image and taste of the kingdom.

The ecclesiological dimension

Eucharistic theology has shared in the general renewal of the theology of the Church in our century. In this connection, a strong influence has been exercised on Western thought by the Orthodox, whose view is typically expressed in N. Afanssieff's designation of the eucharist as 'the sacrament of assembly'. Vatican II went so far as to call the eucharistic assembly of the local Church the 'principal manifestation of the Church' (Constitution on the Sacred Liturgy, 41). The understanding of the eucharist as the fellowship meal of Christ in his Church shines through the works of Catholic authors such as N. Lash, *His Presence in the World*, and J.M. Powers, *Eucharistic Theology*. Protestants who have typically spoken of the sacrament as 'the Lord's Supper' and 'the Holy Communion' can only welcome this development.

But eucharistic theology—particularly in its ecclesiological aspect—must be related to the historical situation of Christianity. The stress on the ecclesiological significance of the eucharist has to be seen within the context of a divided Christendom in which the institutionally separated bodies are nevertheless seeking unity. There is a glaring discrepancy between the 'theological' character of the eucharist as a sacrament of fellowship and the 'historical' situation of mutual excommunication. All Christians wish to overcome this gap. But modern ecumenists have differed on ways and means: should eucharistic communion be a final goal of Christian unity, not to be anticipated meanwhile? or might 'intercommunion' rather be seen as an effective step on the way to fuller unity? In recent years, the second view has been gaining ground and, at least among theologians, appears now to hold the field. Supporters of the first view insisted, among other things, on the need for agreement about the nature of the eucharist. Amid all the pluralism of modern theology, there has in fact been a considerable convergence of thought on the nature of the eucharist: and this is undoubtedly favouring the advance of the 'intercommunion' front.

Ecumenical agreement

The sacraments have occupied the Faith and Order movement from its earliest days. Concerning the eucharist, a remarkable book by J.J. von Allmen both resumed and furthered the work in the World Council of Churches: *The Lord's Supper* (Eng. tr. Lutterworth [1969]). The Swiss Reformed theologian set forth a balanced yet dynamic view of the eucharist, based on the following complementary pairs: the Supper as anamnesis of Christ and epiclesis of the Spirit; the eucharist as revelation of the limits and the fullness of the Church; communion with Christ and with the brethren; the Supper as bread of life and as sacrifice; the Supper as prayer and as response to prayer; the eucharist in the rhythm of the Church's mission and worship. The long years of work in Faith and Order bore fruit in the statement finally agreed at the Accra meeting of the Commission in 1974 and now included, for consideration by the Churches, in *One Baptism, One Eucharist, and a mutually recognized Ministry* (W.C.C. [1975]).

108 Baptism and Eucharist: Ecumenical Convergence in Celebration

Other notable ecumenical agreements include the 'Windsor Statement' of the Anglican/Roman Catholic International Commission [1971] and the text produced by the French Groupe des Dombes in 1972: both documents figure in *Modern Eucharistic Agreement* (S.P.C.K. [1973]).

The eucharist and the world
Eucharistic theology has both affected and been affected by recent ecclesiological reflection on the Church's task of witness and service in human society. The 1960s sought to relate the cult to 'secular life': witness J.G. Davies, *Worship and Mission* (S.C.M. [1966]). Vatican II, with its notion of the Church as the sacrament of the world's salvation and its Pastoral Constitution on the Church in the Modern World, clearly formed the background to N. Lash's *His Presence in the World: a study in eucharistic worship and theology* (Sheed & Ward [1968]). A Latin American interpretation and application of Vatican II lies behind the series 'A Theology for Artisans of a New Humanity' produced by J.L. Segundo, S.J., in Montevideo: volume 4 is entitled *The Sacraments Today* (Orbis [1974]) and situates the sacraments 'functionally' within a view that 'there is only one real finality that combines temporal progress and the growth of the kingdom into one single, supernatural destiny for man'. With something more of a 'perennial' tone, various writings of A. Schmemann have set forth the 'cosmic' dimension of the sacraments in the Orthodox understanding: notably *The World as Sacrament* (D.L.T. [1966]; published in the U.S.A. as *For the Life of the World* and as *Sacraments and Orthodoxy*); the book contains a remarkable exploitation of Feuerbach's dictum that 'man is what he eats'.

The eucharist as blessing
Thanks largely to biblical (J.P. Audet) and liturgical (L. Bouyer; L. Ligier) scholars, recent eucharistic theology has become very much aware of the nature of the central prayer which is the chief verbal expression of the meaning of the sacrament. With its roots in the Jewish *berakah*, the Christian *eucharistia* is the grateful praise of God for his marvellous works in Christ, with the plea—implicit or explict—that he will extend his graciousness into the present and hasten the triumph of his own kingdom. In the recent widespread liturgical revision in the West, one of the most notable features has been the recovery of the great eucharistic prayer.

The revised liturgies in fact now express many of the insights of eucharistic theology which we have outlined: a dynamic sense of memorial, a broadened appreciation of the works of God in Christ, an awareness of the pneumatological, eschatological and ecclesiological dimensions of worship...Just as reflection on the phenomenology of the rite has provided a stimulus to eucharistic theology, so in turn has eucharistic theology helped the churches to bring the meaning of the rite to clearer verbal expression in the liturgy itself.

3. *EUCHARISTIC LIFE RENEWED*

There can be no question about the important contribution which the liturgical movement has made to many churches throughout the world in the twentieth century. Its goals in the renewal of Christian worship have been common, but the steps needed to reach them have naturally varied according to the different positions in which the respective churches found themselves at the outset.

As far as the eucharist is concerned, the chief aim has been the active and regular participation of all Christians in the Lord's Supper. Roman Catholics had retained frequent celebrations of the Mass, but the communion of lay people was lamentably rare; Pope Pius X encouraged a move to more frequent communion. The Protestant churches, on the other hand, had tended to abandon the celebration of the Lord's Supper when insufficient numbers had announced themselves for communion; here it has been a matter of increasing the number of occasions when people are offered the opportunity to share in the Supper. Among both Protestants and Catholics, there has been the need to ensure a more active participation in the whole service by the distribution of roles among the various members of the congregation, instead of acquiescing in a clerical monopoly of the action. On these scores, Catholics and Protestants have been attempting to rectify a condition which set in already in the fourth and fifth centuries and which the sixteenth century had either compounded or at least failed to redress (see G. Dix, *The Shape of the Liturgy*, pp. 18f).

Since the recognition that the worship assembly is the place in which most Christians learn the faith and grow in it (an insight propagated by the Roman Catholic pioneer in the liturgical movement, Dom Lambert Beauduin), intelligibility has required that the Roman Catholic Church turn to the vernacular tongues, while most Protestant churches have sought to provide versions of their rite in more contemporary language. Catholic preachers have learned to expound the scriptures, while Protestant preachers have begun to relate their sermon more directly to the liturgical action. The reading of the Old Testament has been widely re-introduced, while new lectionaries have sought to achieve a thorough and representative use of the whole Bible in all its variety.

Several references have already been made to the recovery of the ancient "shape" of the service of word and sacrament as outlined by Justin Martyr. For Catholics this has often meant a pruning of accretions; for Protestants it has meant an enrichment of significant action and thematic content.

Questions of cultural adaptation have arisen, particularly in other parts of the world than those Western areas in which much of the history of Christianity has unfolded. While it must not be forgotten that the gospel brings both judgment and the offer of transformation to all human culture in so far as human beings need to be liberated from their sin, it may also properly be expected that the Church and its worship will embrace the rich variety of peoples among God's human creation in ways which allow them all to find themselves truly "at home" there and so anticipate the bringing of "the treasures of the nations" into the heavenly city. Styles of speaking and singing, patterns of gesture, posture and movement, the arrangement of space and the employment of time—all these can appropriately affect the way in which the Lord's Supper is celebrated and experienced. A few Protestant and independent churches have tried the use of more local food and drink in places where wheat and grapes are not cultivated; but the overwhelming practice has been to stick with bread and wine on the grounds that they are the two elements with which Jesus himself instituted the Lord's Supper, have many other associations in the scriptures, and figure among the few precious links which have so far bound Christians almost universally together.

Certainly one current in the liturgical movement has been concerned to relate worship to the social realities of the local church. Emblematic is the title of A.G. Hebert's classic work, *Liturgy and Society* (1935). I have heard Indian Christians testify to the contribution made by the holy communion to the breaking down of the caste system. In Latin America, the politically active "base communities" are nourished at the Lord's table. This is not to deny that the eucharist has sometimes been "tamed" into support of conservative and even oppressive systems, or to claim that its explosive potential has yet been fully discovered.

The ways in which the Orthodox churches have become sensitive to many of the issues raised by the liturgical movement can be illustrated from the texts reprinted on pp. 213–221.

GEOFFREY WAINWRIGHT

LITURGICAL TEXTS

Usually the eucharistic prayer alone is given, as this is the clearest expression of the understanding on which the Lord's Supper is being celebrated. Sometimes other prayers are also given, either where these are of particular interest or where they include components which are more customarily part of the eucharistic prayer itself.

Little attempt has been made to standardize typography in the reproduction of these texts from such varied sources. It should be clear who says what. It may help to know that parts spoken by the president of the eucharist are usually in roman type; that rubrics, or directions, are often in italic; and that the people's part may be either roman or italic type.

1. JUSTIN MARTYR

Born in Syria, Justin was writing in Rome about the year 150. In chapter 67 of his *First Apology* he describes the regular Sunday service of the Christians. Some further details are found in connection with his description of a baptismal eucharist in chapters 65 and 66.

The present translation is taken from R.C.D. Jasper and G.J. Cuming, *Prayers of the Eucharist: Early and Reformed.*

67.3. And on the day called Sun-day an assembly is held in one place of all who live in town or country, and the records of the apostles or writings of the prophets are read for as long as time allows.

4. Then, when the reader has finished, the president in a discourse admonishes and exhorts (us) to imitate these good things.

5. Then we all stand up together and offer prayers; and as we said before, when we have finished praying, bread and wine and water are brought up, and the president likewise offers prayers and thanksgivings to the best of his ability, and the people assent, saying the Amen; and there is a distribution, and everyone participates in (the elements) over which thanks have been given; and they are sent through the deacons to those who are not present.

6. And the wealthy who so desire give what they wish, as each chooses; and what is collected is deposited with the president.

7. He helps orphans and widows, and those who through sickness or any other cause are in need, and those in prison, and strangers sojourning among us; in a word, he takes care of all those who are in need.

8. And we all assemble together on Sun-day, because it is the first day, on which God, having transformed the darkness and matter, made the world; and Jesus Christ our Saviour rose from the dead the same day; for they crucified him the day before Saturday; and the day after Saturday, which is Sun-day, he appeared to his apostles and disciples, and taught them these things which we have presented to you for your consideration.

Chapter 65–66:

65.1. After we have thus baptized him who has believed and has given his assent, we take him to those who are called brethren where they are assembled, to make common prayers earnestly for ourselves and for him who has been enlightened[1] and for all others everywhere, that, having learned the truth, we may be deemed worthy to be found good citizens in our actions and guardians of the commandments, so that we may be saved with eternal salvation.

2. When we have ended the prayers, we greet one another with a kiss.

3. Then bread and a cup of water and of mixed wine[2] are brought to him who presides over the brethren, and he takes them and offers praise and glory to the Father of all in the name of the Son and of the Holy Spirit, and gives thanks at some length that we have been deemed worthy of these things from him. When he has finished the prayers and the thanksgiving, all the people present give their assent by saying, 'Amen.'

4. Amen is Hebrew for 'So be it'.

5. And when the pesident has given thanks and all the people have assented, those whom we call deacons give to each one present a portion of the bread and wine and water over which thanks have been given,[3] and take them to those who are not present.

66.1. And we call this food 'thanksgiving';[4] and no one may partake of it unless he is convinced of the truth of our teaching, and has been cleansed with the washing for forgiveness of sins and regeneration, and lives as Christ handed down.

2. For we do not receive these things as common bread or common drink; but just as our Saviour Jesus Christ, being incarnate through the word of God, took flesh and blood for our salvation, so too we have been taught that the food over which thanks have been given by the prayer of the Word who is from him,[5] from which our flesh and blood are fed by transformation, is both the flesh and blood of that incarnate Jesus.

3. For the apostles in the records composed by them which are called gospels, have handed down what was commanded them: that Jesus took bread, gave thanks, and said, 'Do this for my remembrance; this is my body'; and likewise he took the cup, gave thanks, and said, 'This is my blood'; and likewise he

---

[1] i.e., by baptism.
[2] It is not clear whether Justin means one cup or two cups.
[3] Greek: *Eucharistēthentos*.
[4] Greek: *Eucharistia*.
[5] *Or by a word of prayer that is from him or by a prayer of the word that is from him.*

took the cup, gave thanks, and said, 'This is my blood'; and gave to them alone.

4. And the evil demons have imitated this and ordered it to be done also in the mysteries of Mithras. For as you know or may learn, bread and a cup of water are used with certain formulas in their rites of initiation.

67.1. And thereafter we continually remind one another of these things. Those who have the means help all those in need; and we are always together.

2. And we bless the Maker of all things through his Son Jesus Christ and through the Holy Spirit over all that we receive.

2. HIPPOLYTUS: "THE APOSTOLIC TRADITION"

Introduction and text from R.C.D. Jasper and G.J. Cuming, *Prayers of the Eucharist: Early and Reformed.*

The Apostolic Tradition of Hippolytus is generally believed to have survived in the form of an anonymous, untitled work which in the nineteenth century was given the name of *The Egyptian Church Order*. This has come down to us in Latin, Coptic, Arabic, and Ethiopic versions, and in various adaptations such as *The Apostolic Constitutions* and the *Testamentum Domini*. Its identification with the work of Hippolytus was proposed by E. Schwartz (1910) and R. H. Connolly (1916), and implies a date of c.A.D. 215. The work professedly reflects 'the tradition which has remained until now', and so may be taken as a witness to Roman practice some fifty years earlier. This brings it close to the time of Justin, with whose account it agrees quite closely. Like Justin, Hippolytus describes two eucharists, one following the consecration of a bishop, the other after a baptism. He gives us the earliest surviving text of a eucharistic prayer, but this should be regarded as an individual specimen rather than as an invariable form.

BIBLIOGRAPHY
B. Botte, *La Tradition Apostolique de Saint Hippolyte* (1972).
G. Dix, *The Apostolic Tradition of Saint Hippolytus* (1968, ed. H. Chadwick).
R.H. Connolly, 'The Eucharistic Prayer of Hippolytus', in *Journal of Theological Studies*, 39 (1938), pp. 350-69.
G. Dix, *The Shape*, pp. 157-62.
J.A. Jungmann, *The Early Liturgy* (1960), pp. 52-73.
L. Bouyer, *Eucharist* (1970), pp. 158-82.

CHAPTER 4: The eucharist

1. And when he has been made bishop, all shall offer the kiss of peace, greeting him because[1] he has been made worthy.

---

[1] *Or* that.

2. *Then the deacons shall present the offering to him; and he, laying his hands on it with all the presbytery, shall say, giving thanks:*

3. The Lord be with you.[2]
And all shall say:
And with your spirit.
Up with your hearts.[3]
We have them with the Lord.
Let us give thanks to the Lord.
It is fitting and right.
And then he shall continue thus:

4. We render thanks to you, O God, through your beloved child[4] Jesus Christ, whom in the last times you sent to us as saviour and redeemer and angel of your will;

5. Who is your inseparable Word, through whom you made all things, and in whom you were well pleased.

6. You sent him from heaven into the Virgin's womb; and, conceived in the womb, he was made flesh and was manifested as your Son, being born of the Holy Spirit and the Virgin.

7. Fulfilling your will and gaining for you a holy people, he stretched out his hands when he should suffer, that he might release from suffering those who have believed in you.

8. And when he was betrayed to voluntary suffering that he might destroy death, and break the bonds of the devil, and tread down hell, and shine upon the righteous, and fix the limit, and manifest the resurrection,

9. he took bread and gave thanks to you, saying, 'Take, eat; this is my body, which shall be broken for you.' Likewise also the cup, saying, 'This is my blood, which is shed for you;

10. When you do this, you make my remembrance.'

11. Remembering therefore his death and resurrection, we offer to you the bread and the cup, giving you thanks because you have held us worthy to stand before you and minister to you.

12. And we ask that you would send your Holy Spirit upon the offering of your holy Church; that, gathering them into one, you would grant to all who partake of the holy things (to partake) for the fullness of the Holy Spirit for the confirmation of faith in truth;[5]

13. that we may praise and glorify you through your child[6] Jesus Christ, through whom be glory and honour to you, to the Father and the Son with the Holy Spirit, in your holy Church, both now and to the ages of ages. (Amen.)

---

[2] Coptic *adds* all.
[3] *The Latin has no verb.*
[4] *Or* servant.
[5] *The Latin is almost untranslatable at this point. Literally translated,* 'grant' *has no object; hence the addition of* 'to partake'. Testamentum Domini *reads:* 'Grant to all who partake of the holy things to be united with you for filling with Holy Spirit for the confirmation of faith in truth'; *this may be closer to the original.*
[6] Cf. note 4.

A note on fixity and improvization in the eucharistic prayer

In *The Apostolic Tradition*, Hippolytus writes thus:

CHAPTER 10
3. *And the bishop shall give thanks according to what we said above.*
4. *It is not at all necessary for him to say the same words as we said above, as though trying (to say them) from memory, when giving thanks to God; but let each pray according to his ability.*
5. *If indeed he is able to pray sufficiently long with a solemn prayer, it is good. But if, when he prays, he recites a prayer according to a fixed form, no one shall prevent him. Only, let his prayer be correct and orthodox.*

It will be remembered that Justin says that the president prays "to the best of his ability"; this is usually taken to mean that he prayed extempore. As R.P.C. Hanson has shown, it is likely that the eucharistic president prayed *freely* within the guidelines of certain *conventions* ("The liberty of the bishop to improvise prayer in the eucharist" in *Vigiliae christianae* 15, 1961, pp. 173–76; see also L. Bouyer, "L'improvisation liturgique dans l'Eglise ancienne" in *La Maison-Dieu* no. 111, 1972, pp. 7–19). Around the turn of the fourth and fifth centuries, synodical canons start limiting freedom for fear of heretical formulations. "Free churches" in the Protestant tradition have often practised free prayer throughout the Lord's Supper. In modern times, this has started to be done even in churches which had hitherto shown the greatest respect to fixed texts.

Remarks on "variation and fixity" can be found in a book by George Every, which is useful also in a more general way for the understanding of the prayer of thanksgiving: *Basic Liturgy: a Study in the Structure of the Eucharistic Prayer* (London, Faith Press, 1961),

3. ROMAN MISSAL (1970): EUCHARISTIC PRAYER II

The anaphora in Hippolytus' *Apostolic Tradition* has inspired several modern compositions. An example is here offered from the new *Roman Missal* published after Vatican II.

The text is the emended translation proposed by the International Committee on English in the Liturgy (ICEL) in 1980.

The Lord be with you: *And also with you.* Lift up your hearts: *We lift them up to the Lord.* Let us give thanks to the Lord our God: *It is right to give him thanks and praise.*

Father, it is our duty and our salvation, always and everywhere to give you thanks through your beloved Son, Jesus Christ.

He is the Word through whom you made the universe, the Saviour you sent to redeem us. By the power of the Holy Spirit he took flesh and was born of the Virgin Mary.

For our sake he opened his arms on the cross; he put an end to death and revealed the resurrection. In this he fulfilled your will and won for you a holy people.

And so we join the angels and the saints in proclaiming your glory as we sing (say):

Holy, holy, holy Lord, God of power and might, heaven and earth are full of your glory. Hosanna in the highest. Blessed is he who come in the name of the Lord. Hosanna in the highest.

Lord, you are holy indeed, the fountain of all holiness. Let your Spirit come upon these gifts to make them holy, so that they may become for us the body and blood of our Lord, Jesus Christ.

Before he was given up to death, a death he freely accepted, he took bread and gave you thanks. He broke the bread, gave it to his disciples, and said: Take this, all of you, and eat it: this is my body which will be given up for you.

When supper was ended, he took the cup. Again he gave you thanks and praise, gave the cup to his disciples, and said: Take this, all of you, and drink from it: this is the cup of my blood, the blood of the new and everlasting covenant. It will be shed for you and for all, so that sins may be forgiven. Do this in memory of me.

Let us proclaim the mystery of faith:

⟨1 *Christ has died, Christ is risen, Christ will come again.*

OR

⟨2 *Dying you destroyed our death, rising you restored our life. Lord Jesus, come in glory.*

OR

⟨3 *When we eat this bread and drink this cup, we proclaim your death, Lord Jesus, until you come in glory.*

OR

⟨4 *Lord, by your cross and resurrection you have set us free. You are the Saviour of the world.*

In memory of his death and resurrection, we offer you, Father, this life-giving bread, this saving cup. We thank you for counting us worthy to stand in your presence and serve you. May all of us who share in the body and blood of Christ be brought together in unity by the Holy Spirit.

Lord, remember your Church throughout the world; make us grow in love as your people, together with N. our Pope, N. our bishop, and all the ministers of your Gospel.

Remember our brothers and sisters who have gone to their rest in the hope of rising again; bring them and all the departed into the light of your presence.

Have mercy on us all; make us worthy to share eternal life with Mary, the virgin mother of God, with the apostles, and with all the saints who have done your will throughout the ages. May we praise you in union with them, and give you glory through your Son, Jesus Christ.

Through him, with him, in him, in the unity of the Holy Spirit, all glory and honour is yours, almighty Father, for ever and ever.
P: Amen.

4. EASTERN ORTHODOX LITURGY OF ST JOHN CHRYSOSTOM

Introduction and text from R.C.D. Jasper and G.J. Cuming, *Prayers of the Eucharist: Early and Reformed.*

This liturgy became, and has remained, the principal and normal rite of the Orthodox Church. Its structure is of the West Syrian type, with the epiclesis following the Institution Narrative and preceding the Intercessions. It may well have preserved the form used in Antioch during Chrysostom's episcopate (A.D. 370–98). Much of the language can be paralleled from his sermons, in which he often refers to the liturgy familiar to his hearers.

The text translated below is that of the Barberini manuscript, written at the end of the eighth century, with the people's part supplied from modern editions. As far as the anaphora is concerned, the contemporary form differs from the Barberini text only in a few additions from the Liturgy of St Basil, here in angle-brackets, and in the omission of two phrases, here in square brackets.

The anaphora
The priest says: The grace of our Lord Jesus Christ, and the love of the God and Father, and the fellowship of the Holy Spirit be with you all.
People: And with your spirit.
Priest: Let us lift up our hearts.
People: We have them with the Lord.
Priest: Let us give thanks to the Lord.
People: It is fitting and right ⟨to worship the Father, the Son, and the Holy Spirit, the consubstantial and undivided Trinity⟩.
The priest begins the holy anaphora: It is fitting and right to hymn you, ⟨to bless you, to praise you,⟩ to give you thanks, to worship you in all places of your dominion. For you are God, ineffable, inconceivable, invisible, incomprehensible, existing always and in the same way, you and your only-begotten Son and your Holy Spirit. You brought us out of not-being to being; and when we had fallen, you raised us up again; and did not cease to do everything until you had brought us up to heaven, and granted us the kingdom that is to come. For all these things we give thanks to you and to your only-begotten Son and to your Holy Spirit, for all that we know and do not know, your seen and unseen benefits that have come upon us. We give you thanks also for this ministry; vouchsafe to receive it from our hands, even though thousands of archangels and ten thousands of angels stand before you,

cherubim and seraphim, with six wings and many eyes, flying on high (*aloud*) singing the triumphal hymn ⟨proclaiming, crying, and saying:⟩ *People:* Holy,⟨holy, holy, Lord of Sabaoth; heaven and earth are full of your glory. Hosanna in the highest. Blessed is he who comes in the name of the Lord. Hosanna in the highest.⟩

The priest, privately: With these powers, O Master, lover of man, we also cry and say: holy are you and all-holy, and your only-begotten Son, and your Holy Spirit; holy are you all-holy and magnificent is your glory; for you so loved the world that you gave your only-begotten Son that all who believe in him should not perish, but have eternal life.

When he had come and fulfilled all the dispensation for us, on the night in which he handed himself over, he took bread in his holy and undefiled and blameless hands, gave thanks, blessed, broke and gave it to his holy disciples and apostles, saying, (*aloud*) 'Take, eat; this is my body, which is⟨broken⟩for you⟨for forgiveness of sins⟩. ⟨*People:* Amen.⟩ Likewise the cup also after supper, saying, (*aloud*) 'Drink from this, all of you; this is my blood of the new covenant, which is shed for you and for many for the forgiveness of sins.'

People: Amen.

The priest, privately: We therefore, remembering this saving commandment and all the things that were done for us: the cross, the tomb, the resurrection on the third day, the ascension into heaven, the session at the right hand, the second and glorious coming again; (*aloud*) offering you your own from your own, in all and through all,

People: we hymn you,⟨we bless you, we give you thanks, O Lord and pray to you, our God⟩.

The priest says privately: We offer you also this reasonable and bloodless service, and we beseech and pray and entreat you, send down your Holy Spirit on us and on these gifts set forth; and make this bread the precious body of your Christ, [changing it by your Holy Spirit, Amen; and that which is in this cup the precious blood of your Christ, changing it by your Holy Spirit,] Amen;

The priest privately: so that they may become to those who partake for vigilance of soul, for forgiveness of sins, for fellowship with the Holy Spirit, for the fullness of the kingdom⟨of heaven⟩, for boldness towards you; not for judgment or for condemnation.

We offer you also this reasonable service for those who rest in faith, ⟨forefathers⟩, fathers, patriarchs, prophets, apostles, preachers, evangelists, martyrs, confessors, ascetics, and all the righteous ⟨spirits⟩ perfected in faith; (*aloud*) especially our all-holy, immaculate, highly glorious, blessed Lady, Mother of God and ever-virgin Mary; Saint John the⟨prophet,⟩forerunner and Baptist, and the holy⟨glorious⟩and honoured apostles; and this saint whose memorial we are keeping, and all your saints: at their entreaties, look upon us, O God.

And remember all those who have fallen asleep in hope of resurrection to eternal life, and grant them rest where the light of your own countenance looks upon them.

Again we beseech you, remember, Lord, all the orthodox episcopate who rightly divide the word of your truth, all the priesthood, the diaconate in Christ, and every order of the clergy.

We offer you this reasonable service also for the (whole) world, for the holy, catholic, and apostolic Church, for those who live in a chaste and reverend state, [for those in mountains and in dens and in caves of the earth,] for the most faithful Emperor, the Christ-loving Empress, and all their court and army: grant them, Lord, a peaceful reign, that in their peace we may lead a quiet and peaceful life in all godliness and honesty.

Remember, Lord, the city in which we dwell, and all cities and lands, and all who dwell in them in faith.

(*aloud*) Above all, remember, Lord, our Archbishop *N*.

Remember, Lord, those at sea, those travelling, the sick, those in adversity, prisoners, and their salvation.

Remember, Lord, those who bring forth fruit and do good works in your holy churches and remember the poor; and send out your mercies upon us all,

(*aloud*) and grant us with one mouth and one heart to glorify and hymn your all-honourable and magnificent name, the Father, the Son, and the Holy Spirit, now and always and to the ages of ages.

People: Amen.

5. ROMAN MISSAL (1970): EUCHARISTIC PRAYER IV

Modern Western eucharistic prayers have sometimes looked ecumenically to the East for inspiration in structure and style. Eucharistic Prayer IV of the Roman rite is an example.

The text is the emended translation proposed by the International Committee on English in the Liturgy (ICEL) in 1980.

The Lord be with you: *And also with you.* Lift up your hearts: *We lift them up to the Lord.* Let us give thanks to the Lord our God: *It is right to give him thanks and praise.*

Father in heaven, it is right that we should give you thanks and glory: you are the one God, living and true. Through all eternity you live in unapproachable light. Source of life and goodness, you have created all things, to fill your creatures with every blessing and lead them to the joyful vision of your light. Countless hosts of angels stand before you to do your will; they look upon your splendour and praise you, night and day. United with them, and in the name of every creature under heaven, we too praise your glory as we say: *Holy, holy, holy Lord, God of power and might, heaven and earth are full of your glory. Hosanna in the highest. Blessed is he who comes in the name of the Lord. Hosanna in the highest.*

Father, we acknowledge your greatness: all your actions show your wisdom and love. You formed the human race in your own likeness: male and female you created them and set them over the whole world to serve you, their creator, and to rule over all creatures, Even when they disobeyed you and lost your friendship you did not abandon them to the power of death, but helped all people to seek and find you. Again and again you offered them a covenant, and through the prophets taught them to hope for salvation. Father, you so loved the world that in the fullness of time you sent your only Son to be our Saviour.

Conceived through the power of the Holy Spirit and born of the Virgin Mary, he became like us in all things but sin. To the poor he proclaimed the good news of salvation, to prisoners, freedom, and to those in sorrow, joy. In fulfilment of your will he gave himself up to death; but by rising from the dead, he destroyed death and restored life. And that we might live no longer for ourselves but for him, he sent the Holy Spirit from you, Father, as his first gift to those who believe, to complete his work on earth and bring us the fullness of grace.

Father, may this Holy Spirit sanctify these offerings. Let them become the body and blood of Jesus Christ our Lord as we celebrate the great mystery which he left us as an everlasting covenant.

He always loved those who were his own in the world. When the time came for him to be glorified by you, his heavenly Father, he showed the depth of his love. While they were at supper, he took bread, said the blessing, broke the bread and gave it to his disciples, saying: Take this, all of you, and eat it: this is my body which will be given up for you.

In the same way, he took the cup, filled with wine. He gave you thanks, and giving the cup to his disciples, said: Take this, all of you, and drink from it: this is the cup of my blood, the blood of the new and everlasting covenant. It will be shed for you and for all men so that sins may be forgiven. Do this in memory of me.

Let us proclaim the mystery of faith:

⟨1 *Christ has died, Christ is risen, Christ will come again.*

OR

⟨2 *Dying you destroyed our death, rising you restored our life. Lord Jesus, come in glory.*

OR

⟨3 *When we eat this bread and drink this cup, we proclaim your death, Lord Jesus, until you come in glory.*

OR

⟨4 *Lord, by your cross and resurrection you have set us free. You are the Saviour of the world.*

Father, we now celebrate this memorial of our redemption. We recall Christ's death, his descent among the dead, his resurrection, and his ascension to your right hand; and, looking forward to his coming in glory, we offer you his body and blood, the acceptable sacrifice which brings salvation to the whole world.

Lord, look upon this sacrifice which you have given to your Church; and by your Holy Spirit, gather all who share this one bread and one cup into the one body of Christ, a living sacrifice of praise. Lord, remember those for whom we offer this sacrifice, especially N. our Pope, N. our bishop, and bishops and clergy everywhere. Remember those who take part in this offering, those here present and all your people, and all who seek you with a sincere heart.

Remember those who have died in the peace of Christ and all the dead whose faith is known to you alone.

Father, in your mercy grant also to us, your children, to enter into our heavenly inheritance in the company of the Virgin Mary, the Mother of God, and your apostles and saints. Then, in your kingdom, freed from the corruption of sin and death, we shall sing your glory with every creature through Christ our Lord, through whom you give us everything that is good.

Through him, with him, in him, in the unity of the Holy Spirit, all glory and honour is yours, almighty Father, for ever and ever. *P: Amen.*

6. "A COMMON EUCHARISTIC PRAYER" (USA)

Eucharistic Prayer IV of the Roman Missal became the basis of "A Common Eucharistic Prayer" put together by an unofficial ecumenical committee in the USA, and published in 1975. This prayer was taken up by the Consultation on Church Union in its *Word Bread Cup* (1978), was included by the Episcopal Church in its revised *Book of Common Prayer* (1979) as Prayer D in Rite II, and has been recommended for use among Methodists, Lutherans and Presbyterians.

Two main differences are to be noted in comparison with the Roman Eucharistic Prayer IV. The "preliminary epiclesis" and the "epiclesis" are brought together in the position of the epiclesis. The wording concerning what "we offer" in the "anamnesis-oblation" is changed.

The text given here is the version found in the Episcopal *Book of Common Prayer*.

The people remain standing. The Celebrant, whether bishop or priest, faces them and sings or says: The Lord be with you. *People:* And also with you. *Celebrant:* Lift up your hearts. *People:* We lift them to the Lord. *Celebrant:* Let us give thanks to the Lord our God. *People:* It is right to give him thanks and praise.

Then, facing the Holy Table, the Celebrant proceeds: It is truly right to glorify you, Father, and to give you thanks; for you alone are God, living and true, dwelling in light inaccessible from before time and for ever.

Fountain of life and source of all goodness, you made all things and fill them with your blessing; you created them to rejoice in the splendour of your radiance.

Countless throngs of angels stand before you to serve you night and day; and, beholding the glory of your presence, they offer you unceasing praise. Joining with them, and giving voice to every creature under heaven, we acclaim you, and glorify your Name, as we sing (say),

Celebrant and People: Holy, holy, holy Lord, God of power and might, heaven and earth are full of your glory. Hosanna in the highest. Blessed is he who comes in the name of the Lord. Hosanna in the highest.

The people stand or kneel. Then the Celebrant continues: We acclaim you, holy Lord, glorious in power. Your mighty works reveal your wisdom and love. You formed us in your own image, giving the whole world into our care, so that, in obedience to you, our Creator, we might rule and serve all your creatures. When our disobedience took us far from you, you did not abandon us to the power of death. In your mercy you came to our help, so that in seeking you we might find you. Again and again you called us into covenant with you, and through the prophets you taught us to hope for salvation.

Father, you loved the world so much that in the fullness of time you sent your only Son to be our Saviour. Incarnate by the Holy Spirit, born of the Virgin Mary, he lived as one of us, yet without sin. To the poor he proclaimed the good news of salvation; to prisoners, freedom; to the sorrowful, joy. To fulfill your purpose he gave himself up to death; and, rising from the grave, destroyed death, and made the whole creation new.

And, that we might live no longer for ourselves, but for him who died and rose for us, he sent the Holy Spirit, his own first gift for those who believe, to complete his work in the world, and to bring to fulfillment the sanctification of all.

At the following words concerning the bread, the Celebrant is to hold it, or lay a hand upon it; and at the words concerning the cup, to hold or place a hand upon the cup and any other vessel containing wine to be consecrated.

When the hour had come for him to be glorified by you, his heavenly Father, having loved his own who were in the world, he loved them to the end; at supper with them he took bread, and when he had given thanks to you, he broke it, and gave it to his disciples, and said, "Take, eat: This is my Body, which is given for you. Do this for the remembrance of me."

After supper he took the cup of wine; and when he had given thanks, he gave it to them, and said, "Drink this, all of you: This is my Blood of the new Covenant, which is shed for you and for many for the forgiveness of sins. Whenever you drink it, do this for the remembrance of me."

Father, we now celebrate this memorial of our redemption. Recalling Christ's death and his descent among the dead, proclaiming his resurrection and ascension to your right hand, awaiting his coming in glory; and offering to you, from the gifts you have given us, this bread and this cup, we praise you and we bless you.

Celebrant and People: We praise you, we bless you, we give thanks to you, and we pray to you, Lord our God.

The Celebrant continues: Lord, we pray that in your goodness and mercy your Holy Spirit may descend upon us, and upon these gifts, sanctifying them and showing them to be holy gifts for your holy people, the bread of life and the cup of salvation, the Body and Blood of your Son Jesus Christ.

Grant that all who share this bread and cup may become one body and one spirit, a living sacrifice in Christ, to the praise of your Name.

Remember, Lord, your one holy catholic and apostolic Church, redeemed by the blood of your Christ. Reveal its unity, guard its faith, and preserve it in peace.

[Remember (*NN*. and) all who minister in your Church.]

[Remember all your people, and those who seek your truth.]

[Remember⎯⎯⎯⎯.]

[Remember all who have died in the peace of Christ, and those whose faith is known to you alone; bring them into the place of eternal joy and light.]

And grant that we may find our inheritance with [the Blessed Virgin Mary, with patriarchs, prophets, apostles, and martyrs, (with⎯⎯⎯⎯) and] all the saints who have found favour with you in ages past. We praise you in union with them and give you glory through your Son Jesus Christ our Lord.

Through Christ, and with Christ, and in Christ, all honour and glory are yours, Almighty God and Father, in the unity of the Holy Spirit, for ever and ever. *Amen.*

7. SYRIAN ORTHODOX CHURCH OF THE EAST

The following introduction and text come from the Very Rev. Kadavil Paul, *The Eucharist Service of the Syrian Jacobite Church of Malabar* (Mysore, Wesley Press, 1961):

There are eighty-eight versions of the Jacobite Liturgies so far found out, of which about sixty four have their authors identified, and which may be used for celebration. There are slight differences between them. The one given here is that of Mar Dionysius Bar Sleebi the Bishop of Omid, and the author of the famous *Expositio liturgiae.* His text or Thaksa or Anaphora is very simple and brief and hence most popular in the Malabar Church and it is used most often. All Liturgies are supposed to be derived from that of St James. The Syriac version of the St James' Liturgy is supposed to have been brought to Malabar and given to the Church by St Thomas the Apostle who is believed to be the founder of this church in Malabar.

The kiss of peace

Priest: Lord, give us at this moment, love, concord and full tranquillity, that we may raise praise and glory unto thee, unto thy only begotten Son and unto thy Holy Ghost now and ever.

All: Amen.

Priest: Peace be unto you all. (Turns and blesses.)

All: And with thy spirit.

Deacon: Let us give peace one to another (mutually) everyone to his neighbour by a kiss holy and divine, in the love of our Lord and our God.

All: Make us worthy, Lord God, for this, all the days of our lives. (The deacon or server passes the kiss from the celebrant to all the others, by the hands and they give to each other.)

Deacon: The holy and divine kiss being given, before the merciful Lord let us bow our heads.

All: Before thee, Our Lord and our God. (And they bow their heads.)

Priest: O Lord bless us with thy irremovable blessings and make us worthy to do thy will, of thy only begotten Son and of thy Holy Ghost, now and ever more.

All: Amen.

Priest: Lord, by this sacrifice which we offer unto thee, remove from us, every filthy thought: and light our souls and sanctify our bodies, that we may raise praise and glory unto thee, unto thy only begotten Son and unto thy Holy Ghost, now and for ever.

All: Amen.

The lifting of the Anaphora[1]

(The celebrant lifts the Anaphora and waves the holy vessels and he says a silent prayer to himself).

Priest: (Silently) Thou art the hard rock which sent forth the twelve rivers of water, for the twelve tribes of Israel. Thou art the hard rock which was set against the tomb of our Redeemer.

Deacon: (Aloud) Bless my Lord:

Let us stand well in reverence, in modesty, with purity and holiness; let us stand therefore all of us, my brethren, in love and in faith; hence in the fear of God, let us look on this dread and holy Anaphora offered before us by the hands of the respected priest; for in tranquillity and in peace he offers the living sacrifice unto God the Father and Lord of all, in behalf of all of us.

All: Mercy, peace, sacrifice and thanks.

Priest: (Turns and blesses). The love of God the Father, (+) the grace of the only begotten Son (+) and the fellowship and communion (+) of the Holy Ghost be with you all my brethren, for ever.

All: And with thy spirit.

Priest: (Invokes the people to lift their hearts, himself lifting the hands.) Up where Christ sitteth on the right hand of God the Father, there be the thoughts, minds and hearts of all of us at this hour.

All: They are with the Lord God.

Priest: Let us praise the Lord with fear.

All: It is meet and right.

Priest: (Hovering the hands over the holy vessels, he says silently thus:) It is meet and right to glorify and praise the Father, the Son and the Holy Ghost, the one true God.

---

[1] The Anaphora is a thin silken fabric covering the holy vessels together, at time of the Pro-thesis.

Priest: (Aloud) With the thousands of thousands and tens of thousands of the fiery who stand before thee and glorify thee without ceasing, may we be made worthy to praise thee in Trisagion, while crying and saying:

All: Holy, Holy, Holy, Lord God, Mighty by whose praises heaven and earth are full, Hosanna in the highest! Blessed is he that came and cometh in the name of the Lord God, glory in the highest.

Priest: (Hovering the hands, says silently:) Holy is the Father who begetteth and is not begotten, holy is the Son who is begotten and is not begetter, and holy is the Holy Spirit who proceeds from the Father and takes from the Son, the one true God who redeems us by his mercy and kindness.

The consecration

Priest: When He got prepared for the redemptive passion, He took bread and blessed (+ +) and sancti- (+) fied, and brake! and he called it his holy Body for eternal life unto those who receive it. (Some say these words only in Syriac)

All: Amen.

Priest: And also the chalice blended of wine and water, he blessed (+ +) and sancti- (+) fied, and he completed it as his precious Blood for eternal life unto those who receive it. (This too is said in Syriac).

All: Amen.

Priest: While he entrusted these unto the disciples, he ordered them saying; "Thus ye do unto my memorial until I come". (Here he takes the spoon and "gmoortho" together and raises up abruptly with his right hand and places them together on the right hand side and moves the "Kaukbo" from right side to the left.)

All: Thy death our Lord, we commemorate and thy resurrection we confess, and thy second coming we await. Thy mercy be upon us all.

Priest: O Lord hence thy church remembereth the whole of thy redeeming dispensation and thy dreadful second coming, in which everyone shall be rewarded according as he did. Because of this thy Church and thy flock with penitence entreat thee and through thee and with thee unto thy Father saying:

All: Have mercy upon us God, Father almighty. Thee we glorify, thee we bless, thee we worship and thee we beseech, Lord God, spare O Good One, and have mercy upon us.

Priest: (Silently, when the above is said) O my Lord, we thy weak and sinful servants also thank thee and praise thy magnanimity about everything and for every thing.

The invocation of the Holy Ghost

Deacon: Bless my Lord: My beloved ones, how fearful is this hour and how dreadful this moment, in which the living Holy Spirit from the high eminence of heaven glories and descends, and hovers and dwells upon this Eucharist that is offered and sanctifies it; in calmness and fear be ye standing and praying¹

All: Peace be with us and tranquillity to us all.

Priest: Lord answer me, Lord answer me, Lord answer me, spare me and bless me.

All: Kurielaison, Kurielaison, Kurielaison! (Aloud).

Priest: (Blesses the Bread with right hand saying:) And may He perfect this bread as the Body (+ + +) of Christ our God.

All: Amen.

Priest: (Blesses the wine) And this blended cup He may change into the Blood (+ + +) of Christ our God.

All: Amen.

Priest: May these be unto all who partake of these, for the remission of their debts, and may they inherit eternal life by these. They will raise praise and glory unto thee, unto thy only begotten Son and unto thy Holy Ghost, now and ever more.

The main intercessions
(Now the congregation may sit down)
Deacon: Bless my Lord:

Let us pray and beseech our Lord and our God at this great, dread and holy moment for all our holy and reverent spiritual Fathers, our rulers who are over us today in this life and tend and govern the holy churches of God that are in every place; our blessed Patriarch and our Father Mor Ignatius, Mor Baselios, Mor Gregorios and our prelate Mor (N) being appointed by God, with the rest of all bishops and spiritual Fathers of Orthodox and correct faith. Let us beseech the Lord.

Priest: (In silence when the above is being said) O Lord, we offer thee this sacrifice in behalf of thy holy Church in every place and in behalf of thy faithful people and the clerical order.

All: Kurielaison.

Priest: (Aloud) O Lord, give thou tranquillity and peace unto thy holy Church, and good and calm old age to its ministers. Appoint thou in it shepherds who correctly interpret the word of Truth that we may raise praise and glory unto thee, unto thy...etc.

All: Amen.

Deacon: Bless my Lord.

Again hence we remember all our faithful brethren and true Christians who have already bidden and entreated us, weak and infirm though we are, to remember them in this hour and in this moment, Lord, in behalf of all who are fallen into various hard temptations, and are relying on thee, Lord God almighty, for their salvation and for thy speedy visitation of them, and for this church sustained by God, and for concord and prosperity to all her faithful children, that they might be in righteousness; let us beseech the Lord.

Priest: (Silently) O Lord, remember all those who do good, be thou merciful and help all those who call upon thee and depend upon thee in true faith.

All: Kurielaison.

Priest: (Aloud) Lord, while thou givest helps from thee unto all those who wail in need and poverty, protect thou also all those who extend the hand of helps unto them, that we may raise praise and glory ... etc.

All: Amen.

Deacon: Bless my Lord.

Again hence we remember also all the faithful and true Christian kings who have supported and confirmed in the true faith the churches and monasteries of God in all parts; and for the whole of Christendom, and for the clergy and for all the faithful people, that they may be in righteousness. Let us beseech the Lord.

Priest: (S) O Lord, remember those kings who aid thy holy church and those who do good unto thy faithful people.

All: Kurielaison.

Priest: (Aloud) O Lord, abandon from us that invisible enemy and his cruelty. Redeem us from the hands of unkind masters that we may raise praise and etc.

All: Amen.

Deacon: Bless my Lord:

Again hence we remember her who is worthy to be exalted and glorified of all generations of the earth, the spotless, the glorious, the blessed and ever-virgin Mary, the holy Mother of God; with her also let us remember the prophets, the Apostles, the preachers, the evangelists, the martyrs, the confessors and the blessed St John the Baptist the fore-runner of his Master, and the holy and glorious St Stephen, the head of the deacons and the first of the martyrs, and the respected saints Peter and Paul the chief Apostles. Let us remember moreover together all the saintly men and women. May their prayers be a fortress unto us. Let us beseech the Lord.

Priest: (S) O Lord remember all thy saints and the mother of thy only begotten Son, save us and help us by the prayers of those who pacify thee.

All: Kurielaison.

Priest: Lord shelter us under the wings of thy saints and arrange us in their group and with them we will sing unto thee praise and glory ... etc.

All: Amen.

Deacon: Bless my Lord:

Again hence we do remember those already in the place of the saints, who divinely died in holiness and are at rest, who having kept the blameless apostolic and one faith, entrusted that to us; and we proclaim those three sacred and general Synods of Nicea, Constantinople and Ephesus, and those our holy Fathers who were glorious and God-bearing, prelates and doctors present in them; James the first Arch-bishop of Jerusalem, apostle and martyr, with Ignatius, Clemis, Dionysius, Athanasius, Julius, Basalius, Gregorios Dioscoros, Thimothios, Philoxinos, Anthimos, Ivanios, reputably hence St Cyril, the high tower and the true, the explainer who interpreted and showed about the incarnation of our Lord Jesus Christ, that the Word-God took flesh. Again hence also our Patriarch Mor Severius, the crown of the Syrians, the prudent mouth-piece, pillar and teacher of the whole holy Church of God, that meadow full of flowers, who every hour proclaimed that

Mary is undoubtedly Mother of God, and keeper of the true faith; also Mor Ephraim and Mor Jacob, Mor Isaac and Mor Balai and Mor Bar Soumo, the head of the lamenters, Mor Simon the stilite, the elect Mor Ab-hai and those who before them, with them and after them have kept and given and entrusted to us, the one undefiled faith. Let their prayers be a fortress unto us, let us beseech the Lord.

Priest: (S) Lord, remember those true shepherds of ours, the tried holy Fathers and doctors of true faith who preached unto us the true faith.

All: Kurielaison.

Priest: O Lord keep us in the true faith and make us not, Lord, such as slant away and be guilty, that we may raise praise and etc.

All: Amen.

Deacon: Bless my Lord:
Again hence we remember all the faithful departed in love and in the true faith, from this holy Sanctuary and from this church, and from this locality and from all places and parts (the faithful dead who in true faith have already died) and are at rest and have gone to thee, God, Father and Lord of souls and of every flesh. Let us entreat and beseech Jesus our God who received their souls and spirits unto himself, that in his abundant mercy he may make them worthy of the remission of trespasses and the forgiveness of sins; that he may carry us and them to his kingdom of heaven. Let us cry aloud thrice Kurielaison.

Priest: (S) Remember, Lord, those faithful departed who died in thy hope. Pacify thou in thy mercy those who are saved by the blood of thy only begotten Son.

All: Kurielaison, Kurielaison, Kurielaison.[2]

Priest: O Lord while thou lookest upon them mercifully, absolve their debts and pardon their short-comings, because the Body and Blood of thy Only begotten Son are hidden in their limbs. We rely on Him, to find by him mercy and pardon of sins, for us and for them.

All: Amen. O God liberate, absolve and pardon both us and them of the follies committed before thee, wittingly and unwittingly, voluntarily and involuntarily.

Priest: (S) God comfort thou and absolve our faults in thought, word and deed, those which are evident and those which are secret, yet evident unto thee.

Priest: (Aloud) O Lord make us and them worthy of a Christian end, while thou rememberest not our follies and theirs, that even in this, as in everything, thy name respected in all and blessed, may be glorified, praised and adored with that of our Lord Jesus Christ and with that of thy Holy Ghost, now and ever more.

All: Amen, as it was, as it is and shall be from generation to generation and unto all generations, world without end. Amen.

---

[2] Here all rise up and remain standing again.

8. THE ROMAN CANON (EUCHARISTIC PRAYER I)

Introduction and text from R.C.D. Jasper and G.J. Cuming, *Prayers of the Eucharist: Early and Reformed.*

The Roman Canon cannot be dated with precision. Quotations and parallels begin to appear towards the end of the fourth century in such writers as Ambrose and Ambrosiaster, and in the letter of Pope Innocent I to Bishop Decentius (A.D. 416). The text translated below is based on the oldest manuscripts, none older than the eighth century. It differs from the standard text of 1571 only slightly.

The canon

Priest: The Lord be with you.
People: And with your spirit.
Priest: Up with your hearts.
People: We have them with the Lord.
Priest: Let us give thanks to the Lord our God.
People: It is fitting and right.
Priest: It is fitting and right, our duty and our salvation, that we should always and everywhere give you thanks, O Lord, holy Father, almighty eternal God, through Christ our Lord; through whom angels praise, dominions adore, powers fear, the heavens and the heavenly hosts and the blessed seraphim, joining together in exultation celebrate your majesty.
We pray you, bid our voices to be admitted with theirs, beseeching you, confessing you, and saying:
People: Holy, holy, holy, Lord God of Sabaoth. Heaven and earth are full of your glory. Hosanna in the highest. Blessed is he who comes in the name of the Lord. Hosanna in the highest.
Priest: We therefore pray and beseech you, most merciful Father, through your Son Jesus Christ our Lord, to accept and bless these gifts, these offerings, these holy and unblemished sacrifices; above all, those which we offer to you for your holy catholic Church: vouchsafe to grant it peace, protection, unity, and guidance throughout the world, together with your servant *N.* our pope, and *N.* our bishop, and all orthodox upholders of the catholic and apostolic faith.
Remember, Lord, your servants, men and women, and all who stand around (us), whose faith and devotion are known to you, for whom we offer to you or who offer to you this sacrifice of praise for themselves and for their own, for the redemption of their souls, for the hope of their salvation and safety, and pay their vows to you, the living, true and eternal God.
In fellowship with *(here a seasonal clause may follow)* and venerating the memory above all of the glorious ever-virgin Mary, Mother of our God and Lord Jesus Christ, and also of your blessed apostles and martyrs Peter, Paul,

Andrew, James, John, Thomas, James, Philip, Bartholomew, Matthew, Simon and Thaddaeus, Linus, Cletus, Clement, Xystus, Cornelius, Cyprian, Laurence, Chrysogonus, John and Paul, Cosmas and Damian, and all your saints, by whose merits and prayers grant us to be defended in all things by the help of your protection; through Christ our Lord.

[Therefore, Lord, we pray you graciously to accept this offering made by us, your servants, and also by your whole family; and to order our days in peace; and to command that we are snatched from eternal damnation and numbered among the flock of your elect; through Christ our Lord.]

Vouchsafe, we beseech you, O God, to make this offering wholly blessed, approved, ratified, reasonable, and acceptable; that it may become to us the body and blood of your dearly beloved Son Jesus Christ our Lord;

who, on the day before he suffered, took bread in his holy and reverend hands, lifted up his eyes to heaven to you, his almighty God and Father, gave thanks to you, blessed, broke, and gave it to his disciples, saying, "Take and eat from this, all of you; for this is my body." Likewise after supper, taking also this glorious cup in his holy and reverend hands, again he gave thanks to you, blessed, and gave it to his disciples, saying, "Take and drink from it, all of you; for this is the cup of my blood, of the new and eternal covenant, the mystery of faith, which will be shed for you and for many for forgiveness of sins. As often as you do this, you will do it for my remembrance."

Therefore also, Lord, we your servants, and also your holy people, have in remembrance the blessed passion of your Son Christ our Lord, likewise his resurrection from the dead, and also his glorious ascension into heaven; we offer to your excellent majesty from your gifts and bounty a pure victim, a holy victim, an unspotted victim, the holy bread of eternal life and the cup of everlasting salvation.

Vouchsafe to look upon them with a favourable and kindly countenance, and accept them as you vouchsafed to accept the gifts of your righteous servant Abel, and the sacrifice of our patriarch Abraham, and that which your high-priest Melchizedek offered to you, a holy sacrifice, an unblemished victim.

We humbly beseech you, almighty God, to bid them be borne by the hands of your angel to your altar on high, in the sight of your divine majesty, that all of us who have received the most holy body and blood of your Son by partaking at this altar may be filled with all heavenly blessing and grace; through Christ our Lord.

Remember also, Lord, the names of those who have gone before us with the sign of faith, and sleep in the sleep of peace. We beseech you to grant to them and to all who rest in Christ a place of restoration, light, and peace; through Christ our Lord.

To us sinners your servants also, who trust in the multitude of your mercies, vouchsafe to grant some part and fellowship with your holy apostles and martyrs, with John, Stephen, Matthias, Barnabas, Ignatius, Alexander, Marcellinus, Peter, Felicity, Perpetua, Agatha, Lucy, Agnes, Cecilia, Anastasia, and with all your saints: into whose company we ask that you will admit us, not weighing our merit, but bounteously forgiving through Christ our Lord.

Through him, Lord, you ever create, sanctify, quicken, bless and bestow all these good things on us. Through him and with him and in him all honour and glory is yours, O God the Father almighty, in the unity of the Holy Spirit, through all the ages of ages. Amen.

With very small changes, the Roman Canon continues in use as Eucharistic Prayer I in the new Missal issued after Vatican II (the official English translation is there provided by the International Committee on English in the Liturgy = ICEL).

***

Because the controversies at the Reformation concerned not only "the canon" but also "the offertory" which preceded the canon, I will also give some "offertory prayers", first from the old Roman Catholic rite (text again from Jasper and Cuming) and then from the new Missal of 1969/70 (English translation from ICEL).

Offertory prayers
Receive, holy Father, almighty, eternal God, this unblemished offering which I, your unworthy servant, present to you, my living and true God, for my innumerable sins, offences, and negligences; for all who stand round, and for all faithful Christians, alive and dead; that it may avail for my salvation and theirs to eternal life.

O God, who in a wonderful way created human nature in its dignity, and more wonderfully restored it; grant us through the mystery of this water and wine, to share his divinity who vouchsafed to share our humanity, Jesus Christ, your Son, our Lord; who is alive and reigns with you as God in the unity of the Holy Spirit through all the ages of ages.

We offer you, Lord, the cup of salvation, and pray that of your kindness it may ascend in the sight of your divine majesty for our salvation and that of the whole world, in a sweet-smelling savour.

Receive, Lord, our humble spirits and contrite hearts; and may our sacrifice be performed today in your sight so as to please you, Lord God.

Come, Sanctifier, almighty, eternal God, and bless this sacrifice prepared for your holy name.

Through the intercession of blessed Michael the archangel, who stands at the right of the altar of incense, and of all the elect, may the Lord vouchsafe to bless this incense and receive it as a sweet-smelling savour; through Christ our Lord.

While censing the altar, the priest recites Psalm 141:2–4; and while washing his hands, he recites Psalm 25:6–12. Then the prayers continue:

Receive, holy Trinity, this offering which we offer you in memory of the passion, resurrection, and ascension of our Lord Jesus Christ; and in honour of the blessed ever-virgin Mary, and blessed John the Baptist, and the holy apostles Peter and Paul, and of... and all saints; that it may avail to their honour and our salvation. May they vouchsafe to intercede for us in heaven, whose memory we celebrate on earth, through the same Jesus Christ our Lord.

Pray, brothers, that my sacrifice and yours may be acceptable to God, the almighty Father.

People: May God receive the sacrifice from your hands to the praise and glory of his name, and to our benefit, and that of all his holy Church.

From the Roman Missal of 1970

C: Blessed are you, Lord, God of all creation. Through your goodness we have this bread to offer, which earth has given and human hands have made. It will become for us the bread of life.

P: Blessed be God for ever.

C: By the mystery of this water and wine may we come to share in the divinity of Christ, who humbled himself to share in our humanity.

Blessed are you, Lord, God of all creation. Through your goodness we have this wine to offer, fruit of the vine and work of human hands. It will become our spiritual drink.

P: Blessed be God for ever.

C: Lord God, we ask you to receive us and be pleased with the sacrifice we offer you with humble and contrite hearts.

The Priest washes his hands, saying:

C: Lord, wash away my iniquity; cleanse me from my sin.

Pray, brethren, that our sacrifice may be acceptable to God, the almighty Father.

P: May the Lord accept the sacrifice at your hands for the praise and glory of his name, for our good, and the good of all his Church.

The preparation of the gifts concludes with the invitation to pray with the priest, and the prayer over the gifts, which is "proper" to the particular mass.

9. TEXTS FROM LUTHER

Introduction and texts from R.C.D. Jasper and G.J. Cuming, *Prayers of the Eucharist: Early and Reformed.*

In 1520 Luther published his *Babylonish Captivity*, urging the need for a liturgy in the vernacular and attacking the Roman doctrines of transubstantiation and the sacrifice of the Mass. The liturgical expression of his views followed in 1523 in *Formula Missae*. This set out a truncated version of the Roman rite, and all that remained of the canon was the Sursum Corda, Institution Narrative, Sanctus and Benedictus accompanied by an elevation. After considerable experiment he produced his *Deutsche Messe* in 1526, in which the canon was reduced simply to the Institution Narrative. Both

Formulae Missae and *Deutsche Messe* served as models for later Lutheran rites, and those which followed the latter were clearly slighter in content.

A. Formula of Mass and Communion for the Church at Wittenberg 1523

...there follows that complete abomination, into the service of which all that precedes in the Mass has been forced, whence it is called *Offertorium,* and on account of which nearly everything sounds and reeks of oblation. In the midst of these things those words of life and salvation have been placed, just like in times past the ark of the Lord was placed in the temple of idols next to Dagon. And there is no Israelite there who is able either to approach or lead back the ark, until it has made its enemies infamous, smiting them on the back, with eternal shame, and has compelled them to send it away, which is a parable for the present time. Therefore repudiating all those things which smack of sacrifice and of the offertory, together with the entire *canon,* let us retain those things which are pure and holy, and then we will order our Mass in this fashion.

I During the Creed or after the canon[1], let bread and wine be prepared in the customary way for consecration. Except that I am not yet fixed in my mind as to whether or not water should be mixed with the wine, although I incline to the preparation of pure wine, because the indication strikes me as wrong which Isaiah advances in Chapter I, "Your wine," he says, "is mixed with water." For pure wine symbolizes beautifully the purity of the teaching of the Gospel. Then, too, nothing has been poured out for us save the blood of Christ only unmixed with ours, of which we make commemoration here. Neither can the dream of those stand who say that our union with Christ is here symbolized, the commemoration of which union we do not make here. Nor are we united before the shedding of his blood, otherwise at the same time we would be celebrating the pouring out of our own blood with the blood of Christ for ourselves. Nevertheless in opposition to liberty, I will not introduce a superstitious law. Christ will not care very much about this, nor are these matters worthy of contention. Enough foolish contention over this has been engaged in by the Roman and Greek churches as also in many other matters. And because some assert that blood and water flowed from the side of Christ, that does not prove anything. For that water signifies something other than what they wish to be signified by that mixed water. Nor was that mixed with the blood. Moreover the figure proves nothing, and the example does not stand; hence as a human invention it is held to be free.

II The bread and the wine having been prepared, let the order be in this manner:

The Lord be with you.
Response: And with thy spirit.

Lift up (your) hearts.
Response: Let us lift them up to the Lord.

Let us give thanks unto our Lord God.

---

[1] Probably a printer's error for "after the Sermon".

Response: It is meet and right.

It is truly meet and right, just and salutary for us to give you thanks always and everywhere, Holy Lord, Father Almighty, Eternal God, through Christ our Lord.

III Then... Who the day before he suffered took bread, giving thanks, broke and gave to his disciples, saying, Take, eat. This is my body, which is given for you.

Similarly also the cup, after he supped, saying, This cup is the new testament in my blood which is poured out for you and for many in remission of sins. As often as you shall do this, do it in memory of me.

I wish these words of Christ, allowing a moderate pause after the Preface, to be recited in the same tone of voice in which the Lord's Prayer is sung at another place in the canon; so that it will be possible for those standing by to hear, although in all these things liberty is allowed to pious minds to recite these words either silently or audibly.

IV The consecration ended, let the choir sing the Sanctus, and when the Benedictus is sung, let the bread and chalice be elevated according to the rite in use up to this time, chiefly on account of the infirm who might be greatly offended by the sudden change in this more noted rite in the Mass, especially where they have been taught through vernacular sermons what is sought by this elevation.

V After this the Lord's Prayer is read. Thus: *Let us pray: Taught by your saving precepts,* etc., omitting the prayer following: *Deliver us, we beseech,* with all signs, which they were wont to make over the host and with the host over the chalice; nor shall the host be broken or mixed in the chalice. But immediately after the Lord's Prayer shall be said, *The Peace of the Lord,* etc., which is, so to speak, a public absolution of the sins of the communicants, truly the Gospel voice announcing remission of sins, the one and most worthy preparation for the Lord's Table, if it be apprehended by faith and not otherwise than though it came forth from the mouth of Christ himself. On account of this I wish it to be announced with face turned to the people, as the bishops were accustomed to do, which is the sole vestige of the ancient bishops left among our bishops.

VI Then let him communicate himself first, then the people; in the meanwhile let the Agnus Dei be sung. But if he should desire to pray the prayer, *O Lord Jesus Christ, Son of the living God, who according to the will of the Father,* etc. before communicating, he will not pray wrongly, only change the singular number to the plural *ours* and *us* for *mine* and *me.* Likewise the prayer, *The Body of the Lord,* etc. guard my *soul, or* your *soul unto life eternal. And the blood of* our *Lord, guard* your *soul unto life eternal.*

VII If he desires to sing the Communion let it be sung. But in the place of the *ad complendam* or final collect which so frequently savours of sacrifice, let this prayer be read in the same tone: *What we have taken with the mouth, O Lord.* This one also may be read: *Your Body, O Lord, which we have received,* etc. changing to the plural number. *Who live and reign,* etc. *The Lord be with you,* etc. In place of the *Ite missa,* let *Benedicamus domino* be said, adding Alleluia according to its own melodies where and when it is desired; or Benedicamus may be borrowed from Vespers.

VIII Let the customary Benediction be given. Or take that from Numbers 6, which the Lord himself arranged and ordered: *The Lord bless us and guard us: May he show us his face and be merciful to us; The Lord turn his face to us and give us peace.* Or that in Psalm 96, *May God, our God, bless us: May God bless us and all the ends of the earth fear him. Amen.* I believe Christ used something of this kind when, ascending into heaven, he blessed his disciples.

And this, too, should be free to the bishop, namely, by what order he may desire either to receive or to administer both species. For assuredly he may consecrate both bread and wine consecutively before he receives the bread; or between the consecration of the bread and wine he may communicate with the bread both himself and as many as desire it, and thereupon consecrate the wine and at length give to all to drink of it. After which manner Christ seems to have acted, as the words of the Gospel reveal, where he commanded to eat the bread before he blessed the cup. Then is said expressly: *Likewise also the cup after he supped.* Thus you perceive the cup was blessed only after eating the bread. But this quite new rite will not permit the doing of those things following the consecration about which we spoke above, unless they should be changed.

This is the way we think about the Mass, but at the same time taking care in all such matters lest we make binding things which are free, or compel those to sin who either would do some other thing or omit certain things; only let them keep the words of consecration uncorrupted, and let them do this in faith. For these should be the usages of Christians, that is of children of the free woman, who observe these things voluntarily and from the heart, changing them as often as and in whatever manner they might wish. Wherefore it is not right that one should either require or establish some indispensable form as a law in this matter, by which he might ensnare or vex consciences. Whence also we find no complete example of this use in the ancient fathers and in the Primitive Church, save only in the Roman Church. But if they have appointed something as a law in this matter, it should not be observed; because these things neither can nor should be bound by laws...

B. The German Mass 1526

The Office and Consecration follows in this wise:

Example: Our Lord Jesus Christ, in the night in which he was betrayed, took bread; and when he had given thanks, he brake it and gave it to his disciples, saying, Take, eat; this is my body, which is given for you; this do as oft as you do it, in remembrance of me.

After the same manner also, he took the cup, when he had supped, and said, Take and drink you all of it; this is the cup, a new testament in my blood, which is shed for you for the remission of sins; this do, as oft as you drink it, in remembrance of me.

It seems to me that it would be in accord with the institution of the Lord's Supper to administer the sacrament immediately after the consecration of the bread, before the cup is blessed, for both Luke and Paul say: He took the cup after they had supped, etc. During the distribution of the bread the German Sanctus could be sung, or the hymn, *Gott sei gelobet,* or the hymn of John Hus: *Jesus Christus unser Heiland.* Then shall the cup be blessed and administered; while the remainder of the hymns are sung, or the German Agnus Dei. Let there be a chaste and orderly approach, not men and women with each other but the women after the men, wherefore they should also stand separately at allotted places. What should be the attitude in respect to secret confession, I have indicated in other writings and my opinion can be found in the *Betbuechlein.*

We do not want to abolish the elevation but retain it because it goes well with the German Sanctus and signifies that Christ has commanded us to remember him. For as the sacrament is elevated in a material manner and yet Christ's body and blood are not seen in it, so he is remembered and elevated by the word of the sermon and is confessed and adored in the reception of the sacrament. Yet it is all apprehended by faith, for we cannot see how Christ gives his body and blood for us and even now daily shows and offers it before God to obtain grace for us.

10. MODERN LUTHERAN TEXTS

A. Germany (1955/77)

The following form is taken from *Agende für evangelisch-lutherische Kirchen und Gemeinden* I (1955) incorporating revisions from 1976 and 1977 offered for trial use. The English translation is borrowed from the Lutheran/Roman Catholic Joint Commission, *The Eucharist* (Geneva, Lutheran World Federation, 1980).

THE HOLY COMMUNION

Preface (Great Thanksgiving)

President: The Lord be with you.

Congregation: And with your spirit.

P: Lift up your hearts!

C: We lift them to the Lord.

P: Let us give thanks to the Lord, our God.

C: It is estimable and right.

(25 Prefaces for the church year; for example for general use:)

P: It is truly estimable and right, just and salutary, that at all times and in all places we give you thanks, holy Lord, almighty Father, eternal God, through Jesus Christ our Lord. You sent him for the salvation of the world that by his death we might have forgiveness of sins and by his resurrection we might have life. Through him the angels praise your majesty, the heavenly hosts adore you, and the powers tremble; together with the blessed Seraphim all the citizens of heaven praise you in brilliant jubilation. Unite our voices with theirs and let us sing praise in endless adoration:

C: Holy, holy, holy, Lord God, of Sabaoth; heaven and earth are full of your glory. Hosanna in the highest. Blessed is he who comes in the name of the Lord. Hosanna in the highest.

Consecration (using forms A, B, or C, as follows)

(A)

P: Our Father in heaven...deliver us from the Evil One.

C: For yours is the kingdom...for ever. Amen.

P: Our Lord Jesus Christ in the night in which he was betrayed, took bread, gave thanks; broke it, and gave it to his disciples saying: Take and eat; this † is my body, given for you; do this in remembrance of me. In like manner he took the cup, after supper, gave thanks, and gave it to them saying: Take and drink from it, all of you; this cup is the new covenant in † my blood, shed for you for the forgiveness of sins. Do this, as often as you drink it, in remembrance of me.

(B)

(Several alternatives are provided at this point; see below)

P: We praise you, Lord of heaven and earth that you showed your creatures mercy, and that you have sent your only Son in our flesh. We thank you for the salvation you have prepared for us through the holy and all-sufficient sacrifice of his body and blood on the tree of the cross. Gathered in his name and for his remembrance, we pray: Lord, send down upon us the Holy Spirit, sanctify and renew us in body and soul, and grant that under this bread and wine we receive in true faith the very body and blood of your Son to our salvation, since even now we make use of Christ's own testament according to his command.

Our Lord Jesus Christ in the night in which he was betrayed...
(cf. A above)

Therefore we remember, Lord, heavenly Father, the saving passion and death of your dear Son Jesus Christ. We praise his victorious resurrection from the dead and are comforted by his ascension into your heavenly sanctuary where he, our High Priest, continually intercedes for us. And as all of us are one body in Christ through the fellowship of his body and blood, so gather your faithful people from the ends of the earth, that together with all the faithful we may celebrate in his kingdom the marriage feast of the Lamb. Through him be praise and honour, glory and adoration, almighty God, in the Holy Spirit, now and forever, and to the ages of ages.

C: Amen.

P: Our Father in heaven...deliver us from the Evil One.

C: For yours is the kingdom...for ever. Amen.

P: The peace of the Lord be with you all.

C: Amen.

C: Hymn: "O Christ, Lamb of God", *or* "Lamb of God, pure and sinless".

(C)

C: Communion Hymn.

P: Our Saviour, Jesus Christ invites us to his table where he wills to give us that power and comfort which proceed from his death and resurrection. In bread and wine, the signs of his presence, he unites himself with us and draws us together as members of his church.

Our Lord Jesus Christ in the night in which he was betrayed... (cf. A above).

As often as you eat this bread and drink from this cup, you proclaim the Lord's death, until he comes.

In this supper which Jesus Christ shared with his disciples, he wills to be with us with all he has to give. Nothing now can separate us from God any longer, not even those things which may torment us: our doubts, our failures, our guilt. No longer are we left alone.

Merciful God and Father, you sent your Son to us, and you have invited us to return home to you. You are greater than all those things which grieve us and cause us anxiety. Since your Son has given himself for us, receive us. Renew and sanctify our life that nothing is able to separate us from your love.

C: Lord, we believe, help our unbelief!

P: If this is your prayer, join your voice in the petition: O Christ, Lamb of God, who bear the sin of the world, have mercy on us.

C: Hymn: "O Christ, Lamb of God"...

P: Lord, have mercy on us!

C: Lord, have mercy on us!

P: Our Lord Jesus Christ invites you to receive his forgiveness under the bread and wine. Come, for he has made preparations for you. Blessed are those who eat bread in the kingdom of God.

Distribution (communion)

Thanksgiving and dismissal

Five more alternatives are provided for use in Form B:

1.

P: We praise you, Lord of heaven and earth. You have had mercy on your creatures and have sent your Son in human flesh. We thank you for the redemption which he accomplished on the cross. We pray: Send down upon us the Holy Spirit, sanctify and renew us in body and soul, so that under this bread and wine we receive the body and blood of Jesus Christ to our salvation, as we now do what he commanded:

Our Lord Jesus Christ in the night in which he was betrayed...(cf. A above)

C: (may sing or say:) We proclaim your death, O Lord, and we praise your resurrection, until you come again in glory.

P: So we remember, heavenly Father, the suffering and death of your Son. We praise his resurrection and ascension, and we rely on his lordship over all the world. We pray: Just as all who receive his body are *one* body in Christ, so gather together your people from the ends of the earth, and let us with all faithful people celebrate the eternal feast of joy in his kingdom. Through him be praise and honour, glory and adoration, almighty God, in the Holy Spirit, now and forever, and to the ages of ages.

C: Amen.

Our Father in heaven...

2.

P: We glorify you, Lord, and sing your praise. You have not abandoned to sin and death that which you, almighty God, have made. Through Jesus Christ, your word, you summon us all to life. He took our guilt upon himself and made peace between you and all people.

Our Lord Jesus Christ in the night in which he was betrayed... (cf. A above)

C: We proclaim your death, O Lord, and we praise your resurrection, until you come again in glory.

P: Therefore we give you thanks, heavenly Father, for the life and passion of your Son, and for his sacrifice on the cross. We praise his resurrection, the victory over evil and death. Give us, Lord, the Holy Spirit, and renew our life through him. Bring together in the unity of faith all who share the body and blood of Christ; unite them in the fellowship of love and in the hope of your glory.

(*Maranatha!*) Our Lord comes.

C: Amen. Come, Lord Jesus!

Our Father in heaven...

3.

(Without Preface and Sanctus)

P: Lord, our God, Ruler over all. We praise you for the wonder of your creation. You bless human labour and endow us with life and joy. You have given us bread and wine that we may celebrate the supper of your Son. We thank you for the mystery of your love. Receive us anew as your own that our conduct may honour you, through Jesus Christ, our Lord.

Our Lord Jesus Christ in the night in which he was betrayed... (cf. A above)

C: We proclaim your death, O Lord, and we praise your resurrection, until you come again in glory.

P: So we remember, Father, the life he gave up for all people, and his resurrection from the dead. He offered himself for the world's salvation and is established as Lord over all the powers. Send us the Holy Spirit, that through these gifts he would fill us with new life. Bind together in the fellowship of the faith all those who belong to your people. Have mercy upon your church and give it unity in this supper of joy. O God, we await your great day.

(*Maranatha!*) Our Lord comes.

C: Amen. Come, Lord Jesus!

Our Father in heaven...

4.

(After Preface and Sanctus)

P: We praise the eternal, holy God: who wonderfully preserves his creation;

who governs the course of the world according to his counsel; and who elected his people to be the witness of his mercy. We thank him that he sent us his Son, the messenger of his love, who supports us and our guilt, and stands by us in every need; who loved us to the end.

Our Lord Jesus Christ in the night in which he was betrayed... (cf. A above)

Deacon: As often as you eat this bread and drink from this cup, you proclaim the Lord's death, until he comes.

C: We proclaim your death, O Lord, and we praise your resurrection, until you come again in glory.

P: Therefore we remember his suffering and death, his resurrection and his future. At his table he gives us fellowship with God and love for all humankind.

Deacon: Our thoughts and our deeds belong to him. He sets us on the way of peace. May he bless us in his supper, and sanctify our life through his Spirit.

C: Hymn: "Come, Holy Spirit, and fill the hearts of the faithful" *or another hymn of invocation of the Holy Spirit.*

5.

P: We praise you, almighty God, that you gave your Son over [to death], Jesus Christ, our Saviour, who was obedient even unto death.

Our Lord Jesus Christ in the night in which he was betrayed... (cf. A above)

So we remember his death, and we pray: Fill us with your Spirit. Bless to us these gifts. Through this bread which we share with one another give us fellowship with Jesus Christ. Through this cup from which we drink unite us with him. Remember your church scattered throughout the world, and bring us together into your kingdom. To you be all honour forever.

Our Father in heaven...

B. Sweden (1975)

The following was approved by the Synod of the Church of Sweden in 1975 as an alternative to the order of 1942. The English translation is from the Lutheran/Roman Catholic Joint Commission, *The Eucharist* (Geneva, Lutheran World Federation, 1980).

Sursum corda

P: Lift up your hearts.
C: We lift them to the Lord.
P: Let us give thanks to the Lord our God.
C: He alone is worthy of our praise.

Preface

P: Indeed, you alone are worthy of our praise, almighty Father, holy God. Your will we praise and bless through Jesus Christ, our Lord.

(Here follows one of ten Proper Prefaces, concluding with:)
P: Therefore with all your faithful through all times, and with all the company of heaven, we praise your name and devoutly sing:

Sanctus

C: Holy, holy, holy Lord, God of Sabaoth. Heaven and earth are full of your glory. Hosanna in the highest. Blessed is he that comes in the name of the Lord. Hosanna in the highest.

The Thanksgiving continued (One of the following prayers is said:)

A.

P: Praise be to you, Lord of heaven and earth, who have shown mercy towards mankind and given your only Son so that all who believe in him shall not perish but have everlasting life. We thank you for the salvation you have prepared for us through Jesus Christ. Send your Spirit in our hearts that he might work in us a living faith. Sanctify also through your Spirit this bread and wine, fruits of the earth and the toil of people which we bear unto you, so that we, through them, partake of the true body and blood of our Lord Jesus Christ.

In the night he was betrayed, he took bread, gave thanks, broke it and gave it to his disciples, and said: Take and eat. This is my body which is given for you. Do this in remembrance of me. Likewise he took the cup, gave thanks, and gave it to the disciples and said: Drink this, all of you. This cup is the new covenant in my blood which is shed for many for the remission of sins. Do this, so often as you drink it, in remembrance of me.

Therefore, Holy Father, we celebrate this meal in remembrance of the passion and death of your Son, his resurrection and ascension. We eat the bread of life and drink the cup of salvation until the day of his glorious return. We pray:

Look upon the perfect and everlasting sacrifice (or offering) through which you reconciled us to yourself in Christ. Through the Holy Spirit let us all be joined in one body and perfected to a living sacrifice in Christ.

Through whom and with whom and in whom, in the unity of the Holy Spirit, all honour and glory is yours, almighty God and Father for ever and ever.

C: Amen.

B.

P: We praise you, God, who hold heaven and earth in your hands. In you we live, move and have our being. Your mercy is better than life. Our lips shall praise you. We thank you for sending your Son to save the world. You let him suffer death upon the cross in order to exalt him and give him that name which is above all other names. Let your spirit touch us and these our gifts of bread and wine so that we, through them, share in Christ's body and blood.

In the night he was betrayed...

C: We proclaim his death, we confess his resurrection until the day he returns in glory.

P: Holy Father, when we celebrate the remembrance of our Saviour, you give us a part in his life, his death and resurrection, his heavenly glory. Here is his body and blood which has reconciled us with you. Through your Spirit make us all one in him, to reveal his life in the world. Let the day come soon when you create new heavens and a new earth where righteousness reigns. We praise you and glorify you through Jesus Christ in the Holy Spirit, now, always and forever.

C: Amen.

C.

P: We thank you, Lord of heaven and earth, for opening your hand and satisfying all things living with your grace. You give us our daily bread, health and strength. From the wheat of the field and the grapes of the hillside you prepare bread and wine. You spread your table for us. Let your Spirit come to us and these gifts, so that we partake of the heavenly bread and the blessed cup that are the body and blood of Christ.

In the night he was betrayed...

C: We proclaim his death, we confess his resurrection until the day he returns in glory.

(The prayer continues with one of the following alternatives:)

P: Here we see your Son's passion and death, his resurrection from the dead and his life with you in glory. Here we meet him who prays for us and who shall come to judge the living and dead on the day that you decide. God, we thank you for your promise of new heavens and a new earth where righteousness reigns. We thank you for the hope of a blessed resurrection through your Son, our Saviour.

C: Amen.

OR

P: Let all those who share this bread and this cup be joined through the Holy Spirit in a single body and perfected to a living sacrifice in Christ.

C: Amen.

C. USA (1978)

The following is taken from the *Lutheran Book of Worship* (1978), which was prepared by the churches participating in the Inter-Lutheran Commission on Worship, namely Lutheran Church in America, The American Lutheran Church, the Evangelical Lutheran Church of Canada, and The Lutheran Church-Missouri Synod.

28. THE GREAT THANKSGIVING is begun by the minister standing at the altar.

P: The Lord be with you.

C: And also with you.

P: Lift up your hearts.

C: We lift them to the Lord.

P: Let us give thanks to the Lord our God.

C: It is right to give him thanks and praise.

29. The preface appropriate to the day or season is sung or said.

P: It is indeed right and salutary...we praise your name and join their unending hymn:

C: Holy, holy, holy Lord, God of power and might: Heaven and earth are full of your glory. Hosanna. Hosanna. Hosanna in the highest. Blessed is he who comes the name of the Lord. Hosanna in the highest.

30. The minister continues, using one of the sections below

31. The minister may say:

Holy God, mighty Lord, gracious Father: Endless is your mercy and eternal your reign.
You have filled all creation with light and life;
heaven and earth are full of your glory.
Through Abraham you promised to bless all nations.
You rescued Israel, your chosen people.
Through the prophets you renewed your promise;
and at this end of all the ages, you sent your Son,
who in words and deeds proclaimed your kingdom
and was obedient to your will, even to giving his life.
In the night in which he was betrayed, our Lord Jesus took bread, and gave thanks; broke it, and gave it to his disciples, saying: Take and eat; this is my body, given for you.
Do this for the remembrance of me.
Again, after supper, he took the cup, gave thanks, and gave it for all to drink, saying: This cup is the new covenant in my blood, shed for you and for all people for the forgiveness of sin.
Do this for the remembrance of me.
For as often as we eat of this bread and drink from this cup, we proclaim the Lord's death, until he comes.

C: Christ has died. Christ is risen. Christ will come again.

P: Therefore, gracious Father, with this bread and cup we remember the life our Lord offered for us.
And, believing the witness of his resurrection, we await his coming in power to share with us the great and promised feast.

C: Amen. Come, Lord Jesus.

P: Send now, we pray, your Holy Spirit, the spirit of our Lord and of his resurrection, that we who receive the Lord's body and blood may live to the praise of your glory and receive our inheritance with all your saints in light.

C: Amen. Come, Holy Spirit.

P: Join our prayers with those of your servants of every time and every place, and unite them with the ceaseless petitions of our great high priest until he comes as victorious Lord of all.

C: Through him, with him, in him, in the unity of the Holy Spirit, all honour and glory is yours, almighty Father, now and forever. Amen

OR

32. The minister may say:

P: In the night in which he was betrayed, our Lord Jesus took bread, and gave thanks; broke it, and gave it to his disciples, saying: Take and eat; this is my body, given for you.
Do this for the remembrance of me.
Again, after supper, he took the cup, gave thanks, and gave it for all to drink, saying: This cup is the new covenant in my blood, shed for you and for all people for the forgiveness of sin.
Do this for the remembrance of me.

OR

33. The minister may say:

P: Blessed are you, Lord of heaven and earth.
In mercy for our fallen world you gave your only Son, that all those who believe in him should not perish, but have eternal life.
We give thanks to you for the salvation you have prepared for us through Jesus Christ.
Send now your Holy Spirit into our hearts, that we may receive our Lord with a living faith as he comes to us in his holy supper.

C: Amen. Come, Lord Jesus.

P: In the night in which he was betrayed our Lord Jesus took bread, and gave thanks: broke it, and gave it to his disciples, saying: Take and eat; this is my body, given for you.
Do this for the remembrance of me.
Again, after supper, he took the cup, gave thanks, and gave it for all to drink, saying: This cup is the new covenant in my blood, shed for you and for all people for the forgiveness of sin.
Do this for the remembrance of me.

11. REFORMED TEXTS FROM THE SIXTEENTH CENTURY

Introductions and texts taken from R.C.D. Jasper and G.J. Cuming, *Prayers of the Eucharist: Early and Reformed.*

A. Zwingli

Zwingli's first liturgical work appeared in the pamphlet *De Canone Missae Epicheiresis (An Attack upon the Canon of the Mass)* in 1523. It was written in Latin and, despite its title, contained his proposals for the revision of the whole of the Roman rite. While he was prepared to retain most of the liturgy of the word, he replaced the canon after the Sanctus and Preface with four prayers of his own composition. His *Action oder Bruch des Nachtmals (Action or Use of the Lord's Supper)* published two years later was much more radical and, apart from the Institution Narrative, the canon had disappeared completely. This became the norm for all later Zwinglian rites. The translations here are from the texts provided in Bretschneider's *Corpus Reformatorum*, vols. 39 and 40.

I. An attack on the canon of the mass (1523)

Sursum corda
Preface
Sanctus

The Canon is then replaced by the four following prayers:

1 Most merciful and thrice holy Father, you created man in the beginning to enjoy paradise here and then afterwards to enjoy yourself. From this state of grace man fell through his own fault and was deemed worthy of death: he tainted all those who came after him; and then there was simply no hope of life, unless you, who alone are good, decided to relieve man's distress. You promised his seed that he would bruise the head of the evil seducer, so that man would not waste away in perpetual despair. In accordance with this promise, when the appointed time was fulfilled, you offered your Son, our Lord Jesus Christ, who took our flesh through the pure and ever-virgin Mary, that he might become for us perfect priest and perfect victim, unique among the human race. He gave himself to be the sacrifice for those who were lost: and not content with this, so that we might lack for nothing, he gave himself to be our food and drink. So, most blessed Father, we pray that your goodness may be constantly on our lips: and, although our deepest gratitude can never match your kindness, we pray that in your constant and unfailing goodness you will make us worthy to sing your praises continually with our hearts and lips and in our deeds, and to ask for nothing that would be alien to you. In confidence, therefore, we shall offer you prayer and praise in accordance with your will, as we have been taught by your most dearly beloved Son, Jesus Christ our Lord. Guided therefore by his precepts, we are bold to say:

Our Father...

2 O God, you fed not only man from his youth but also every living creature. Feed our hungry souls, we pray, with heavenly food: for you are he who fills the hungry with good things. Our souls are spiritual, made in your image; therefore they can only be refreshed with spiritual food, and that food can only be given by your word. Your word is truth: for you are truth, and from you nothing can come save that which is genuine, holy, steadfast and unspotted. Never deprive us of the food of your word, but ever feed us in your goodness. That is the true bread, which gives life to the world. We would eat the flesh and drink the blood of your Son in vain, if we did not firmly believe above all things through the faith of your word, that your Son our Lord Jesus Christ was crucified for us and atoned for the sins of the whole world. He himself said that the flesh profits nothing, but it is the Spirit which gives life. Quicken us, therefore, by your Spirit and never deprive us of your word; for your word is the vehicle of your Spirit, and assuredly it will never return to you empty. By that one thing, and that alone, is the human mind set

free, for it is the truth; and you have promised through your Son that if the truth sets us free, then indeed we shall be truly free. So we pray that we may never lack the food of your word, for by that one thing we are granted the freedom and security of salvation. Through your Son, Jesus Christ our Lord, who is alive and reigns with you in the unity of the Holy Spirit, God, through all the ages of ages. Amen.

3 Therefore, O Lord, as you have taught us by your word that heaven and earth shall pass away rather than your word, so we firmly believe that not even the least particle will ever fall. And as we believe that your Son, once offered for us, made reconciliation to the Father, so we also firmly believe that he offered himself to be the food of our souls under the forms of bread and wine; so that the memory of his generous deed may never be abolished. Increase our faith, if it falters in any way; and grant that as your Son brought us back into your grace through the shame and bitterness of the cross and provided us with everlasting delights, so with him as leader and protector may we overcome the hardships and afflictions of this world, while we eat his body and drink his blood. For he gave himself to us as food, so that just as he himself vanquished the world, we, nourished by him, might hope to vanquish it in turn. In vain do we say that we make remembrance of him and what he did, if we do it by word alone. Grant us, therefore, merciful Father, through Christ your Son our Lord, through whom you give life to all things, and through whom you renew and sustain all things, that we may show him forth in our lives; so that the likeness which we lost in Adam may be restored. And in order that this may take place in us the more effectively and surely, grant that all we who partake of the body and blood of your Son may have one hope and purpose, and be ourselves one in him, as he is one with you. Through the same Christ our Lord.

4 O God, among those born of women none has arisen greater than your Son, and you have deigned to reveal that he is the lamb to take away our sins. Through him be ready to hear our cry, "O Lamb of God, you take away the sins of the world, have mercy on us." In your kindness forgive all our faults. For he suffered, that through him we might have perpetual access to you: he wished to be clothed with our weakness, that in him we might have strength: he gave himself as food, that we might be nourished by him and grow into the fullness of his perfect life. O Lord, draw our hearts by your gracious light, that we may worthily and faithfully join in the sacred banquet of your Son, of which he himself is both our host and our most delectable food.

For on the night on which he was betrayed, he took bread, and giving thanks, he blessed and broke it, and gave it to his disciples, and said:

Take and eat. This is my body, which is given for you. Do this in remembrance of me.

Likewise the cup, after they had eaten; he took it, offered thanks, and gave it to them, saying:

Drink of this, all of you. For this is my blood of the new testament which is shed for you in the remission of sins. Do this, as often as you drink it, in remembrance of me.

For as often as you eat this bread and drink this cup, you proclaim the death of the Lord, until he comes.

Therefore come to me, all you who labour and are heavy laden, and I will give you rest.
The body of our Lord Jesus Christ preserve you to everlasting life.
The blood of our Lord Jesus Christ preserve you to everlasting life.

Brief Thanksgiving
Nunc Dimittis
Blessing

II. Action or use of the Lord's Supper (1525)
The way Christ instituted this supper
The minister reads as follows: On the night when he was betrayed and given up to death, Jesus took bread; and when he had given thanks he broke it, and said, "Take, eat; this is my body: do this in remembrance of me." In the same manner also, he took the cup after supper, said thanks, and gave it to them, saying, "Drink this, all of you: this cup is the new testament in my blood. Do this as often as you drink it, in remembrance of me. For as often as you eat this bread and drink this cup, you proclaim and glorify the Lord's death."

Then the designated servers carry around the unleavened bread, from which each one of the faithful takes a morsel or mouthful with his hand, or has it offered to him by the server who carries the bread around. And when those with the bread have proceeded so far that everyone has eaten his small piece, the other servers then follow with the cup, and in the same manner give it to each person to drink. And all of this takes place with such honour and propriety as well becomes the Church of God and the Supper of Christ.

Afterwards, the people having eaten and drunk, thanks is given according to the example of Christ, by the use of Psalm 112.

B. Calvin, Form of Church Prayers

John Calvin's rite first appeared when he was minister to the congregation of French exiles at Strasbourg from 1538 to 1541. Impressed by Bucer's German rite which he found in use there, he adopted it almost word for word in French. His Geneva rite was first published in 1542 after his recall. It was a slightly simplified form of his Strasbourg rite; but the matter was essentially the same. In structure it also resembled Farel's rite, which it replaced at Geneva.

The rite was intended to recover the eucharist in its primitive simplicity as the weekly worship of the Church. Such a service, Calvin believed, would "manifest God's glory and allow the sweetness of consolation to fill the hearts of the faithful better than all the childish and theatrical follies of the mass".

The canon was replaced by the Narrative of the Institution, followed by a reminder of God's promises, an excommunication of those forbidden to communicate and a prayer for worthy reception.

After the Prayer and the Confession of Faith, to testify in the name of the people that all wish to live and die in the doctrine of Christ, he (the minister) says aloud: Let us listen to the institution of the Holy Supper by Jesus Christ, as narrated by St Paul in the eleventh chapter of the first epistle to the Corinthians:

For I have received from the Lord what I also delivered to you, that the Lord Jesus, on the night when he was betrayed, took bread, and when he had given thanks, he broke it, and said, "This is my body, which is broken for you. Do this in remembrance of me." In the same way also the cup, after supper, saying, "This cup is the new covenant in my blood. Do this, as oft as you drink it, in remembrance of me." For as often as you eat this bread and drink the cup, you proclaim the Lord's death until he comes. Whoever, therefore, eats the bread or drinks the cup of the Lord in an unworthy manner will be guilty of profaning the body and blood of the Lord. Let a man examine himself, and so eat of the bread and drink of the cup. For anyone who eats and drinks without discerning the body eats and drinks judgement upon himself.

We have heard, brethren, how our Lord celebrated his Supper with his disciples, and thereby indicating that strangers, namely those who are not of the company of the faithful, ought not to be admitted. Therefore, in accordance with this rule, in the name and by the authority of the Lord Jesus Christ, I excommunicate all idolaters, blasphemers, despisers of God, heretics, and all who form private sects to break the unity of the Church, all perjurers, all who rebel against parents or their superiors, all who are seditious, mutinous, quarrelsome or brutal, all adulterers, fornicators, thieves, misers, ravishers, drunkards, gluttons, and all who lead a scandalous life. I declare that they must abstain from this holy table, for fear of defiling and contaminating the holy food which our Lord Jesus Christ gives only to his household and believers.

Therefore, in accordance with the exhortation of St Paul, let each man prove and examine his conscience, to see whether he has truly repented of his faults, and is satisfied with himself, desiring to live henceforth a holy life and according to God. Above all, let each man see whether he puts his trust in the mercy of God, and seeks his salvation entirely in Jesus Christ; and whether, renouncing all hatred and rancour, he truly intends and resolves to live in peace and brotherly love with his neighbours.

If we have this testimony in our hearts before God, let us have no doubt at all that he claims us for his children, and that the Lord Jesus Christ addresses his words to us, to invite us to his table, and to present us with this holy sacrament which he communicated to his disciples.

And although we may feel within ourselves much frailty and misery from not having perfect faith, and from being inclined to unbelief and distrust, as well as from not being devoted to the service of God so entirely and with such zeal as we ought, and from having to war daily against the lusts of our flesh, nevertheless, since our Lord has graciously permitted us to have his gospel imprinted on our hearts, in order to withstand all unbelief, and has given us the desire and longing to renounce our own desires, in order to follow righteousness and his holy commandments, let us all be assured that the sins and imperfections which remain in us will not prevent him from receiving us, and making us worthy to partake of this spiritual table; for we do not come to declare that we are perfect or righteous in ourselves; but, on the contrary, by seeking our life in Christ, we confess that we are in death. Let us therefore understand that this sacrament is a medicine for the spiritually poor and sick, and that the only worthiness which our Saviour requires in us is to know ourselves, so as to be dissatisfied with our vices, and have all our pleasure, joy and contentment in him alone.

First, then, let us believe in those promises which Jesus Christ, who is the unfailing truth, has pronounced with his own lips, namely, that he is indeed willing to make us partakers of his own body and blood, in order that we may possess him entirely and in such a manner that he may live in us, and we in him. And although we see only bread and wine, yet let us not doubt that he accomplishes spiritually in our souls all that he shows us outwardly by these visible signs; in other words, that he is heavenly bread, to feed and nourish us unto eternal life.

Next let us not be unmindful of the infinite goodness of our Saviour, who displays all his riches and blessings at this table, in order to give them to us; for, in giving himself to us, he bears testimony to us that all which he has is ours. Moreover, let us receive this sacrament as a pledge that the virtue of his death and passion is imputed to us for righteousness, just as if we had suffered it in our own persons. Let us never be so perverse as to hold back when Jesus Christ invites us so gently by his word. But, reflecting on the dignity of the precious gift which he gives us, let us present ourselves to him with ardent zeal, in order that he may make us capable of receiving him.

With this in mind, let us raise our hearts and minds on high, where Jesus Christ is, in the glory of his Father, and from whence we look for him at our redemption. Let us not be bemused by these earthly and corruptible elements which we see with the eye, and touch with the hand, in order to seek him there, as if he were enclosed in the bread or wine. Our souls will only then be disposed to be nourished and vivified by his substance, when they are raised above all earthly things, and carried as high as heaven, to enter the kingdom of God where he dwells. Let us therefore be content to have the bread and the wine as signs and evidences, spiritually seeking the reality where the word of God promises that we shall find it.

This done, the ministers distribute the bread and cup to the people, having warned them to come forward with reverence and in order. Meanwhile some psalms are sung, or some passage of scripture read, suitable to what is signified by the sacrament.

12. MODERN TEXTS FROM THE REFORMED CHURCHES

A. The Reformed Church of France

The first text is taken from the *Liturgie* of 1963. It is followed by the second and fourth of the five eucharistic prayers contained in the proposed new liturgy emanating from the official liturgical commission and authorized for publication, in 1982, by the National Council of the Reformed Church of France.

The liturgy of 1963

Coming down from the pulpit, the celebrant moves to a position behind the communion table. The linen covers are removed from the bread and the wine.

The celebrant may say: Will you please stand.

The congregation stands.

Either the celebrant says: Let us lift our hearts to the Lord!

Or the celebrant says: Let us lift up our hearts:

Congregation: We lift them up to the Lord.

Celebrant: Let us give thanks to the Lord our God.

Congregation: It is right and fitting so to do.

Preface

Celebrant: It is indeed right and fitting, it is our joy and salvation to give Thee thanks at all times and in all places, Almighty God, Eternal and Holy Father, through Jesus Christ our Lord, for the glory of Thy creation and for Thy redeeming love.

Therefore with the whole Church, with the angels and all the heavenly host, with the great cloud of witnesses, we joyfully praise and magnify Thy glorious name:

(A version of the Sanctus is said or sung.)

Celebrant: Let every creature keep silence in the presence of God!

The congregation kneels or bows the head, in silence.

Institution

Celebrant: On the night when he was delivered up, the Lord Jesus took bread and, having given thanks, he broke it and said: "TAKE, EAT, THIS IS MY BODY GIVEN FOR YOU. DO THIS IN REMEMBRANCE OF ME!" In the same manner, after supper, he took the cup and said: "THIS CUP IS THE NEW COVENANT IN MY BLOOD. DO THIS, WHENEVER YOU DRINK OF IT, IN REMEMBRANCE OF ME!"

Whenever, therefore, you eat this bread and drink from this cup, you are proclaiming the Lord's death until he come.

(Here, when necessary, the celebrant may add: Wherefore, anyone who shall eat the bread or drink of the cup of the Lord Jesus unworthily will be guilty of the Lord's body and blood. Let all therefore examine themselves, and then eat of this bread and drink of this cup.)

Prayer

Celebrant: Let us pray:

Holy and Righteous Father, as we commemorate here the one perfect sacrifice offered once and for all upon the cross by our Lord Jesus Christ, rejoicing in his resurrection and looking forward to his coming, we offer ourselves to Thee as a living and holy sacrifice.

(Pause)

Thou who knowest our hearts: cleanse us and renew Thy grace and pardon in us. By the life of Thy risen Son, make us alive; may he abide in us and we in him.

(Pause)

Send Thy Holy Spirit upon us so that, in receiving this bread and this cup, we may be privileged to partake of the body and blood of our Lord Jesus Christ. For it is through him that Thou dost create, sanctify, quicken, bless and bestow on us every gift.[1]

(Pause)

As the corn once scattered in the fields and the grapes dispersed on the hillsides are now reunited on this table in this bread and wine, so, Lord, may Thy whole Church soon be gathered together from the ends of the earth in Thy kindgom. Come, Lord Jesus! Amen.[1]

(The "Agnus Dei" is sung.)

Invitation

Celebrant: Blessed are they that hunger and thirst for righteousness, for they shall be filled!

Blessed are they whom Thou dost take with Thee to feed them with the blessings of Thy house!

Blessed are they that are invited to the marriage feast of the Lamb!

Come, says Jesus, for everything is prepared!

Fraction

At the breaking of the bread, the celebrant says: The bread we break is the communion in the body of our Lord Jesus Christ, which was given for us.

At the lifting up of the cup, the celebrant says: The cup of blessing for which we give thanks is the communion in the blood of our Lord Jesus Christ, the blood of the new covenant which was poured out for our sakes.

Communion

After each serving, the celebrant pronounces one of the following dismissals:

Go in peace, in the grace of your Lord.
Go in peace, in the joy of your Lord.
Go in peace in the strength of your Lord.

The communicants return to their seats.

Eucharistic prayer II (1982)

(The Lord be with you:
   And with your spirit.
Let us lift up our hearts:
   We lift them to the Lord.

---

[1] If the Lord's Prayer has not already been said after the intercessions, it may be said at one of these points.

Let us give thanks to the Lord our God:
    It is right and good so to do.)
Yes, it is our joy,
O God of love and holiness, our Creator and our Father,
to give you thanks always and everywhere.
In your image you made us all;
your universe you put in our care;
your creation you entrust to our hands,
with all its wonders and its travail.
You make us partners in your labours
and invite us to share in your rest,
through Christ our Lord,
whom the earth and the heavens
with all the angels and archangels
acclaim for ever and ever, singing:
    Holy, holy, holy Lord,
    God of the universe!
    Heaven and earth are filled with your glory.
    Hosanna in the highest.
    Blessed is he who comes in the name of the Lord.
    Hosanna in the highest.
Lord, send upon us and upon this thanksgiving meal the Spirit of life,
who spoke through Moses and the prophets,
who descended upon Jesus at the river Jordan,
and upon the apostles at the first day of Pentecost.
Send this same Spirit of fire,
that its coming may transfigure our humanity
by the power of Christ's body and blood.
During the supper, Jesus took bread
and, having said the blessing, broke it,
and gave it to the disciples saying:
"Take, this is my body."
Then he took a cup
and, having given thanks, he gave it to them,
and they all drank from it.
And he told them:
"This is my blood,
the blood of the covenant, shed for the many.
Truly I declare to you, I will never again drink
of the fruit of the vine until the day I drink it new
in the kingdom of God."
Great is the mystery of the faith:
    Lord Jesus,
    we proclaim your death,
    we celebrate your resurrection,
    we await your coming in glory.
As we celebrate before you the memorial of the death
and resurrection of your Son,
we offer you thanks, Lord,
for having chosen us to serve in your presence.

We humbly ask for your Holy Spirit,
to make us partakers of
Christ's body and blood
and unite us in a single body.
We pray for your goodness upon us all:
grant that we, too, with the witnesses of your people,
with Peter, Paul and the other apostles,
with Mary and the faithful of all times,
may have a share in eternal life
and sing your praises
through Jesus Christ, your beloved Son.
Through him, with him, and in him,
be all honour and glory to you,
God the Father Almighty,
in the unity of the Holy Spirit,
for ever and ever. Amen.
The Lord's Prayer follows.

Eucharistic prayer IV (1982)

(The Lord be with you;
   And with your spirit.
Let us lift up our hearts:
   We lift them to the Lord.
Let us give thanks to the Lord our God:
   It is right and good so to do.)

Truly it is right and good,
Holy Father, Almighty and Eternal God,
to give you thanks always and everywhere
through Christ our Lord.

For he is your living Word,
through whom you created all things;
whom you sent to us as our Saviour,
to do your will to the very end,
and to gather together from our human race
a holy people for your own possession.

Therefore with the angels and all your witnesses
we proclaim your glory:
   Holy, holy, holy Lord,
   God of the universe!
   Heaven and earth are filled with your glory.
   Hosanna in the highest.
   Blessed is he who comes in the name of the Lord.
   Hosanna in the highest.
Send, Lord, your Holy Spirit
upon us and upon this thanksgiving meal,
that this bread and this cup
may give us communion in the body and blood of your Son.

During the supper, Jesus took bread
and, having said the blessing, broke it,
and gave it to the disciples saying:
"Take, eat, this is my body."
Then he took a cup
and, having given thanks, he gave it to them, saying:
"Drink from it, all of you, for this is my blood,
the blood of the covenant, shed for the many,
for the remission of sins.
Truly I declare to you, I will no longer drink of the fruit of the vine until the
  day I drink it new with you in my Father's kingdom."
Great is the mystery of the faith:
  Lord Jesus, we proclaim your death,
  we celebrate your resurrection,
  we await your coming in glory.
Therefore, Lord, we make before you the memorial
of the incarnation and passion of your Son,
of his resurrection from the dead,
of his ascension in glory,
of his perpetual intercession;
we await and earnestly pray for his return,
rejoicing in the Holy Spirit
whom you have given to your Church.
O God our Father, we remember that the Crucified
ever lives to intercede for us;
we therefore pray you to transform our lives,
that they may be consecrated to you;
grant us the joy of your presence,
and fill our hearts with your Spirit,
through Christ our Saviour.
Through him, with him, and in him,
be all honour and glory to you,
God the Father almighty,
in the unity of the Holy Spirit,
for ever and ever. Amen.

The Lord's Prayer follows.

B. United Church of Christ, USA: Service of Word and Sacrament I (1969)

This church dates from the union in 1957 between the Congregationals and the Evangelical and Reformed Church. The latter tradition was the home of the liturgically significant "Mercersburg Movement" in the nineteenth century.

Invitation

The people standing, the minister shall say: Luke the Evangelist records that on the evening of the first day of the week, the same day on which our Lord rose from the dead, when he was at table with two of the disciples, he took bread and blessed and broke it, and gave it to them, and their eyes were opened, and they knew him.

Beloved, this is the joyful feast of the people of God. Come from the East and the West, and from the North and the South, and gather about the table of the Lord.

Behold how good and pleasant it is when brothers dwell in unity.

The peace of our Lord Jesus Christ be with you all. Amen.

The great thanksgiving

Lift up your hearts. *We lift them up to the Lord.* Let us give thanks to the Lord our God. *It is meet and right so to do.*

We give thanks to you, O holy Lord, Father Almighty, everlasting God, for the universe which you have created, for the heavens and the earth, and for every living thing. We thank you that you have formed us in your own image and made us for yourself. We bless you that when we rebelled against you, you did not forsake us, but delivered us from bondage, and revealed your righteous will and steadfast love by the law and the prophets.

Above all, we thank you for the gift of your Son, the Redeemer of all men, who was born of Mary, lived on earth in obedience to you, died on the cross for our sins, and rose from the dead in victory; who rules over us, Lord above all, prays for us continually, and will come again in triumph.

We thank you for your Holy Spirit and for your holy church, for the means of grace and for the promise of eternal life. With patriarchs and prophets, apostles and martyrs, with your church on earth and with all the company of heaven, we magnify and praise you, we worship and adore you, O Lord Most Holy:

Holy, holy, holy, Lord God almighty,
your glory fills all heaven and earth.
Hosanna in the highest.
Blessed is he who comes in the name of the Lord.
Hosanna in the highest.

        OR

Holy, holy, holy,
Lord God of Sabaoth,
Heaven and earth are full of the majesty of your glory
Hosanna in the highest!
Blessed is he who comes in the name of the Lord.
Hosanna in the highest!

We thank you that the Lord Jesus on the night when he was betrayed took bread, and, when he had given thanks, broke it and said, "Take, eat, this is my body which is for you"; and that he also took the cup, saying, "Drink of it, all of you; this is the new covenant in my blood. Do this in remembrance of me."

Obeying the commandment of our Lord Jesus Christ, we, your people, offer you this bread and this cup, recalling his incarnate life, his atoning death, his resurrection and ascension until he come.

Bless and sanctify by your Holy Spirit both us and these your gifts of bread and wine, that in this holy communion of the body and blood of Christ we may be made one with him and he with us, and that we may remain faithful members of his body until we feast with him in your heavenly kingdom.

Here we offer ourselves in obedience to you, through the perfect offering of your Son Jesus Christ, giving you thanks that you have called us to be a royal priesthood, a holy nation, your own people; and to you, O Father, as to the Son and the Holy Spirit, be ascribed blessing and honour and glory and power forever and ever. Amen.

C. The Church of Scotland: Book of Common Order (1979)

In the 1979 revision of its *Book of Common Order* the Church of Scotland included three different orders for the Holy Communion. The first corresponded in linguistic style to the King James' Version of the Bible, the second to the Revised Standard Version, the third to the New English Bible. It is the second of these that is given here.

Prayer of the veil and offertory prayer when the minister shall unveil the elements.

Let us pray.

O God, who by the blood of thy dear Son hast consecrated for us a new and living way into the holiest of all; help us in faith to enter with him and grant that being pure in heart by grace, we may have part in his true, pure, immortal sacrifice; through Jesus Christ our Lord. Amen.

Almighty and most merciful Father, out of the fullness of thy gifts, we offer to thee this bread and this cup. Blessed be thy holy name for ever; through Jesus Christ our Lord. Amen.

If the words of institution included in the prayer of consecration below are not to be used there, the warrant may be read here.

[Beloved in the Lord, attend to the words of the institution of the holy supper of our Lord Jesus Christ, as they are delivered by Saint Paul:

I have received of the Lord that which also I delivered unto you, that the Lord Jesus, the same night in which he was betrayed, took bread; and when he had given thanks, he brake it, and said, Take, eat: this is my body, which is broken for you; this do in remembrance of me. After the same manner also he took the cup, when he had supped, saying, This cup is the new testament in my blood; this do ye, as oft as ye drink it, in remembrance of me. For as often as ye eat this bread, and drink this cup, ye do shew the Lord's death till he come.]

The eucharistic prayer

The Lord be with you; *And with thy spirit.* Lift up your hearts; *We lift them up unto the Lord.* Let us give thanks unto our Lord God. *It is meet and right so to do.*

Truly at all times and in all places we should give thanks to thee, O holy Lord, Father Almighty, everlasting God: who didst create the heavens and the earth and all that is therein; who didst make man in thine own image and whose tender mercies are over all thy works.

We praise thee for Jesus Christ whom thou hast sent to be the Saviour of the world.

Blessed be the hour in which he was born and the hour in which he died.

Blessed be the dawn of his rising again and the high day of his ascending.

We praise thee that he, having ascended up on high and sitting at thy right hand, sent forth the Holy Spirit upon the Church to be the light and guide of all those who put their trust in thee.

Blessed be the Spirit, the Giver of Life, enabling thy people to proclaim the gospel among all nations and to fulfill with Christ their royal priesthood until he comes again.

Thee mighty God, heavenly King, we magnify and praise. With angels and archangels and with all the company of heaven, we worship and adore thy glorious name; evermore praising thee and saying:

> Holy, holy, holy, Lord God of hosts,
> heaven and earth are full of thy glory;
> Glory be to thee, O Lord Most High.
> Blessed is he that cometh in the name of the Lord:
> Hosanna in the highest.

Truly holy and blessed is thy Son Jesus Christ, blessed in all his gifts, blessed in that most holy mystery which he did institute, who in the same night in which he was betrayed took bread and when he had blessed and given thanks he broke it and said, "Take, eat; this is my body, which is broken for you: do this in remembrance of me." In the same manner also after supper he took the cup, saying, "This cup is the new covenant in my blood: do this, as often as you shall drink it, in remembrance of me."

Therefore, having in remembrance his work and passion, we now plead his eternal sacrifice and set forth this memorial which he has commanded us to make. Send down thy Holy Spirit to sanctify both us and these thine own gifts of bread and wine which we set before thee, that the bread which we break may be the communion of the body of Christ, and the cup which we bless the communion of the blood of Christ; that we may receive them to our spiritual nourishment and growth in grace, and to the glory of thy most holy name.

These things, O Lord, we seek not only for ourselves but for all in the communion of thy Church and especially for... *[here the minister may pray for the sick, and the poor, and for the needs of particular persons; or a short period of silence may be kept].*

Accept this our duty and service, O Father, and graciously accept us also as, in fellowship with all the faithful in heaven and on earth, we pray thee to fulfill in us, and in all men, the purpose of thy redeeming love; through Jesus Christ our Lord, in whose words we are bold to pray and to say,

Our Father...

The breaking of bread

[Here may be said:] Holy things to the holy: *One only is holy, Jesus Christ, in whom are we to the glory of God the Father.* O taste and see that the Lord is good: *Blessed is the man that trusteth in him.*

Here the minister shall say: In obedience to our Lord Jesus Christ, and for a memorial of him we do this: who, the same night in which he was betrayed, took bread (*here the minister shall take the bread into his hands*), and when he had blessed, and given thanks, he broke it (*here he shall break the bread*), and said, "Take, eat: this is my body, which is broken for you: do this in remembrance of me."

After the same manner also, he took the cup (*here he shall raise the cup*) saying, "This cup is the new covenant in my blood: do this, as often as you shall drink it, in remembrance of me."

Lamb of God, that takest away the sins of the world: Have mercy upon us.
Lamb of God, that takest away the sins of the world: Have mercy upon us.
Lamb of God, that takest away the sins of the world: Grant us thy peace.

The communion

13. ANGLICAN TEXTS FROM THE REFORMATION PERIOD

Introduction and texts are taken from R.C.D. Jasper and G.J. Cuming, *Prayers of the Eucharist: Early and Reformed.*

The preparation of the first Book of Common Prayer was undertaken by Archbishop Cranmer and "certain of the most learned and discreet bishops and other learned men of this realm", known as the Windsor Commission. It was meant to be a congregational book, written in the vernacular and grounded in scripture. The eucharist kept the structure of the Roman rite, preserved prayers of traditional English usage and included the Order of the Communion of 1548. It required communion in both kinds, and made no provision for private Masses. The Act of Uniformity of January 1549 ordered that it should come into use on the Feast of Pentecost (9 June), or if copies were available earlier, three weeks after the copy had been procured. The earliest existing copies, printed by Edward Whitchurche, were dated 7 March.

The 1549 Prayer Book was not well received: traditionalists objected to the changes in the Mass; while the Reformers, such as Hooper and Ridley, did not regard the changes as far-reaching enough. A thorough-going criticism of the Book was submitted by Martin Bucer in his *Censura* in 1551: and in the spring of 1552 a second Prayer Book, much more Protestant in tone, appeared. Under a new Act of Uniformity its use was required by All Saints Day. It had a short life, however; for on the death of Edward VI in July 1553 and the accession of Mary, the Roman rite was restored as the official use.

In the 1662 Prayer Book the changes made in the 1552 rite were small, but none the less significant:
a. The title "The Prayer of Consecration" was used.
b. Manual acts accompanied the recitation of the Institution Narrative.
c. "Amen" was inserted after the Institution Narrative.
d. The addition of the 1549 words of administration to those of 1552, first made in 1559, was retained.
e. Provision for additional consecration was made by the recitation of the Institution Narrative over further supplies of bread and wine.
f. The consecrated elements remaining after communion were to be veiled until they were consumed at the end of the service.

A. The Book of Common Prayer (1549)

Then shall the Minister take so much bread and wine as shall suffice for the persons appointed to receive the holy communion, laying the bread upon the corporal, or else in the paten, or in some other comely thing prepared for that purpose: and putting the wine into the chalice, or else in some fair or convenient cup prepared for that use (if the chalice will not serve) putting thereto a little pure and clean water, and setting both the bread and wine upon the altar. Then the Priest shall say: The Lord be with you.

Answer: And with thy spirit.

Priest: Lift up your hearts.

Answer: We lift them up unto the Lord.

Priest: Let us give thanks to our Lord God.

Answer: It is meet and right so to do.

The Priest: It is very meet, right, and our bounden duty that we should at all times and in all places give thanks to thee, O Lord, holy Father, almighty everlasting God.

Here shall follow the proper Preface, according to the time (if there be any specially appointed), or else immediately shall follow,

Therefore with angels and archangels, and with all the holy company of heaven, we laud and magnify thy glorious name; evermore praising thee, and saying,

Holy, holy, holy, Lord God of hosts: heaven and earth are full of thy glory. Hosannah in the highest. Blessed is he that cometh in the name of the Lord. Glory to thee, O Lord, in the highest.

This the Clerks shall also sing.

When the Clerks have done singing, then shall the Priest or Deacon turn him to the people, and say: Let us pray for the whole state of Christ's Church.

Then the priest, turning him to the altar, shall say or sing, plainly and distinctly, this prayer following: Almighty and everliving God, which by thy holy apostle hast taught us to make prayers, and supplications, and to give thanks for all men; We humbly beseech thee most mercifully to receive these our prayers, which we offer unto thy divine Majesty; beseeching thee to inspire continually the universal church with the spirit of truth, unity, and concord: and grant, that all they that do confess thy holy name may agree in the truth of thy holy world, and live in unity and godly love. Specially we beseech thee to save and defend thy servant Edward our king; that under him we may be godly and quietly governed; and grant unto his whole council, and to all that be put in authority under him, that they may truly and indifferently minister justice, to the punishment of wickedness and vice, and to the maintenance of God's true religion and virtue. Give grace (O heavenly Father) to all bishops, pastors and curates that they may both by their life and doctrine set forth thy true and lively word, and rightly and duly administer thy holy sacraments. And to all thy people give thy heavenly grace; that with meek heart and due reverence, they may hear and receive thy holy word; truly serving thee in holiness and righteousness all the days of their life. And we most humbly beseech thee of thy goodness (O Lord) to comfort and succour all them, which in this transitory life be in trouble, sorrow, need, sickness, or any other adversity. And especially we commend unto thy merciful goodness this congregation, which is here assembled in thy name, to celebrate the commemoration of the most glorious death of thy Son. And here we do give unto thee most high praise, and hearty thanks, for the wonderful grace and virtue declared in thy saints, from the beginning of the world; and chiefly in the glorious and most blessed Virgin Mary, mother of thy Son Jesus Christ our Lord and God; and in the holy patriarchs, prophets, apostles and martyrs, whose examples (O Lord) and stedfastness in thy faith, and keeping thy holy commandments, grant us to follow. We commend unto thy mercy (O Lord) all other thy servants, which are departed hence from us with the sign of faith, and now do rest in the sleep of peace: grant unto them, we beseech thee, thy mercy, and everlasting peace; and that, at the day of the general resurrection, we and all they which be of the mystical body of thy Son, may altogether be set on his right hand, and hear that his most joyful voice, Come unto me, O ye that be blessed of my Father, and possess the kingdom, which is prepared for you from the beginning of the world. Grant this, O Father, for Jesus Christ's sake, our only Mediator and Advocate.

O God, heavenly Father, which of thy tender mercy didst give thine only Son Jesu Christ to suffer death upon the cross for our redemption; who made there (by his one oblation once offered) a full, perfect, and sufficient sacrifice, oblation, and satisfaction, for the sins of the whole world; and did institute, and in his holy gospel command us to celebrate a perpetual memory of that his precious death, until his coming again: hear us (O merciful Father) we beseech thee; and with thy Holy Spirit and word vouchsafe to ble + ss and sanc + tify these thy gifts and creatures of bread and wine, that they may be unto us the body and blood of thy most dearly beloved Son Jesus Christ, who, in the same night that he was betrayed, took bread;[1] and when he had blessed, and given thanks, he brake it, and gave it to his disciples, saying, Take, eat; this is my body which is given for you; do this in remembrance of me.

Likewise after super he took the cup,[2] and when he had given thanks, he gave it to them, saying, Drink ye all of this; for this is my blood of the new

---

[1] Here the priest must take the bread into his hands.
[2] Here the priest shall take the cup into his hands.

Testament, which is shed for you and for many for remission of sins. Do this, as oft as you shall drink it, in remembrance of me.

These words before rehearsed are to be said, turning still to the altar, without any elevation or shewing the sacrament to the people.

Wherefore, O Lord and heavenly Father, according to the institution of thy dearly beloved Son our Saviour Jesu Christ, we thy humble servants do celebrate and make here before thy divine Majesty, with these thy holy gifts, the memorial which thy Son hath willed us to make; having in remembrance his blessed passion, mighty resurrection, and glorious ascension; rendering unto thee most hearty thanks for the innumerable benefits procured unto us by the same; entirely desiring thy fatherly goodness mercifully to accept this our sacrifice of praise and thanksgiving; most humbly beseeching thee to grant, that by the merits and death of thy Son Jesus Christ and through faith in his blood, we and all thy whole church may obtain remission of our sins, and all other benefits of his passion. And here we offer and present unto thee (O Lord) our self, our souls and bodies, to be a reasonable, holy and lively sacrifice unto thee; humbly beseeching thee, that whosoever shall be partakers of this holy communion may worthily receive the most precious body and blood of thy Son, Jesus Christ, and be fulfilled with thy grace and heavenly benediction, and made one body with thy Son Jesu Christ, that he may dwell in them, and they in him. And although we be unworthy (through our manifold sins) to offer unto thee any sacrifice, yet we beseech thee to accept this our bounden duty and service, and command these our prayers and supplications, by the ministry of thy holy angels, to be brought up into thy holy tabernacle, before the sight of thy divine Majesty; not weighing our merits, but pardoning our offences, through Christ our Lord; by whom, and with whom, in the unity of the Holy Ghost, all honour and glory be unto thee, O Father Almighty, world without end. Amen.

B. The Book of Common Prayer (1662)

After which the Priest shall proceed, saying: Lift up your hearts.

Answer: We lift them up unto the Lord.

Priest: Let us give thanks unto our Lord God.

Answer: It is meet and right so to do.

Then shall the Priest turn to the Lord's Table, and say: It is very meet, right, and our bounden duty, that we should at all times and in all places, give thanks unto thee, O Lord, Holy Father, Almighty everlasting God.

Here shall follow the proper Preface, according to the time, if there be any specially appointed: or else immediately shall follow: Therefore with Angels and Archangels, and with all the company of heaven, we laud and magnify thy glorious Name, evermore praising thee, and saying, Holy, holy, holy, Lord God of Hosts, heaven and earth are full of thy Glory: Glory be to thee, O Lord most High. Amen.

Then shall the Priest kneeling down at the Lord's Table, say in the name of all them that shall receive the Communion, this Prayer following.

We do not presume to come to this thy Table, O merciful Lord, trusting in our own righteousness, but in thy manifold and great mercies. We are not worthy so much as to gather up the crumbs under thy Table. But thou art the same Lord, whose property is always to have mercy: grant us therefore, gracious Lord, so to eat the flesh of thy dear Son Jesus Christ, and to drink his blood, that our sinful bodies may be made clean by his body, and our souls washed through his most precious blood, and that we may evermore dwell in him and he in us. Amen.

When the Priest, standing before the Table, hath so ordered the Bread and Wine, that he may with the more readiness and decency break the Bread before the people, and take the Cup into his hands, he shall say the Prayer of Consecration, as followeth:

Almighty God, our heavenly Father, who of thy tender mercy didst give thine only Son Jesus Christ to suffer death upon the Cross for our redemption; who made there (by his one oblation of himself once offered) a full, perfect, and sufficient sacrifice, oblation, and satisfaction, for the sins of the whole world; and did institute, and in his holy Gospel command us to continue, a perpetual memory of that his precious death, until his coming again; Hear us, O merciful Father, we most humbly beseech thee; and grant that we receiving these thy creatures of bread and wine, according to thy Son our Saviour Jesus Christ's holy institution, in remembrance of his death and passion, may be partakers of his most blessed Body and Blood: who in the same night that he was betrayed,[1] took Bread; and, when he had given thanks,[2] he brake it, and gave it to his disciples, saying, Take, eat;[3] this is my Body which is given for you: Do this in remembrance of me. Likewise after supper[4] he took the Cup; and, when he had given thanks, he gave it to them, saying, Drink ye all of this: for this[5] is my Blood of the New Testament, which is shed for you and for many for the remission of sins: Do this, as oft as ye shall drink it, in remembrance of me. *Amen.*

14. MODERN ANGLICAN PRAYERS

A. Church of England: Alternative Service Book (1980)

Holy Communion, rite A

The eucharistic prayer

THE TAKING OF THE BREAD AND CUP AND THE GIVING OF THANKS

The president takes the bread and cup into his hands and replaces them on the holy table.

---

[1]Here the priest is to take the paten into his hands.
[2]And here to take the Bread.
[3]And here to lay his hands upon all the Bread.
[4]Here he is to take the Cup into his hand.
[5]And here to lay his hand upon every vessel (be it Chalice or Flagon) in which there is any Wine to be consecrated.

The president uses one of the four EUCHARISTIC PRAYERS which follow.

First Eucharistic Prayer

President: The Lord be with you   or   The Lord is here.
All: and also with you.   His Spirit is with us.
President: Lift up your hearts.
All: We lift them to the Lord.
President: Let us give thanks to the Lord our God.
All: It is right to give him thanks and praise.
President: It is indeed right, it is our duty and our joy, at all times and in all places to give you thanks and praise, holy Father, heavenly King. almighty and eternal God, through Jesus Christ your only Son our Lord.

For he is your living Word; through him you have created all things from the beginning, and formed us in your own image.

Through him you have freed us from the slavery of sin, giving him to be born as man and to die upon the cross; you raised him from the dead and exalted him to your right hand on high. Through him you have sent upon us your holy and life-giving Spirit, and made us a people for your own possession.

PROPER PREFACE, when appropriate.

Therefore with angels and archangels, and with all the company of heaven, we proclaim your great and glorious name, for ever praising you and saying:
All: Holy, holy, holy Lord, God of power and might, heaven and earth are full of your glory. Hosanna in the highest.

This ANTHEM may also be used.
Blessed is he who comes in the name of the Lord. Hosanna in the highest.

President: Accept our praises, heavenly Father, through your Son our Saviour Jesus Christ; and as we follow his example and obey his command, grant that by the power of your Holy Spirit these gifts of bread and wine may be to us his body and his blood;

Who in the same night that he was betrayed, took bread and gave you thanks; he broke it and gave it to his disciples, saying, Take, eat; this is my body which is given for you; do this in remembrance of me. In the same way, after supper he took the cup and gave you thanks; he gave it to them, saying, Drink this, all of you; this is my blood of the new covenant, which is shed for you and for many for the forgiveness of sins. Do this, as often as you drink it, in remembrance of me.

All: Christ has died: Christ is risen: Christ will come again.

President: Therefore, heavenly Father, we remember his offering of himself made once for all upon the cross, and proclaim his mighty resurrection and glorious ascension. As we look for his coming in glory, we celebrate with this bread and this cup his one perfect sacrifice.

Accept through him, our great high priest, this our sacrifice of thanks and praise; and as we eat and drink these holy gifts in the presence of your divine majesty, renew us by your Spirit, inspire us with your love, and unite us in the body of your Son, Jesus Christ our Lord.

Through him, and with him, and in him, by the power of the Holy Spirit, with all who stand before you in earth and heaven, we worship you, Father almighty, in songs of everlasting praise:
All: Blessing and honour and glory and power be yours for ever and ever. Amen.

Since the formulation of the anamnesis-oblation has been one of the most delicate matters in Anglican revisions of the eucharist, that section is also reproduced here from the second, third and fourth eucharistic prayers in rite A of the *Alternative Service Book*.

From the second eucharistic prayer:
President: Therefore, Lord and heavenly Father,
having in remembrance his death once for all upon the cross,
his resurrection from the dead,
and his ascension into heaven,
and looking for the coming of his kingdom,
we make with this bread and this cup
the memorial of Christ your Son our Lord.
Accept through him this offering of our duty and service;
and as we eat and drink these holy gifts
in the presence of your divine majesty,
fill us with your grace and heavenly blessing;
nourish us with the body and blood of your Son,
that we may grow into his likeness
and, made one by your Spirit,
become a living temple to your glory.

From the third eucharistic prayer:
President: And so, Father, calling to mind his death on the cross,
his perfect sacrifice made once for the sins of all men,
rejoicing at his mighty resurrection and glorious ascension,
and looking for his coming in glory,
we celebrate this memorial of our redemption;
We thank you for counting us worthy
to stand in your presence and serve you;
we bring before you this bread and this cup;
We pray you to accept this our duty and service,
a spiritual sacrifice of praise and thanksgiving.
Send the Holy Spirit on your people
and gather into one in your kingdom
all who share this one bread and one cup,
so that we, in the company of all the saints,
may praise and glorify you for ever,
through him from whom all good things come,
Jesus Christ our Lord;

From the fourth eucharistic prayer:
President: Therefore, Lord and heavenly Father,
in remembrance of the precious death and passion,

the mighty resurrection and glorious ascension
of your dear Son Jesus Christ,
we offer you through him this sacrifice of praise and thanksgiving.
Grant that by his merits and death,
and through faith in his blood,
we and all your Church may receive forgiveness of our sins
and all other benefits of his passion.
Although we are unworthy, through our many sins,
to offer you any sacrifice,
yet we pray that you will accept this,
the duty and service that we owe;
do not weigh our merits, but pardon our offences,
and fill us all who share in this holy communion
with your grace and heavenly blessing.

B. The Episcopal Church in the USA: Book of Common Prayer (1979)

Reproduced here is Eucharistic Prayer C from the Holy Eucharist rite II.

This is followed by an outline "Order for Celebrating the Holy Eucharist", which allows many of the parts to be freely formulated within the indicated limits.

Holy Eucharist II: Eucharistic prayer C

The Lord be with you. *And also with you.* Lift up your hearts. *We lift them to the Lord.* Let us give thanks to the Lord our God. *It is right to give him thanks and praise.*

Then, facing the Holy Table, the Celebrant proceeds: God of all power, Ruler of the Universe, you are worthy of glory and praise.

Glory to you for ever and ever.

At your command all things came to be: the vast expanse of interstellar space, galaxies, suns, the planets in their courses, and this fragile earth, our island home.

By your will they were created and have their being.

From the primal elements you brought forth the human race, and blessed us with memory, reason, and skill. You made us the rulers of creation. But we turned against you and betrayed your trust: and we turned against one another.

Have mercy, Lord, for we are sinners in your sight.

Again and again, you called us to return. Through prophets and sages you revealed your righteous Law. And in the fullness of time you sent your only Son, born of a woman, to fulfill your Law, to open for us the way of freedom and peace.

By his blood, he reconciled us.
By his wounds, we are healed.

And therefore we praise you, joining with the heavenly chorus, with prophets, apostles, and martyrs, and with all those in every generation who have looked to you in hope, to proclaim with them your glory, in their unending hymn:

Celebrant and People: Holy, holy, holy Lord, God of power and might, heaven and earth are full of your glory. Hosanna in the highest. Blessed is who comes in the name of the Lord. Hosanna in the highest.

The Celebrant continues: And so, Father, we who have been redeemed by him, and made a new people by water and the Spirit, now bring before you these gifts. Sanctify them by your Holy Spirit to be the Body and Blood of Jesus Christ our Lord.

At the following words concerning the bread, the Celebrant is to hold it, or lay a hand upon it; and at the words concerning the cup, to hold or place a hand upon the cup and any other vessel containing wine to be consecrated.

On the night he was betrayed he took bread, said the blessing, broke the bread, and gave it to his friends, and said, "Take, eat: This is my Body, which is given for you. Do this for the remembrance of me."

After supper, he took the cup of wine, gave thanks, and said, "Drink this, all of you: This is my Blood of the new Covenant, which is shed for you and for many for the forgiveness of sins. Whenever you drink it, do this for the remembrance of me."

Remembering now his work of redemption, and offering to you this sacrifice of thanksgiving,

We celebrate his death and resurrection, as we await the day of his coming.

Lord God of our Fathers; God of Abraham, Isaac, and Jacob; God and Father of our Lord Jesus Christ: Open our eyes to see your hand at work in the world about us. Deliver us from the presumption of coming to this Table for solace only, and not for strength; for pardon only, and not for renewal. Let the grace of this Holy Communion make us one body, one spirit in Christ, that we may worthily serve the world in his name.

Risen Lord, be known to us in the breaking of the Bread.

Accept these prayers and praises, Father, through Jesus Christ our great High Priest, to whom, with you and the Holy Spirit, your Church gives honour, glory, and worship, from generation to generation. *Amen.*

An order for celebrating the Holy Eucharist

This rite requires careful preparation by the Priest and other participants.

It is not intended for use at the principal Sunday or weekly celebration of the Holy Eucharist.

The people and priest

Gather in the Lord's Name

Proclaim and respond to the Word of God

The proclamation and response may include readings, song, talk, dance, instrumental music, other art forms, silence. A reading from the Gospel is always included.

Pray for the world and the Church

Exchange the peace
Either here or elsewhere in the service, all greet one another in the name of the Lord.

Prepare the table
Some of those present prepare the table; the bread, the cup of wine, and other offerings, are placed upon it.

Make Eucharist
The Great Thanksgiving is said by the Priest in the name of the gathering, using one of the eucharistic prayers provided.
The people respond—Amen!

Break the bread

Share the gifts of God
The Body and Blood of the Lord are shared in a reverent manner; after all have received, any of the Sacrament that remains is then consumed.

When a common meal or Agapé is a part of the celebration, it follows here.

At the great thanksgiving

In making Eucharist, the Celebrant uses one of the Eucharistic Prayers from Rite One or Rite Two, or one of the following forms:

Form 1

Celebrant: The Lord be with you.

People: And also with you.

Celebrant: Lift up your hearts.

People: We lift them to the Lord.

Celebrant: Let us give thanks to the Lord our God.

People: It is right to give him thanks and praise.

The Celebrant gives thanks to God the Father for his work in creation and his revelation of himself to his people;

Recalls before God, when appropriate, the particular occasion being celebrated;

Incorporates or adapts the Proper Preface of the day, if desired.

If the Sanctus is to be included, it is introduced with these or similar words

And so we join the saints and angels in proclaiming your glory, as we sing (say),

Celebrant and People: Holy, holy, holy Lord, God of power and might, heaven and earth are full of your glory. Hosanna in the highest. Blessed is he who comes in the name of the Lord. Hosanna in the highest.

The Celebrant now praises God for the salvation of the world through Jesus Christ our Lord.

The Prayer continues with these words: And so, Father, we bring you these gifts. Sanctify them by your Holy Spirit to be for your people the Body and Blood of Jesus Christ our Lord.

At the following words concerning the bread, the Celebrant is to hold it, or lay a hand upon it; and at the words concerning the cup, to hold or place a hand upon the cup and any other vessel containing wine to be consecrated.

On the night he was betrayed he took bread, said the blessing, broke the bread, and gave it to his friends, and said, "Take, eat: This is my Body, which is given for you. Do this for the remembrance of me."

After supper, he took the cup of wine, gave thanks, and said, "Drink this, all of you. This is my Blood of the new Covenant, which is shed for you and for many for the forgiveness of sins. Whenever you drink it, do this for the remembrance of me."

Father, we now celebrate the memorial of your Son. By means of this holy bread and cup, we show forth the sacrifice of his death, and proclaim his resurrection, until he comes again.

Gather us by this Holy Communion into one body in your Son Jesus Christ. Make us a living sacrifice of praise.

By him, and with him, and in him, in the unity of the Holy Spirit all honour and glory is yours, Almighty Father, now and for ever. *Amen.*

Form 2

Celebrant: The grace of our Lord Jesus Christ and the love of God and the fellowship of the Holy Spirit be with you all.

People: And also with you.

Celebrant: Lift up your hearts.

People: We lift them to the Lord.

Celebrant: Let us give thanks to the Lord our God.

People: It is right to give him thanks and praise.

The Celebrant gives thanks to God the Father for his work in creation and his revelation of himself to his people;

Recalls before God, when appropriate, the particular occasion being celebrated;

Incorporates or adapts the Proper Preface of the day, if desired.

If the Sanctus is to be included, it is introduced with these or similar words.

And so we join the saints and angels in proclaiming your glory, and we sing (say),

Celebrant and People: Holy, holy, holy Lord, God of power and might, heaven and earth are full of your glory.

Hosanna in the highest.

Blessed is he who comes in the name of the Lord.

Hosanna in the highest.

The Celebrant now praises God for the salvation of the world through Jesus Christ our Lord.

At the following words concerning the bread, the Celebrant is to hold it, or lay a hand upon it; and at the words concerning the cup, to hold or place a hand upon the cup and any other vessel containing wine to be consecrated.

On the night he was handed over to suffering and death, our Lord Jesus Christ took bread; and when he had given thanks to you, he broke it, and gave it to his disciples, and said, "Take, eat: This is my Body, which is given for you. Do this for the remembrance of me."

After supper he took the cup of wine; and when he had given thanks, he gave it to them, and said, "Drink this, all of you: This is my Blood of the new Covenant, which is shed for you and for many for the forgiveness of sins. Whenever you drink it, do this for the remembrance of me."

Recalling now his suffering and death, and celebrating his resurrection and ascension, we await his coming in glory.

Accept, O Lord, our sacrifice of praise, this memorial of our redemption. Send your Holy Spirit upon these gifts. Let them be for us the Body and Blood of your Son. And grant that we who eat this bread and drink this cup may be filled with your life and goodness.

The Celebrant then prays that all may receive the benefits of Christ's work, and the renewal of the Holy Spirit.

The Prayer concludes with these or similar words: All this we ask through your Son Jesus Christ. By him, and with him, and in him, in the unity of the Holy Spirit all honour and glory is yours, Almighty Father, now and for ever. Amen.

15. METHODIST EUCHARISTIC PRAYERS

John Wesley's adaptation of the Anglican *Book of Common Prayer,* or variants thereof, were long customary in Methodism. Two results of Methodist participation in the modern liturgical movement are printed here: first, from the British *Methodist Service Book* (1975), and second from the "alternate rite" of the United Methodist Church in the USA as revised in *We Gather Together* (1980)

A. The British "Methodist Service Book" (1975): "The Sunday Service"

The Thanksgiving

All stand.

The Minister says the great prayer of thanksgiving:

Lift up your hearts.

We lift them to the Lord.

Let us give thanks to the Lord our God.

It is right to give him thanks and praise.

Father, all-powerful and ever-living God,
it is indeed right, it is our joy and our salvation,

always and everywhere to give you thanks and praise
through Jesus Christ your Son our Lord.
You created all things and made us in your own image.
When we had fallen into sin, you gave your only Son to
be our Saviour.

He shared our human nature, and died on the cross.
You raised him from the dead, and exalted him to your
right hand in glory, where he lives for ever to pray for us.
Through him you have sent your holy and life-giving
Spirit and made us your people, a royal priesthood,
to stand before you to proclaim your glory and
celebrate your mighty acts.
And so with all the company of heaven we join in
the unending hymn of praise:

Holy, holy, holy Lord, God of power and might,
heaven and earth are full of your glory. Hosanna in the highest.
Blessed is he who comes in the name of the Lord.
Hosanna in the highest.

We praise you, Lord God, King of the universe,
through our Lord Jesus Christ
who, on the night in which he was betrayed
took bread, gave thanks, broke it, and gave it to his disciples, saying,
"Take this and eat it. This is my body given for you.
Do this in remembrance of me."
In the same way, after supper,
he took the cup, gave thanks, and gave it to them, saying,
"Drink from it all of you.
This is my blood of the new covenant,
poured out for you and for many, for the forgiveness of sins.
Do this, whenever you drink it, in remembrance of me."

Christ has died. Christ is risen. Christ will come again.

Therefore, Father, as he has commanded us,
we do this in remembrance of him,
and we ask you to accept our sacrifice of praise and thanksgiving.

Grant that by the power of the Holy Spirit
we who receive your gifts of bread and wine
may share in the body and blood of Christ.

Make us one body with him.

Accept us as we offer ourselves to be a living sacrifice,
and bring us with the whole creation to your heavenly kingdom.

We ask this through your Son, Jesus Christ our Lord.

Through him, with him, in him,
in the unity of the Holy Spirit,
all honour and glory be given to you, almighty Father,
from all who dwell on earth and in heaven
throughout all ages. Amen.

B. The United Methodist Church, USA (1980)

The great thanksgiving

The Lord be with you.
And also with you.
Lift up your hearts.
We lift them to the Lord.
Let us give thanks to the Lord our God.
It is right to give him thanks and praise.

Father, it is right that we should always
and everywhere give you thanks and praise.

Only you are God. You created all things and called them good.
You made us in your own image.
Even though we rebelled against your love you did not desert us.
You delivered us from captivity,
made covenant to be our Sovereign God,
and spoke to us through your prophets.

Therefore, we join the entire company of heaven
and all your people now on earth
in worshipping and glorifying you:

Holy, holy, holy Lord, God of power and might,
heaven and earth are full of your glory.
Hosanna in the highest.
Blessed is he who comes in the name of the Lord.
Hosanna in the highest.

We thank you, holy Lord God,
that you loved the world so much
you sent your only Son to be our Saviour.
The Lord of all life came to live among us.

He healed and taught, ate with sinners,
and won for you a new people by water and the Spirit.
We saw his glory.
Yet he humbled himself in obedience to your will,
freely accepting death on a cross.
By dying, he freed us from unending death;
by rising from the dead, he gave us everlasting life.
On the night in which he gave himself up for us,
the Lord Jesus took bread.
After giving you thanks, he broke the bread,
gave it to his disciples, and said:
Take, eat; this is my body which is given for you.
When the supper was over, he took the cup.
Again he returned thanks to you,
gave the cup to his disciples, and said:
Drink from this, all of you,
this is the cup of the new convenant in my blood,
poured out for you and many,

for the forgiveness of sins.
When we eat this bread and drink this cup,
we experience anew the presence of the Lord Jesus Christ
and look forward to his coming in final victory.

Christ has died, Christ has risen, Christ will come again.

We experience anew, most merciful God,
the suffering and death,
the resurrection and ascension of your Son,
asking you to accept this our sacrifice of praise and thanksgiving,
which we offer in union with Christ's offering for us,
as a living and holy surrender of ourselves.

Send the power of your Holy Spirit on us,
gathered here out of love for you, and on these gifts.
May the Spirit help us know in the breaking of this bread
and the drinking of this wine the presence of Christ
who gave his body and blood for all.
And may the Spirit make us one with Christ,
one with each other, and one in service to all the world.

Through your Son Jesus Christ
with the Holy Spirit in your holy Church,
all glory and honour is yours, Almighty Father
now and for ever. Amen.

16. BAPTISTS

The following account has been supplied by Dr W.M.S. West, Principal of Bristol Baptist College, England.

English Baptist practice in the Eucharist

Twenty years ago it would have been possible to say that there was a typical English Baptist Service of the Lord's Supper. It took the form of an "appendage" to the traditional Baptist "hymn sandwich", occurring once a month after morning worship and once a month after evening worship. Following the conclusion of the first service, including the benediction, a number of the congregation would leave; and the service of the Lord's Supper would then be very simple, with a hymn, words of institution, prayer of thanksgiving, distribution and sharing of the elements, offertory for "the poor and needy", and benediction. This particular form of worship is still practised, but in a diminishing number of Baptist churches.

Since about 1960, the Baptist practice of the Lord's Supper has been influenced by the Liturgical Movement, with the result that more and more churches have included the celebration of the Lord's Supper within the total framework of worship. Liturgically there has been fairly extensive "borrowing" from recent liturgies of other churches, and this practice was also influenced by the publication of *Orders and Prayers for Church Worship* compiled by Ernest A. Payne and Stephen F. Winward (1960). The more recently published *Praise God,* compiled by Alec Gilmore and others (1980), may be taken as a reflection of this new liturgical practice among English Baptists.

However, over the last few years another influence has entered into the practice of the Lord's Supper among English Baptists, namely the charismatic influence. In the judgment of many, this has had the effect of "enlivening" the eucharistic practice. What follows is a narrative of an English Baptist service which shows the influence both of the liturgical tradition and of the charismatic renewal. It is impossible to say that this is typical because there is now a far greater variety of practice of the Lord's Supper among Baptists than there has been for decades.

An order of service for preaching and Eucharist

The service opens with a sequence which may be entitled "A call to worship". This includes a brief invitation to worship based upon a psalm, e.g. Psalm 92 or 95, followed by a hymn of praise. There is then a prayer of adoration, confession and invocation.

The next section may be entitled "The Word" and contains Scripture reading from Old and New Testament, probably a brief hymn related to the Word and Spirit, and the preaching of the Word in the sermon. The sermon will certainly show awareness that the service is proceeding towards a eucharistic celebration. Following the sermon there is a hymn which seeks to link word and sacrament. During the singing of this hymn opportunity is given to leave, to those who feel unable to partake of the Lord's Supper, but before the hymn it is made plain that any who wish to remain in worship and not to partake should feel quite free to allow the elements to pass them by.

For "The Lord's Supper" itself, an invitation is issued to the Lord's Table. This is usually extemporary and makes clear that all who are in good standing in their churches (and/or who sincerely believe in the Lord Jesus Christ) are welcome to participate. It is stated that the invitation is being offered by the church on behalf of the Lord. At this point there is a growing practice of "passing the peace", signifying first the assurance of the peace as a gift of God to us all (shalom), and second an act of reconciliation prior to eucharist between the fellowship (cf. Matt. 5:23f.). Where this happens, there is often movement throughout the congregation as people seek each other out. There then follow the words of institution, usually from 1 Corinthians 11, and a prayer of thanksgiving offered sometimes by a layperson (usually a Baptist deacon). There is increasing care taken about this particular prayer, as it is recognized to incorporate also a simple form of epiclesis. After the prayer of thanksgiving, the bread (growingly one loaf) is broken in quarters and placed upon plates for distribution to the congregation where they sit. Each person breaks a piece off and then, where possible, holds the plate for his or her neighbour. Following the return of the bread to the Table, the cup is distributed. Among smaller congregations there is a movement to return to a common cup and in this case the distribution is similar to that of the bread; but where individual cups are used, the participation in the cup usually takes place together when all have been served. Then follow prayers of response, petition and intercession for the church and the world. In these prayers members of the fellowship are often mentioned by name, and in some churches there is an invitation to those who feel particularly in need to come forward in order to have hands laid on them for healing in body, spirit or mind. Often an offering is taken, which is devoted specifically to love gifts to any within or without the fellowship who may be in particular need. The final hymn is normally one of dismissal into the world, and the concluding benediction is one of blessing and dismissal.

17. DISCIPLES OF CHRIST

The Christian Church (Disciples of Christ) celebrates the Lord's Supper every Sunday.

Two brief prayers are given from their *Handbook for Christian Worship* (St Louis, Bethany Press, 1970).

(FOR THE BREAD) All glory and praise be unto thee, O God, our Father, who of thy tender mercy, gave thine only Son, Jesus Christ our Lord, to suffer death upon the cross for us all. Mercifully grant that thy Holy Spirit and Word may sanctify us and this bread, which thou hast given to be the symbol of the body of our Lord, that it may be for us spiritual food, that by faith we may feed in our hearts on him who is our only Saviour and Lord. For his name's sake. *Amen.*

(FOR THE CUP) We give thanks, O God, for this cup, symbol of the most precious blood of our Lord. We commemorate his Last Supper with his disciples, his death upon the cross, his glorious resurrection and exaltation, and his coming again to receive us to share in his heavenly banquet. We pray thee to grant that thy Holy Spirit and Word may so sanctify us and this cup that we may feed in our hearts by faith upon the blood of our Lord, and that this cup may be for us the cup of fellowship and salvation. Let thy grace be upon us now and bless us beyond our asking. Through Jesus Christ our Lord. *Amen.*

A fuller order of service is suggested by the Rev. Keith Watkins:

Sursum corda

Then shall the minister say: Lift up your hearts
We lift them up unto the Lord.

Holy art thou, eternal Father; holy in thy redeeming Son; holy in thy life-giving Spirit. Therefore with Angels and Archangels, and with all the company of heaven, we laud and magnify thy glorious Name; evermore praising thee, and saying,

Holy, Holy, Holy, Lord God of hosts, heaven and earth are full of thy glory. Glory be to thee, O Lord most high. Amen.

Let us give thanks unto our Lord God.
It is meet and right so to do.

Or, he may read suitable sentences from Scripture such as: Worthy is the Lamb who was slain, to receive power and wealth and wisdom and might and honour and glory and blessing.

The great thanksgiving

Then shall the elder or minister offer the communion prayer (or prayers) in words such as,

Holy Lord, Father Almighty, Everlasting God, we lift up our hearts and praise thee for all thy mercies....

We bless thee that through Jesus Christ our Lord thou, the Creator of heaven and earth, didst make us in thine own image; and that, when we had fallen away from thee through sin, thou of thine infinite mercy and love didst send thy Son to be our Saviour. We thank thee that we have redemption through his blood, the forgiveness of our sins; that by him we have access to the throne of thy majesty on high, and are made thy children by adoption and grace; and that we are called this day to eat and to drink at his table.

For these, and all thy mercies, we laud and magnify thy holy name; and with thy whole church in heaven and on earth, we praise and adore thee.

O God our Father, grant unto us, we humbly beseech thee, thy glorious presence, and the powerful working of thy Spirit in us; and so sanctify these elements of bread and wine, and bless thine own ordinance, that we may receive by faith the body and blood of Jesus Christ, crucified for us, and so feed upon him, that he may be one with us, and we with him.

Most Gracious God, accept our sacrifice of praise and thanksgiving, and receive the offering and consecration which we now make of ourselves, our souls and bodies, unto thee; through Jesus our Lord, by whom and with whom, in the unity of the Holy Spirit, all honor and glory be unto thee, O Father Almighty, world without end. Amen.

The Lord's Prayer *The Minister and people together.*

Then shall the minister say: According to the holy institution and command of our Saviour Jesus Christ, we do this: who on the night when he was betrayed took bread (*here the minister shall take the bread into his hands*), and when he had given thanks, he broke it, and gave it to the disciples (*here he shall break the bread*) and said, "Take, eat; this is my body which is broken for you. Do this in remembrance of me."

In like manner shall he raise the cup in his hands, saying: In the same way he also took the cup, saying, "This cup is the new covenant in my blood. Do this, as often as you drink it, in remembrance of me."

Silence shall be kept for a time.

The minister, having received the Communion with those assisting him, shall invite the people: Brethren, this is the joyful and holy feast of the people of God.

The distribution and receiving of bread and wine

When all have been served, a brief prayer of thanksgiving may be offered; or, suitable words of Scripture may be read.

18. THE OLD CATHOLIC CHURCH

The following eucharistic prayer comes from the Second Order of the Mass according to the use of the Old Catholic Church in the Netherlands. This rite came into use around 1968, the First Order of the Mass being an adaptation of the Tridentine rite.

Eucharistic prayer

The congregation stand.
The Lord be with you.
And with thy spirit.
Life up your hearts.
We lift them up unto the Lord.
Let us give thanks unto the Lord our God.
It is meet and right so to do.
With our whole heart do we give thanks continually,
Lord, holy Father, almighty, everlasting God,
who art worthy to receive honour and power.

For heaven and earth and all that is,
the visible and the invisible,
thou hast created through thy Word.

As the crown of thy creation
thou didst make man in thine own image,
and hast given him to share wondrously
in thy greatness.

We thank thee that thy merciful kindness is over us
by day and by night,
and that thou wilt be with us in all our ways.

Blessed art thou for all
that thou in thy great mercy hast done for us.
Thy mercy endures from generation to generation.

In our forefather Abraham thou hast given us
the promise of thy salvation,
and upon Israel thy servant thou hadst mercy.

By the prophets thou hast spoken to us.
Thou hast visited thy people
and declared their redemption.

And in fulfilment of thy promises
thou didst send unto us thy beloved Son,
Jesus Christ, our Redeemer and Saviour.

Through him we glorify and praise thee
with all the heavenly hosts,
and with all thy chosen, who stand around thy throne,
confessing in deep reverence:
Holy, holy, holy, Lord God of hosts,

Heaven and earth are full of thy glory.
Hosanna in the highest.
Blessed + is he that cometh in the Name of the Lord.
Hosanna in the highest.

Blessed art thou, Lord of all majesty
and King of eternal glory,
through Jesus Christ, thine only begotten Son.

In him thy Word was made flesh
and the fullness of thy grace shone forth splendidly.
In all things he fulfilled thy will and glorified thy Name.

He proclaimed thy kingdom to us
and broke for us the power of darkness.

Our guilt he took upon himself,
he reconciled us to thee and unlocked the new paradise for us.

As the way, the truth and the life
has he revealed us thy love.

And therein was he obedient to thee unto the end,
even unto the Cross,
that he might destroy death by his death
and by his rising restore our life.

On the night in which of his own free will
he gave himself up,
he took the bread in his hands
and with his eyes lifted up to thee his heavenly Father
he gave thanks, blessed it, broke it
and gave it to his disciples, saying:
Take, eat; this is my body,
which is given for you +.

Likewise after supper he took the cup;
gave thanks to thee, blessed it
and gave it to his disciples, saying:
Drink ye all of this;
This is my blood of the new covenant,
which is shed for you and for many
for the remission of sins +.
As oft as ye do this,
Ye shall do it in remembrance of me.
Therefore, O Lord, remembering his saving passion,
his glorious resurrection
and his exaltation to thy right hand,
and looking for his coming in the fullness of majesty,
we here set forth this sign of our faith in him,
who offered the perfect sacrifice to thee
and gained an eternal salvation for us.
Send then, we pray thee, thy Holy Spirit,
the giver of all life and sanctification,
upon us and upon these thy gifts:
bread and wine of eternal life.

And take them from our hands
as a sacrifice acceptable to thee,
by which we offer ourselves to thee,
so that the bread which we break
is a sharing of the body of thy Son
and the cup which we bless
is a sharing of the blood of thy Son.
Grant that all who partake of thy heavenly altar,
may evermore remain united with thee,
together with all thy saints and chosen ones,
with thy blessed and glorious handmaiden
Mary, the mother of our Lord,
(with St...., whose memory we keep today)
with thy prophets and apostles,
with thy martyrs and confessors
and with all, who in thy kingdom
stand around thy throne in praise and prayer.
(Grant, Lord, also a share in the glory
to the departed, whom each of us wishes
to remember before thee...
Deal with them and with all men according
to thy merciful kindness
and let perpetual light shine upon them.
Remember also thy servants on earth
for whom we invoke thy mercy...)

Bless thy Church throughout the world and grant it unity and peace.
Renew the earth according to thy promise,
remember all peoples and grant that all men
may give thee thanks and worship and laud thy holy name.

Through thy beloved Son, our Lord, Jesus Christ
with whom and in whom, almighty Father,
in the unity of the Holy Spirit,
all honour and majesty, power and glory be unto thee,
now and throughout all ages, world without end. *Amen.*

19. SOME ECUMENICAL TEXTS

A. The Church of South India

Since 1947 the Church of South India has united Christians from the Anglican, Congregational, Methodist and Presbyterian traditions. The Church soon produced its *Order for the Lord's Supper,* which has proved important both for the contribution it has made to the internal growth of unity in the CSI and for the influence it exercised on liturgical revisions in the English-speaking world. The story of liturgical discovery in the CSI is told in T.S. Garrett, *Worship in the Church of South India* (London, Lutterworth, revised edition 1965). The text reproduced below is from the 1972 revision.

The Lord's Supper

The Peace may be given here. The manner of giving the Peace is according to the local custom.

A lyric or hymn is sung and the offerings of the people including the bread and the wine are brought forward and placed on the Table.

All standing, the presbyter says: Holy Father, you have opened a new living way for us to come to you through the self-offering of Jesus. We are not worthy to offer gifts to you, but through him we ask you to accept and use us and our gifts for your glory. Amen.

The bearers of the offertory return to their places.

The presbyter and the people say together: Be present, be present, O Jesus, our good High Priest, as you were with your disciples, and make yourself known to us in the breaking of the bread. Amen.

The presbyter says:
The Lord be with you:
And also with you.
Lift up your hearts:
We lift them up to the Lord.
Let us give thanks to the Lord, our God.
It is right to give him thanks and praise.
It is good and right, always and everywhere to give you thanks, O Lord, Holy Father, Almighty and ever-living God;

*Through Jesus Christ, your Son, our Lord, for through him, you created all things from the beginning, and made us men in your own image; through him you redeemed us from the slavery of sin; through him you have sent out your Holy Spirit to make us your own people, the first-fruits of your new creation.

And so we join the angels and the saints in proclaiming your glory as we sing (say):

Holy, Holy, Holy Lord, God of power and might, heaven and earth are full of your glory. Hosanna in the highest.

The presbyter remains standing, the people may kneel.

The presbyter says: Truly holy are you, our Father. In your love for us you gave your Son Jesus Christ to be one of us and to die on the cross for us. By that one perfect sacrifice, he took away the sins of the whole world and commanded us to remember his death until he comes again. So, on the night he was betrayed, he took bread, gave thanks to you, broke it and gave it to his disciples, saying: Take, eat; this is my body given for you; do this in remembrance of me. So also after supper he took the cup, gave thanks to you, gave it to them and said: Drink it, all you, for this is my blood of the new covenant, shed for you and for all men, to forgive sin. Do this, whenever you drink it, in remembrance of me.

Amen. Your death, O Lord, we remember, your resurrection we proclaim, your final coming we await. Christ, to you be glory.

---

* Instead of the words, 'through Jesus Christ...your new creation', another Preface proper to the season of the Christian year or to the occasion may be said.

And so Father, remembering that Jesus, your Son and our Lord, was born and lived among us, suffered and died, rose again and ascended, we, your people, are doing this to remember him as he commanded us until he comes again, and we thank you for reconciling and restoring us to you in him.

O Lord, our God, we give you thanks, we praise you for your glory.

And we humbly ask you Father, to take us and this bread and wine, that we offer to you, and make them your own by your Holy Spirit, so that our breaking of the bread will be a sharing in Christ's body and the cup we bless a sharing in his blood. Join us all together in him. Make us one in faith. Help us to grow up as one body, with Jesus as our head. And let us all together, in the Holy Spirit, bring glory to you, our Father. Amen.

B. The Taizé Community

Two eucharistic prayers are given from the 1972 revision of *Eucharistie à Taizé*. Eucharistic Prayer I remains closest to the older Taizé prayers; the present translation is adapted from *Eucharist at Taizé* (1962), to bring the text into harmony with the revised version. The English translation of Eucharistic Prayer VII has been made for the present occasion.

Eucharistic prayer I

President: The Lord be with you.

All: And with thy spirit.

President: Let us lift up our hearts.

All: We lift them to the Lord.

President: Let us give thanks to the Lord our God.

All: It is right and good so to do.

President: Truly it is right and good to give thee glory, to offer thanks to thee always and everywhere, most holy Father, almighty, everlasting God...

(variable text)

Therefore with angels and martyrs we proclaim thy glory as we sing (say) together:

All: Holy, holy, holy is the Lord, God of the universe. Heaven and earth are full of thy glory. Hosanna in the highest. Blessed be he that comes in the name of the Lord. Hosanna in the highest.

President: Our Father, God of the universe, fill with thy glory our sacrifice of praise. Bless, perfect and accept this eucharist as the figure of the one and only sacrifice of our Saviour.

Send the Holy Spirit upon us and our eucharist: consecrate this bread to be the body of Christ and this cup to be the blood of Christ; that the creator Spirit may accomplish the word of thy beloved Son:

Who, in the same night that he was betrayed, took bread, blessed it by thanksgiving, broke it, and gave it to his disciples, saying: Take, eat from this, all of you; this is my body given for you. Likewise, at the end of the meal, he took the cup, blessed it by thanksgiving, and gave it to his disciples, saying:

Take, drink from this, all of you; for this is the cup of my blood, the blood of the new and eternal covenant, which will be shed for you and for many for the remission of sins. Do this as the memorial of me.

Great is the mystery of the faith.

All: We proclaim thy death, Lord Jesus, we celebrate thy resurrection, we await thy coming in glory.

President: Wherefore, O Lord, we make before thee the memorial of the incarnation and passion of thy Son, his resurrection from the dead, his ascension into glory, his perpetual intercession; we await and pray for his return.

All things come of thee, and our only offering is to recall thy gifts and marvellous works. Therefore we present to thee, O Lord of glory, as our thanksgiving and intercession, the signs of the eternal sacrifice of Christ, unique and perfect, living and holy, the bread of life and the cup of the kingdom.

In thy love and mercy, accept our praise and prayers in Christ, as thou wast pleased to accept the gifts of thy servant Abel the righteous, the sacrifice of our father Abraham, and the gifts of Melchizedek thy high priest, as types of the perfect sacrifice.

Almighty God, we beseech thee that this prayer may be borne by thy angel to thy altar in thy presence on high; and when we receive, communicating at this table, the body and blood of thy Son, may we all be filled with the Holy Spirit and endowed with thy grace and blessings through Christ our Saviour.

By whom, O Lord, thou dost ever create, sanctify, quicken, bless and give us all thy benefits.

By whom, with whom, and in whom be unto thee, O Father almighty, in the unity of the Holy Spirit, all honour and glory, world without end.

All: Amen.

Eucharistic prayer VII

President: The Lord be with you.

All: And with your spirit.

President: Let us lift up our hearts.

All: We lift them to the Lord.

President: Let us give thanks to the Lord our God.

All: It is right and good so to do.

President: Truly it is right and good to give thanks to you, most holy Father, through Jesus Christ our Lord. Through him you created the whole universe, visible and invisible; you made humanity in your own image and established your covenant with us; you revealed to us your promises through the mouth of the prophets.

Therefore with angels and martyrs we proclaim your glory as we sing (say) together:

All: Holy, holy, holy is the Lord, God of the universe! Heaven and earth are full of your glory. Hosanna in the highest. Blessed be he who comes in the name of the Lord. Hosanna in the highest.

President: Truly you are holy, God our Father, and you so loved the world that you sent your Son: he took flesh of the Virgin Mary by the Holy Spirit.

May that Spirit of power today consecrate our eucharist and thus fulfill the word of your beloved Son who wills to give us his body and his blood.

In the night that he was betrayed, he took bread, blessed it by thanksgiving, broke it, and gave it to his disciples, saying: Take, eat from this, all of you; this is my body given for you.

Likewise, at the end of the meal, he took the cup, blessed it by thanksgiving, and gave it to his disciples, saying: Take, drink from this, all of you; for this is the cup of my blood, the blood of the new and eternal covenant, which will be shed for you and for many for the remission of sins. Do this as the memorial of me.

All: Great is the mystery of the faith. We proclaim your death, Lord Jesus, we celebrate your resurrection, we await your coming in glory.

President: Therefore, gracious God, making before you the memorial of the passion, resurrection and ascension of Christ our great high priest who ever lives to intercede for us, we present to you, as a pure offering, his unique and perfect sacrifice.

Sanctify your Church as on the day of Pentecost: let the Spirit of holiness lead her into all truth, strengthen her in her mission to the ends of the earth, and prepare her for your eternal kingdom, where we shall share the inheritance of your saints in light, with the Virgin Mary, with the apostles, prophets and martyrs, (with Saint N.); all of us together await the return of your beloved Son: "Come, Lord Jesus!"

All: Maranatha, the Lord is coming!

President: Through him, with him and in him, be to you, God the Father almighty, in the unity of the Holy Spirit, all honour and glory, world without end.

All: Amen.

C. The British Joint Liturgical Group

Formed in 1963, the semi-official Joint Liturgical Group has exercised great influence on liturgical reforms in Great Britain. Its members come from the Church of England, the Church of Scotland, the Baptist Union, the Episcopal Church in Scotland, the Methodist Church, the Churches of Christ, the Roman Catholic Church, and the United Reformed Church. In 1978 the group published a "eucharistic canon". The notes below the text are supplied by the group itself.

The eucharistic canon

Almighty God, Eternal Father, it is our duty and delight at all times and in all places to give you thanks and praise. You are the creator of all things and the source of all life, in whom we live and move and have our being. You have given us your only Son, Jesus Christ, to free us from the slavery of sin and to make us heirs of eternal life. He was born as one of us, was obedient to your will, and accepted death upon the cross: you raised him from the dead and have made him Lord of all. You send us your Spirit to guide us into the truth, to bring us reconciliation and peace, and to renew us as the Body of your Son.

(And now we give you thanks...)

We praise you, for you are God.

All: We acclaim you, for you are the Lord. We worship you, eternal Father: and with the whole company of heaven we sing in endless praise: Holy, holy, holy Lord, God of power and might. Heaven and earth are full of your glory. Hosanna in the highest.

[Blessed is he who comes in the name of the Lord. Hosanna in the highest.]

Heavenly Father, we offer you this praise through Jesus Christ, your only Son, our Lord, who hallowed your name, accomplished your will, established your kingdom, and gave himself to be our spiritual food. And now we pray that by the power of your Holy Spirit these gifts of bread and wine may be to us his body and his blood. For on the night when he was betrayed he took bread, and when he had given thanks, he broke it, and said, "Take, eat: this is my body which is for you. Do this in remembrance of me." In the same way after supper, he took the cup, saying, "This cup is the new covenant in my blood, Do this, as often as you drink it, in remembrance of me." Therefore, heavenly Father, obeying the command of your dear Son, and looking for his coming again in glory, we celebrate the perfect sacrifice of his death upon the cross, his mighty resurrection and his glorious ascension.

All: Christ is Victor. Christ is King. Christ is Lord of all.

Father, accept through Christ our sacrifice of thanks and praise: and as we eat and drink these holy gifts, kindle in us the fire of your Spirit that with the whole Church on earth and in heaven we may be made one in him. Count us worthy to stand before you as your people and to offer without ceasing our adoration and service, through Jesus Christ our Lord. Through him, with him, and in him, in the unity of the Holy Spirit, all honour and glory are yours, Father Almighty, now and for ever.

All: Amen.

NOTES

[1] This Canon is primarily intended for use on ecumenical occasions, although it may be used at any time.

[2] The Preface. As far as possible the mighty acts of God are expressed in terms of present activity rather than as past events. At the same time the ideas are borrowed from Scripture, e.g. the reference to creation is borrowed from Acts 17:28.

[3] The Sanctus. This, with its introduction, has been taken from the Te Deum. Not only is it eminently suitable, but it is supported by the theory expressed by some scholars that this hymn was originally the Preface, Sanctus and Post-sanctus of a Mass for the Easter Vigil (cf. P. Cagin, *Te Deum ou Illatio,* Solesmes 1906; E. Kähler, *Studien zum Te Deum,* Göttingen 1956).

[4] Benedictus. It is recognized that some people may not wish to use the Benedictus at this point. It may therefore be used at other appropriate points or omitted.

[5] Post-Sanctus. An unusual feature has been the use of material from the Lord's Prayer at this point: but it is thought to be singularly "appropriate".

[6] Institution Narrative. This is substantially the RSV version of 1 Corinthians 11, and can be regarded as a legitimate scriptural warrant.

⁷The Acclamation. Doubts have been expressed as to the desirability of placing the Acclamation immediately after the Institution Narrative. Some feel that this puts undue emphasis on the Narrative, implying that this is *the* consecration formula. It seems logical, however, to place the Acclamation at the conclusion of the Anamnesis, providing congregational endorsement of what has just been said.

This particular acclamation is not in common use; and other acclamations may be used in its place.

D. Consultation on Church Union (USA)

Constituted in 1962, COCU includes the following churches in its membership: African Methodist Episcopal Church, African Methodist Episcopal Zion Church, Christian Church (Disciples of Christ), Christian Methodist Episcopal Church, Episcopal Church, National Council of Community Churches, Presbyterian Church in the United States, United Church of Christ, United Methodist Church, United Presbyterian Church in the USA.

Reproduced here is Eucharistic Prayer II from *Word Bread Cup* (Cincinnati, Forward Movement Publications, 1978). This text is followed by some guidelines for a eucharistic prayer said extemporaneously.

Minister: The Lord be with you.

People: And also with you.

Minister: Lift up your hearts.

People: We lift them to the Lord.

Minister: Let us give thanks to the Lord our God.

People: It is right to give him thanks and praise.

Minister: [It is truly right to glorify you, Father, and to give you thanks; for you alone are God, living and true, dwelling in light inaccessible from before time and for ever.

Fountain of life and source of all goodness. You made all things and fill them with your blessing: you created them to rejoice in the splendour of your radiance.

Countless throngs of angels stand before you to serve you night and day; and, beholding the glory of your presence, they offer you unceasing praise. Joining with them, and giving voice to every creature under heaven, we acclaim you, and glorify your Name, as we sing (say)]*

Minister and People: Holy, holy, holy Lord, God of power and might, heaven and earth are full of your glory. Hosanna in the highest. Blessed is he who comes in the name of the Lord. Hosanna in the highest.

Minister: We remember with joy the grace by which you created all things and made us in your own image.

We rejoice that you called a people in covenant to be a light to the nations.

---

*Local congregations and eucharistic communities are encouraged to make their own decisions about the content and style of this portion of the prayer, focusing on general themes stressing the creation, the season or day in the Church year, or a local occasion. The preface of "A Common Eucharistic Prayer" is included here as an example.

Yet we rebelled against your will. In spite of prophets and pastors sent forth to us, we continued to break your covenant. In the fullness of time, you sent your only son to save us. Incarnate by the Holy Spirit, born of your favoured one, Mary, sharing our life, he reconciled us to your love.

At the Jordan your Spirit descended upon him, anointing him to preach the good news of your reign. He healed the sick and fed the hungry, manifesting the power of your compassion. He sought out the lost and broke bread with sinners, witnessing the fullness of your grace. We beheld his glory.

On the night before he died for us, Jesus took bread; giving thanks to you, he broke the bread and offered it to his disciples, saying:

"Take this and eat, this is my body which is given for you, do this in remembrance of me."

Taking a cup, again he gave thanks to you, shared the cup with his disciples and said: "This is the cup of the new covenant in my blood. Drink from this all of you. This is poured out for you and for many, for the forgiveness of sins."

After the meal our Lord was arrested, abandoned by his followers and beaten. He stood trial and was put to death on a cross. Having emptied himself in the form of a servant, and being obedient even to death, He was raised from the dead and exalted as Lord of heaven and earth.

Through him you bestow the gift of your Spirit, uniting your Church, empowering its mission, and leading us into the new creation you have promised. Gracious God, we celebrate with joy the redemption won for us in Jesus Christ. Grant that in praise and thanksgiving we may be a living sacrifice, holy and acceptable in your sight, that our lives may proclaim the mystery of faith:

Minister and People: Christ has died, Christ is risen, Christ will come again.

Minister: Loving God, pour out your Holy Spirit upon us and upon these gifts, that they may be for us the body and blood of our Saviour Jesus Christ. Grant that we may be for the world the body of Christ, redeemed through his blood, serving and reconciling all people to you.

Remember your Church, scattered upon the face of the earth; gather it in unity and preserve it in truth. Remember the saints who have gone before us [especially ＿＿＿＿ and ＿＿＿＿ (here may occur special names)].

In communion with them and with all creation, we worship and glorify you always;

All: Through your Son Jesus Christ, with the Holy Spirit in your Holy Church, all glory and honour is yours, Almighty God, now and forever. Amen.

***

Eucharistic prayer offered extemporaneously: guidelines

(a) The decision to offer the eucharistic prayer extemporaneously is to be made only after giving due regard to pastoral considerations and liturgical policies and disciplines of the churches represented in the service.

(b) The prayer is for the blessing of the bread and cup through giving thanks to God over them.

(c) The prayer is to include these themes which reflect aspects of the eucharistic prayer commonly expressed by the Church from ancient times:
  (1) thanks for God's creation and redemption of the world in Christ;
  (2) thanks for the gift of this sacrament expressed in a way that recalls Christ's words of institution;
  (3) thanks for the gift of the Holy Spirit whose presence is invoked.

20. TEXTS IN NEW CONTEXTS

A. New Orders of the Mass for India

These are taken from the publication of the National Biblical Catechetical and Liturgical Centre, Bangalore (1974).

Because of the unusual character of these eucharistic prayers, the presentation and the notes provided in the original publication have been retained. Only the longer version of the eucharistic prayer has been reproduced, however.

Introduction

Two versions of the Eucharistic prayer are proposed here: a long version and a short one. The Indian tradition is fond of long development and flowery phraseology. The long version tries to meet this characteristic feature of the Indian religious soul, especially through an elaborate development of salvation history in the proclamation and long responses. The version however is clearly not meant for daily use, but for solemn occasions; moreover, it supposes a familiarity with the Indian and the biblical tradition which cannot be presumed in every congregation. Though it is proposed here as one piece, it could also serve as source material for the composition of various shorter anaphoras. A short version is also proposed, considerably reduced in length and much simplified in content. A true pastoral concern for each congregation must guide the choice between the two versions.

The long version

It begins with a solemn introductory dialogue, where an effort has been made to transpose to the context of Indian sacred rites the substance of the ancient introductory dialogue of the Apostolic tradition of Hippolytus, in use even today in the Roman rite.

The content of the proclamation is fundamentally the same as in the Eucharistic prayers of the liturgical tradition: it gives praise and thanks to God for his creation, and subsequently for his deeds of salvation in history, the climax of which is found in the Christ-event and the Paschal Mystery. In the Indian context, it is appropriate to elaborate on the marvels of God's creation; moreover, the Indian approach to them seems to require that the immanence of God in the universe, His pervasive presence in the whole cosmos and his providence be emphasized. Special reference to the

Noah-covenant and its application to the age-long Indian quest for God also recommends itself. Hence the division of the proclamation into seven stanzas (I—VII).

Each stanza consists of two parts: the proclamation proper made by the celebrant, and the corresponding acclamation by the congregation. The celebrant expresses the theme of each particular section and elaborates on it. The congregation bursts forth into an acclamation, marking the response in faith of the people. Each acclamation takes up the theme of the proclamation of God's deeds made by the priest. All are filled with the spirit of the traditional "Sanctus", that is, the idea of the all-pervading glory of God; this is why the "Sanctus" need not have been preserved. For the sake of rhythm, each acclamation is made up of three lines. When advisable for pastoral reasons, a leader can say the first two lines, while the people join together in the third, which is the same in all the stanzas.

The structure of the proclamation is as follows. Stanzas I to III are dedicated to God's creative action. The first stanza mentions the five elements as God's gift to man and the power by which God himself is present in them. Planets have been included here because they are considered to exercise a great influence in the life of the Indians. The theme of Indian spirituality expressed in this stanza can be summed up in the words of the Bhagavad Gita:

"Whatever being shows wider power prosperity or strength, Be sure that this derives from a fragment of my glory" (X, 41).

The second stanza brings out the theme of life as gift of God. God has given life and power to the mountains, rivers and seas (sacred to the Hindus). He himself is the source of life in all living things. The third stanza on creation brings out the theme of the glory of God in man, who is the crown of God's creative activity. Man, endowed with intellect, speech and love, is called to share in the life of God, who is in himself "Saccidananda".

The following stanzas (IV—VII) recall the history of salvation with its progressive unfolding in three successive covenants. First comes the cosmic covenant with all men (stanza IV), where reference is made to Noah, Job and Melchisedech. Stanza V applies the cosmic covenant to the Indian context. After the search for God as Power present in nature in the animistic religions, mention is made successively of the Hindu religion with its three characteristic margas (Karma, Jnana, bhakti), of Buddhism, Jainism and Islam. Stanza VI is devoted to the historical covenant which God made with Israel through Abraham and Moses. He spoke to Israel and saved it; He instilled in his chosen people a longing for the Messiah. Stanza VII ends with the proclamation of the Christ-event as the fulfilment of salvation-history. The longings of the nations and of Israel are fulfilled in Christ, the God-man. In the narration of Christ's public life, special reference is made to his role as Teacher and Master, in view of the importance of the Guru-chela relationship in the Indian religious tradition. Christ's earthly career culminates in the Paschal Mystery, by which He becomes the source of all life and fills the world with joy by sending the Holy Spirit.

Thus the proclamation ends with the outpouring of the Spirit over the Church in the Mystery of Pentecost. This leads naturally to the first epiclesis (Stanza VIII) with the first epicletic motif where God is called upon to send the Spirit over the gifts of the Church; their change into the Body and Blood of Christ will make the paschal Mystery sacramentally present among us. The double-institution narrative occupies Stanza IX. The anamnesis is found in Stanza X. It contains the twofold idea of the celebration of the memorial of Christ and the sacramental offering of his sacrifice (cf. in the Roman Canon "memores... offerimus... ").

The intercessions-commemorations occupy Stanza XI. (These could eventually be omitted, if provision is made for a litany of intercession led by a deacon between the Eucharistic prayer and the rite of communion, as is the practice in several Eastern liturgies). The intercessions comprise, in order, an ecumenical prayer for Church unity, a prayer for India in its present context of development, for the absent brethren and for the dead. The commemorations of the saints (where St Thomas and St Francis Xavier are specially mentioned as Patrons of India) bring out the idea of the communion of saints between the pilgrim Church and the Church triumphant. There follows in stanza XII the second epiclesis, with the specific motif of the fruits of unity and life to be derived by the Church from its partaking in the Eucharistic banquet. The Trinitarian doxology with which the Eucharistic prayer ends (Stanza XIII) has purposely been made very solemn and has been given a definite Indian flavour.

Some remarks may be made regarding the recitation of the long version of the Eucharistic prayer in concelebration. The main celebrant alone must lead in the introductory dialogue. The concelebrants join with him from the first epiclesis to the second epiclesis included, but the intercessions-commemorations are said by one of the concelebrants. The proclamation (stanzas I to VII) can be said by the main celebrant alone; however, in view of its length, it may be better to distribute the various stanzas among the concelebrants, with the proviso that the main celebrant says stanzas I and VII. For the doxology, it is foreseen that the recitation of the words is combined with the arati or with some similar gesture more in keeping with a particular cultural tradition (cf. infra: rubric and note). It may be more appropriate that the main celebrant alone recites the words of the doxology; the concelebrants can however join with him in the recitation. It is suggested that, after the doxology, all the priests, main celebrant and concelebrants, prostrate in a protracted moment of silent adoration in the posture of "panchanga-pranam".

The short version

The introductory dialogue of the long version has been preserved, as seems advisable for pastoral reasons. The Proclamation is substantially reduced. It consists of three stanzas only. These are distributed as follows: stanza I is devoted to God's creation of the world and of man; stanza II to the Noah-covenant applied to India and to the Mosaic covenant; stanza III to the Christ-event. The first Epiclesis remains the same (stanza IV). In the institution-narrative (stanza V) the preamble with the mention of the washing of the feet at the Last Supper has been suppressed. The Anamnesis is shortened, while keeping the double idea of the memorial and the offering of sacrifice (stanza VI). Two acclamations are proposed; either one or the other is said by the people.

The response which follows in the long form is left out here. The intercessions and commemorations (stanza VII) are shortened, though reference is still made to Christian unity, to the absent brethren, the nation, the dead and the communion of saints. (Here as in the long version the intercession and commemorations can be left out, if provision is made for a litany of intercession led by the deacon after the Eucharistic prayer). The Second Epiclesis remains the same (stanza VIII). The doxology keeps the same solemnity; for this as for the introductory dialogue it seems pastorally advisable to keep the same text as in the long version. For all explanations of the text of this version, the relevant notes which accompany the long version can be consulted.

Eucharistic prayer

Long version

Introductory dialogue (Mangalacaranam)[23]

Cel.: May your Holy Spirit, O God, enlighten our minds, and open our lips that we may sing the wonders of your love![24]

Cong.: Help us, Spirit divine, to proclaim God's mercy!

Cel.: Let us praise and thank the Lord, our God, whose majesty pervades the universe![25]

Cong.: Great is his name and worthy of praise![26]

Cel.: Let us celebrate the glory of the Lord whose splendour shines in the depths of our hearts![27]

Cong.: Glory to Him in whom we have our being![27bis]

Proclamation

I. Cel.: O Supreme Lord of the Universe, You fill[28] and sustain everything around us; You turned, with the touch of your hand, chaos into order, darkness into light.[29] Unknown energies You hid in the heart of matter. From you bursts forth the splendour of the sun and the mild radiance of the moon.[30] Stars and planets without number[31] you set in ordered movement.[32] You are the source of the fire's heat and the wind's might, of the water's coolness[33] and the earth's stability.[34] Deep and wonderful, the mysteries of your creation.

Cong.: We adore you, who are beyond all form![35] You give form[36] to everything, Lord of all creation![37] We praise you,[38] we thank you, we proclaim your glory!

II. c.: God of all that lives, through countless ages you have peopled the seas and rivers, the mountains and plains,[39] with beings innumerable. With power from you the seed buds forth in blossom, the tender shoot grows into a mighty tree, bird and beast multiply and fill the earth. You are the life of all that lives.[40]

Cong.: We adore you, O Source of Life![41] All creatures look to you, Lord of Power![42] We praise you, we thank you, we proclaim your glory!

III. c.: God of all salvation, You formed men[43] in your own image.[44] You created them male and female,[45] you willed their union and harmony. You

●Notes on page 192.

entrusted the earth to their care[46] and promised your blessing to all their descendants. You gave them the spirit of discernment to know you,[47] the power of speech to celebrate your glory,[48] the strength of love to give themselves in joy to you.[49] In this wondrous way, O God, you called them to share in your own being, your own knowledge, your own bliss.[50]

Cong.: We adore you, O Lover of Men![51] In you is the source of our life. We praise you, we thank you, we proclaim your glory!

IV. c.: Lord of all ages, Father most kind and merciful, You want all men to reach the shores of salvation.[52] Even when they fail to respond to your call, you do not abandon them to themselves.[53] In your unchanging fidelity[54] you wish your love for them to stand forever. Your covenant with Noah shows your providence through the constant cycles of nature.[55] In the tempest of Job's affliction, You revealed the mystery of human life.[56] You chose Melchisedech. A priest from among the nations, to bless Abraham your servant.[57]

Cong.: We adore you, Lord of all ages! You are ever at work to shape the destinies of men. We praise you, we thank you, we proclaim your glory!

V. c.: God of the nations, You are the desire and hope of all who search for you with a sincere heart.[58] You are the Power almighty adored as Presence hidden in nature.[59] You reveal yourself to the seers in their quest for knowledge,[60] to devout who seek you through sacrifice and detachment,[61] to every man approaching you by the path of love.[62] You enlighten the hearts that long for release by conquest of desire and universal kindness.[63] You show mercy to those who submit to your inscrutable decrees.[64]

Cong.: We adore you, Light divine! You shine bright in the hearts of those who seek you. We praise you, we thank you, we proclaim your glory!

VI. c.: God of the covenant, in your gracious love for all men[65] You called Abraham to be the father of a great nation.[66] Through Moses your servant You gathered your scattered children into a people.[67] Despite their infidelity,[68] you never failed to speak to them through the Prophets[69] and to save them through your mighty deeds.[70] You instilled into their hearts an eager hope for that awaited day of the Saviour to come,[71] the day of peace and favour for all men.

Cong.: We adore you, God of the Promise! Your erring people you pursue with love. We praise you, we thank you, we proclaim your glory!

VII. c.: O God invisible,[72] at the favourable time[73] you were pleased to become visible to us.[74] Your Word,[75] your only-begotten Son,[76] took on our human condition[77] and was born of the Virgin Mary.[78] As Supreme Teacher and Master,[79] he imparted the words of eternal life[80] to the poor and humble of heart,[81] and went about doing good.[82] When his hour had come,[83] of his own accord he laid down his life[84] as sacrifice[85] for our sins.[86] Raised from the dead by you,[87] Father, he became for us the source of life[88] and sent the Holy Spirit[89] to fill the world with joy and peace.[90]

First epiclesis

VIII. cc.: Now we pray you, Father send this same Spirit to fill these gifts of bread and wine with his divine power,[91] and to make present among us the great mystery of our salvation.[92]

Cong.: Come, O Spirit Supreme, Come, O Spirit all holy, Come, O Spirit who fill the universe.

Institution narrative

IX. cc.: At the Supper which he longed to share with his disciples,[93] Your Son, Jesus Christ, showed the depth of his love.[94] Though Lord and Master,[95] he did the humble work of a slave by washing their feet.[96] During the meal[97] he took bread in his sacred hands, gave you praise and thanks, broke the bread and gave it to his disciples, saying: Take this, all of you, and eat it: This is my body which will be given up for you. Do this to celebrate the memorial of me.[98]

Cong.: Amen.[99]

cc.: In the same way after Supper,[100] he took the cup. Again he gave you praise and thanks, gave the cup to his disciples, saying: Take this, all of you, and drink from it: This is the cup of my blood, the blood of the new and everlasting covenant. It will be shed for you and for all men so that sins may be forgiven. Do this to celebrate the memorial of me.[101]

Cong.: Amen.

Anamnesis

X. cc.: And so, Father, in gratitude we celebrate the memorial of the obedient death of Your Son,[102] of his glorious resurrection from the dead, his triumphant ascension into heaven and his outpouring of the Spirit in whom the Church is born.[103] While in glory he intercedes for us before your throne of mercy,[104] we on earth await his return. When he comes, he will gather up the fruits of redemption, hold them together in his fulness[105] and place them at your feet.[106] United with Him in this mystery of salvation, we offer you His unique and holy sacrifice.

Cong. : 1. We announce your death and proclaim your resurrection, Lord Jesus; gather all your people into your kingdom when you come in glory.[107]

2. We announce your death, Lord Jesus, and proclaim your resurrection and ascension until you come in glory.[108]

3. We proclaim your death, Lord Jesus, until you come in glory; Your resurrection is the hope of our salvation.[109]

4. We proclaim your death, Lord Jesus, until you come in glory.[110]

Intercessions and commemorations

XI. c.: Merciful Father, bring together all your people in the Holy Spirit,[111] help them live in unity and fellowship[112] with Paul, our Pope, N., our Bishop, the patriarchs and pastors of all the Churches.[113]

c.: We pray you, Father, crown the yearnings of this our ancient land[114] with the knowledge and love of your Son. Bless the efforts of all those who labour to build our country into a nation where the poor and the hungry will have their fill, where all people will live in harmony, where justice and peace, unity and love will reign.[115] Bless also all our brethren who are not present at this Eucharist.[116]

c.: Grant to our departed brothers and sisters and all who longed for you a share in your bliss.[117] Welcome them into your Kingdom, where[118] Mary the Virgin Mother of God, the Saints of all lands and ages, St Thomas, St Francis Xavier[119] and St N. unceasingly pray for us and help us share[120] in the riches of your Son, our Lord, Jesus Christ.

Second epiclesis

XII. cc.: Loving Father, send down your Spirit, the fulness of your bliss,[121] to fill with joy and peace[122] all of us who share in the Body and Blood of Christ, that we may be one in Him,[123] and manifest our unity[124] in loving service.[125] May he be the pledge of our resurrection and lead us in hope to the shore of eternal life with all the just in the Kingdom of Heaven.

Cong.: Supreme Spirit, Spirit divine, awaken us to your loving presence.[126]

Doxology

(The celebrant lifts the oblata; doxology and arati are synchronised)[127]

XIII. Cel.: In the Oneness of the Supreme Spirit[128] through Christ who unites all things in his fulness[129] we and the whole creation give to you, God of all, Father of all,[130] honour and glory, thanks and praise, worship and adoration, now and in every age,[131] for ever and ever.

Cong.: Amen. You are the Fulness of Reality,[132] One without a second,[133] Being, Knowledge, Bliss![134] Om, Tat, Sat!

---

[23]Mangalacaranam is a prayer for God's blessing on a religious rite. God is called upon to help us so that our action may be rightly performed. This seems to be the most appropriate way of transposing to the Indian context the introductory dialogue.

[24]Inspired from Rig Veda 3. 62. 10, the Gayatri mantra.

[25]Ps. 8; 1. 10; 104, 1; Isa. Up. 1; cf Agnipurana I, pp. 217–218.

[26]Ps. 95, 4.

[27]Bhagavad Gita (B.G.), 15.15: "I make my dwelling in the hearts of all".

[27]bis. Acts 17, 28; cf. B.G. 7, 12.

[28]Svet. Up. 1, 15–16.

[29]Gen. 1, 2; 1:4.

[30]B.G. 7, 8; cf. B. G, 15, 12.

[31]Bar 3, 34–35

[32]Eccles. 42, 21.

[33]Amos 5, 8; 9, 6.

[34]B.G. 7, 9; 15, 13; cf. Bar 3, 32; Jer 10, 12.

[35]Katha Up. 6, 9; "His form is not something that can be seen". Mait. Up. 7, 1; "Unformed". B.G. 8, 9; "In form unthinkable".

[36]Prasna Up. 2, 12.

[37]Pras. Up. 2, 7: "Lord of creatures"; cf. also Svet. Up. 4, 2; B.G.; 3, 10; 3, 20; 2 Mac. 7, 28; Ps. 19.

[38]Ps. 94.

[39]Amos 4, 13.

[40]B.G. 15, 13; Svet. Up. 1, 6.

[41]B.G. 10, 8; "The source of all am I. From Me all things proceed"; Rg. Veda 10, 121. 2: "Giver of life (Atman)".

⁴²Ps. 144, 15.

⁴³Eccles. 15, 14.

⁴⁴Gen. 1, 27; cf. Eccles. 17, 3.

⁴⁵Gen. 1, 27.

⁴⁶Gen. 2, 15.

⁴⁷Eccles. 16, 24; B.G. 7, 10; 10, 4–5.

⁴⁸Isa. 43, 7; cf. B.G. 10, 9; 11, 36.

⁴⁹B.G. 10, 10.

⁵⁰From the Upanishadic texts down to the theological commentaries, 'Saccidananda' describes the nirguna Brahman in His absolute attributes. God is by himself (sat), in himself (cit), for himself (ananda); this doctrine, primarily philosophical in character, seems strictly identical to that of Christian metaphysics; it applies to God in the infinite degree the transcendental perfections of being; esse, verum, bonum. The Hindu metaphysical formula, however, as that of the Christian metaphysics, can become a valid enunciation of the Christian Trinitarian dogma in a twofold way. First the process of appropriation of God's transcendental perfections esse, verum, bonum (in themselves really identical) to the three divine persons respectively, is entirely legitimate and is thus found frequently in the Christian tradition. Thus, in view of their personal character in the divine life, a specific role in the order of creation and salvation is applied, by theological appropriation, to each of the divine persons respectively, creation (sat) to the Father; revelation (cit) to the Son; sanctification (ananda) to the Spirit. Moreover, understood in a Christian way, Saccidananda becomes a valid expression of the Trinitarian life itself: Sat refers then to the Father as the Person from whom the other two proceed (principium sine principio); Cit to the Son as one who proceeds from the Father per modum actus intellectionis (the fruit of God's self-knowledge); Ananda to the Spirit as proceeding from the Father through the Son per modum actus amoris (the fruit of God's love of Himself the divine Bliss the togetherness of Father and Son).

⁵¹B.G. 9.18.

⁵²Cf. Theme of Liberation (Moksha) to Indian Scriptures.

⁵³Ps. 102, 8–10; 17–18.

⁵⁴Ps. 116, 2.

⁵⁵Gen 9,12–17.

⁵⁶Job. 42, 1–3, 5.

⁵⁷Gen. 14, 18–20; cf. Heb. 7, 1–3.

⁵⁸Vatican II: Declaration on non-Christian Religions. 2.

⁵⁹This very Christian idea is inserted here with reference to animistic religions. Cf. Vat II: Declaration...2; Rg Veda 10, 90. Cf. Is 45, 15–25.

⁶⁰Reference is made to the three paths (marga) towards salvation in the Indian Scriptures. For the path of knowledge cf. Chand. Up. 4, 9, 1–2; 4; 14, 1–2.

⁶¹Chand. Up 2, 23, 1.

⁶²B.G. 11, 54.

⁶³Reference is made here to Buddhism and Jainism; cf. Declaration...2.

⁶⁴Reference is made here to Islam; cf. Declaration...3.

⁶⁵I Tim. 2, 1–6.

⁶⁶Gen. 12, 1–3; Gen. 18, 18; Deut. 7, 7–8

⁶⁷Ex. 3, 7–12.

⁶⁸Deut. 32, 20; Ezek. 16, 43.

⁶⁹Is. 6, 6–9; Jer. 1, 9.

⁷⁰Deut. 29, 3; Ps. 105–106.

⁷¹2 Sam. 7, 1–17; Isa. 9, 5; 11, 1–5; Jer. 23, 5–6.

⁷²1 John 4, 12; Jn 6, 46. In the Indian tradition, cf. Svet. Up. 1, 8. B.G. 2, 25; 8, 18.21; 9, 4.

⁷³Gal. 4, 4–5, Heb. 1, 1.

[74] 1 John 1, 1–4.

[75] John 1, 1. 14; in the Indian tradition, cf. the concept of 'sabda'.

[76] John 1, 14. 18; 3, 16.

[77] All the connotation of Paul's "morphe" and John's "sarx" must be taken into account. Cf. Phil. 2, 7; John 1, 14.

[78] Matt. 1, 18–25.

[79] Mark 10, 17–22; John 13, 13–15; 18, 20. In the Indian tradition of the Guru–chela relationship: the Guru is both "Teacher and Master": he does not only impart knowledge of the Vedas but guides the disciple through life.

[80] John 6, 68.

[81] The notion of 'hanawim' in the O.T...cf. Mt. 11, 5, 5, 3 cf. in the Indian tradition the qualification of the true disciples, the various sadhanas which he needs to listen profitably to the guru.

[82] Acts 10, 38; 1, 1.

[83] John 13, 1; also cf. John 17, 1.5; Rom. 5, 6

[84] John 10, 15–18, the parable of the Good Shepherd.

[85] Isa. 53: the servant of Yahweh, victim for the sins of the people; cf. Chand. Up. 3, 16, 1: Purusa of great sacrifice (yajna).

[86] Rom. 8, 3; 1 Cor. 15, 3; Rom. 5, 6–11.

[87] Rom. 6, 4; Rom. 8, 11; Phil. 2, 9.

[88] Heb. 5, 9; Rom. 8, 9–11; Gal. 5, 16.

[89] John 14, 26; 15, 26; 16, 7.

[90] Gal. 5, 22; the fruits of the Holy Spirit. N.B. At this point, it seems more appropriate to have NO acclamation by the people so that the movement be not interrupted between the recital of the outpouring of the Spirit and the invocation of the Spirit in the epiclesis.

[91] See the anaphora in the Eucholoy of Serapion of Thmuis (Deiss, l., Early Sources of the Liturgy, p. 115; cf. Agnipurana, 1, pp. 217–218).

[92] This formula is preferred to "that they may become the Body and Blood of Our Lord Jesus Christ." Not only does the Body and Blood of Christ become really and substantially present by transubstantiation, but the Paschal Mystery is sacramentally re-presented in the Church. This representation implies, but is broader than, the substantial presence of Christ's Body and Blood.

[93] Luke 22, 15.

[94] John 13, 1.

[95] John 13, 13–14.

[96] John 13, 12.

[97] Matt 26, 26; Mk 14, 22.

[98] The commission to celebrate the memorial is omitted in the Roman Eucharistic Prayers after the institution under the species of bread; yet it is explicitly mentioned in Luke 22, 19 and 1 Cor 11, 24. It is found in the Eucharistic Prayer of the Taize Community. "Do this in memory of Me" is a poor translation, for it does not bring out the full meaning of the biblical term zikkaron (memorial) "Do this as the memorial of Me" (used in the English translation of the Eucharistic Prayer of the Taize Community) may not sound well in English; on the other hand "Do this as a memorial of Me" weakens the text where the definite article "ten" is found. In order therefore to render fully the meaning of "touto poieite eis ten emen anamnesin" (Luke 22, 19) (eis with the accusative case indicates the end of the action), the best translation may be: "Do this to celebrate the memorial of Me."

[99] "Amen" said by the congregation immediately after each of the two parts of the institution-narrative is a deep profession of faith, commonly found in the Eastern liturgies.

[100] Luke 22, 20; 1 Cor. 11, 25.

[101] 1 Cor. 11, 25.

[102] Phil. 2, 8; Heb. 5, 8.

[103] The mystery of Pentecost an *historical* event can be considered as part of the Paschal mystery;

the outpouring of the Spirit which brings the Church into existence is the seal of the New Covenant established by God through Christ with His new people. It seems, therefore, legitimate to mention it in the *anamnesis* as an integral part of the salvific event of which the Eucharist celebrates the memorial. Though there is little evidence for this in the liturgical tradition, the mystery of Pentecost is explicitly mentioned in the anamnesis of the *Anaphora Dioscori Alexandrini* (cf. Hänggi-Pahl, Prex Eucharistica, p. 199). To include the mystery of Pentecost here is not without significance in the context of the dialogue with the Oriental Churches who stress the economy of the Spirit.

On the contrary it is more difficult to see how the *future event* of Christ's second coming can be celebrated in memorial; hence it seems more logical not to mention it *directly* in the anamnesis as belonging to the event of which the memorial is made, though there is some evidence for this procedure in the liturgical tradition. Here the eschatological dimension of the Eucharistic celebration is purposely brought in *indirectly:* "while in glory he intercedes for us...(a lasting function of the Glorified Christ) we on earth await..."

[104] 1 John 2, 1; Heb. 10, 12; 7, 25.

[105] Eph. 1, 23; 2, 21; Col. 1, 19; notion of 'pleroma' in St. Paul. Cf. also the notion of 'purnam' in Brhad. Up 5, 1.1.

[106] 1 Cor. 15, 28.

[107] The acclamation by the people, which in the Roman Eucharistic Prayer is found immediately after the institution-narrative, seems to find its place more naturally after the anamnesis. The anamnesis explains what the Church is doing by repeating the ritual of the Lord's Supper; this explanation quite naturally calls for the acclamation by the People. On the contrary, if the acclamation precedes the anamnesis, it anticipates what the celebrant is about to say in the anamnesis, (cf. Kavanagh, A., *Worship* 1969, 12; Dupuis, J., *Clergy Monthly* 1969, 495, note 19). Notice how the people's acclamation takes up the themes of the anamnesis prayer in the various formulas proposed. For the first form proposed here, cf. Anaphora of the Twelve Apostles, Hänggi-Pahl. *Prex Eucharistica*, p. 266.

[108] Cf. the anamnesis in the Anaphora of Cyril of Alexandria, Hänggi Pahl, op. cit. p. 339.

[109] cf. Irenaeus, Adv. Haer. IV, 18; 5.

[110] cf. 1 Cor. 11, 26.

[111] This intercessory prayer means to be fully ecumenical. It prays for the unity of all the Christian Churches into one Church of Christ. See the *Decree on Ecumenism* of Vatican II, no. 3 where the Christian communities separated from Rome are recognized as 'Churches'.

[112] cf. Vatican II: *Constitution on the Church*, 4; 'koinonia' in Phil. 2; 1.

[113] Note 95 explains why to all the patriarchs and pastors of all the Churches have been added.

[114] cf. Pope Paul VI, addresses at the Bombay Eucharistic Congress; *Clergy Monthly Supplement* 7, 183ff.

[115] cf. Pope John XXIII, Prayer for the Ecumenical Council.

[116] Those "who are not present at this Eucharist" refers primarily to the absent members of the local community, whose absence is due to sickness or to any other reason; even negligence. More broadly, the expression indicates the union of the Eucharist celebrated by a particular community with all those celebrated in the Church.

[117] Cf. Vatican II: *Pastoral Constitution on the Church in the Modern World*, 18.

[118] The intercession of the Saints is purposely introduced indirectly so as not to obscure the uniqueness of the mediation of Christ. This "great discretion" in the way of mentioning the intercession of the Saints is found in the Roman Canon (cf. Communicantes), notwithstanding the fact that the Saints occupy there a prominent place. Cf. Roguet, A., *La Messe d'aujourd' hui;* p. 180–182.

[119] Special mention is made of St. Thomas the Apostle and of St. Francis Xavier, as patrons of India.

[120] Cf. the theology of the communion of Saints in the *Constitution on the Church*, 49.

[121] The concept of the Holy Spirit as Divine Bliss is especially appropriate in the Indian context. (cf. note 50). It is also in order in the epicletic motif where the Church prays that it may derive fruits of unity and life from its partaking in the sacred banquet of Christ's Body and Blood.

[122] Gal. 5, 22; Rom. 14, 17.

[123] John 17, 21; 1 Cor. 12, 12-13.

[124] Acts 2, 46.

[125] John 13, 35; 13, 15; John 15.

[126] This acclamation seems quite appropriate here. What we receive through the sacramental partaking of the Body and Blood of Christ is the Spirit of Christ, transforming us into the image of Christ. Charity and love are derived from the presence of the Spirit within us (cf. Rom. 5, 5). This applies also to the Eucharistic banquet (cf. Tillard, J.M.R.; "L'Eucharistie et le Saint-Esprit". *Nouvelle Revue Theologique* 1968, 363ff);

[127] In the Hindu puja, the pujari makes the arati while reciting the mantras. It seems appropriate therefore that the arati be made *during* the doxology, not after. To this effect, while the consecrated gifts are lifted by the celebrant, representatives of the congregation do the arati with flowers, incense and camphor. The bell also is rung. The arati should be done in such a way that it is seen to be addressed to God, not to the sacred species; to this effect, it is suggested to make a threefold (clock-wise) circular revolution.

[128] The Holy Spirit is referred to here as Supreme Spirit (paramatman). For the structure of the doxology, see Eph. 2: 18: in the Spirit *through* Christ we make our way to the Father. It is specific of Christian prayer that it is normally (not exclusively) addressed in the Spirit through Christ to the Father. This is especially true where liturgical prayer is concerned. Hence the basic structure of the doxology, already found in the *Apostolic Tradition* of Hippolytus: through Christ the Chuch living in the Spirit gives glory to the Father. Trinity is directly intended and the mediation of Christ is stressed. This form has been preserved in the doxology proper, while the response by the congregation which follows sums up with the 'immanent' Trinity (Being, Knowledge, Bliss).

[129] Eph. 1, 10.

[130] Rev. 4, 8; B.G. 11, 40.

[131] Rev. 4, 11; cf. B.G. 11, 39-44.

[132] 1 Cor. 15, 28; cf. Brhad. Up. 5; 1. 1.

[133] Deut. 32, 39; Isa. 46, 9; cf. Chand. Up. 6; 2; 1-2.

[134] Cf Note 28.

B. The Church of Christ in Thailand

The text of this "Order for the Lord's Supper" has been translated and supplied by Mrs Kamol Arayaprateep.

Invitation to the Lord's table

This is the Lord's table. Our Saviour invites those who trust him to share the feast.

People will come from east and west, and from north and south, and sit at table in the kingdom of God.

According to Luke, when our risen Lord was at table with his disciples, he took the bread, and blessed and broke it, and gave it to them, and their eyes were opened and they recognized him.

Paul said, "The cup of blessing which we bless, is it not a participation in the blood of Christ? The bread which we break, is it not a participation in the body of Christ? Because there is one bread, we who are many are one body, for we all partake of the one bread."

Passing the blessing

Minister: Let us open our hearts to receive one another with love; let us forgive each other with the sincere desire that everyone will receive peace.

People: Peace be with you.

The people greet the persons on their left and right by saying these words and then by bowing in the Thai manner: put the two hands together, lift them to the level of the chin and bow the head.

Prayer of thanksgiving

Minister: Lift up your hearts.
People: We lift them to the Lord.
Minister: Let us glorify the Lord.
People: For all his grace and goodness.
Minister: Eternal God, Creator of the universe, all glory belongs to you. We praise you for the world, our life in it, your gift of the breath of life, all the beauty that we have, and all the wonderful things to come. Lord, your living word has led and shaped us since the beginning. Your prophets have called us from our stubbornness, and have prepared us for the coming of your Son. We praise you for Christ who humbled himself to become human like us, to live among us as a poor man, to suffer, to be crucified on the cross, to be buried for the sake of all of us. In Christ we experience forgiveness, and the release from heavy burdens. Christ gives light to our thinking and opens our eyes to see your glory. You raised Christ from the dead and by your Holy Spirit you placed him above all your creation. Hence we are the members of the Church, the body of Christ, the heirs of the promise of eternal life. With gratitude in our hearts we join the fellowship of the faithful in all ages and places praising your name.
People: Holy Holy Holy, God of power and majesty. Heaven and earth are full of your glory, O God most high.
Minister: Holy Father, we thank you for what Christ did on the night when he was betrayed. We remember Christ's commandment in breaking the bread and drinking the wine. We believe firmly that you put the seal of the new covenant upon our hearts.

Holy Spirit, you are the one who leads us all to come here, to proclaim the good news of Christ's resurrection, and you are the one who gathers all of us into one body of Christ, who loved us and died for us.
Together: O God, who called us from death to life; we dedicate ourselves to you, and with the Church through all ages we thank you for your love in Jesus Christ our Lord.
Together: (Lord's Prayer)

The feast of bread and wine

Minister: On the night when Jesus was betrayed, he took bread and when he had given thanks, he broke it and said, "This is my body which is for you. Do this in remembrance of me."
While saying these words the minister shall take the loaf of bread and lift it up to give thanks, then break the bread and put it back on the plate. The minister shall give the bread to the elders to distribute to the people. All shall hold the bread until the minister finishes saying:

The Lord Jesus said, "I am the bread of life; anyone who comes to me shall not hunger, and anyone who believes in me shall never thirst."
All shall eat the bread.
Minister: In the same way also the cup, after supper, the Lord Jesus said, "This cup is the new covenant in my blood. Do this, as often as you drink it, in remembrance of me." For as often as you eat this bread and drink this cup, you proclaim the Lord's death until he comes.
While saying these words the minister shall lift up the cup in the same manner as with the bread, then shall distribute the wine to the elders to give to the people. All shall hold the cup until the minister finishes saying:
The Lord Jesus said, "This is my blood of the covenant which is poured out for many, for the forgiveness of sins. Drink of it, all of you." Let us drink with respect.
All shall drink the cup.
Minister: Let us pray:
Almighty and Eternal God, we thank you for the spiritual feast that you have given to us, because of your love, at this table. This sacrament makes us to be firm in your grace and to be one with the Church and with those who inherit the eternal kingdom of heaven. O Heavenly Father, by your grace help us to have a part in your holiness, so that from now on we are enabled to live our life to glorify you. We pray and give thanks in the name of Jesus Christ your Son. Amen.
People: Amen.

Symbols in the service

The minister or ministers will sit or stand behind the table. When the elders come forward to receive the elements, they will stand around the table. The table will be placed on the same level as the congregation to symbolize that the Lord is in the midst of his people.

There should be an unbroken loaf of bread and a large cup for use during the words of institution. The people will be served from plates of small pieces of bread and from individual cups. Unfermented grape juice is to be used for the wine.

C. Eucharistic Prayer for Australian Aboriginals (1973)

This prayer was prepared in connection with the Roman Catholic international eucharistic congress held at Melbourne in 1973. It was explained thus:

This liturgy is an attempt to express the Eucharistic Act in cultural and thought patterns of the Aboriginal peoples. We must be mindful of a number of factors here.

Firstly, there is an extremely complex series of cultural patterns covering Aboriginal groups throughout Australia. The signs and symbols that are used to express themselves are also complex with a degree that varies so much that what is a symbol in one area is sometimes a contradictory symbol in another.

Secondly, there is a complexity of language which lacks a common substratum. However, we have tried to develop a language pattern that would find common acceptance.

In tribal Aboriginal societies, which no longer exist in their pure form, traditional and cultural social communication are made through the use of specific signs and symbols. Traditions, myths, religious beliefs, for example, are handed down from one generation to another by the use of the spoken word, in song or formal ceremonial conversation and through the use of mime acting. Many of these are pure story telling. Some of them have a sacramental element in that the principle of efficiency operates, that is, if a particular ceremony is performed certain results will follow.

There is also in this cultural context a strong consciousness of the transcendental element of religious experience and belief. There are rich symbols, some of which also have a sacramental efficiency about them, which are strongly used in the religious sphere.

The point must be made also that the religious element of traditional Aboriginal life cannot in reality be separated from the total perspective of life as lived.

Another factor which must be taken into account is a psychological one. Aboriginal thought processes do not cater for the abstract philosophical or theological type concept. The trained mental processes are such that there must be an immediately realistic connection between the mental abstract and the concrete reality. Consequently, such words as heaven are very difficult for Aborigines to apprehend and use.

We have tried to base this Liturgy upon these and other anthropological principles. We look upon this Liturgy as an archetype. It would be used satisfactorily in situations where the tribal tradition is still intact, as in some Catholic missions in Western Australia and the Northern Territory. Many of these groups requested an Aboriginal Liturgy with which they can identify themselves.

Eucharistic prayer

Preface
Cel: May the Father in heaven make you good in your hearts.

All: May he make you good in your heart.

Cel: Listen to the word of the Lord Jesus.

All: We will listen.

Cel: Father in heaven, you love us. You made all things.

All: Father, you are good.

Cel: Father, you made the rivers that gave us water and fish. You made the mountains and the flat country. You made the kangaroos and goannas and birds for us.

All: Father, you are good.

Cel: Father, you send the sun to keep us warm, and the rain to make the grass grow, and to fill the waterholes.

All: Father, you are good.

Cel: Father, you made us your people.

All: Father, you are good.

Cel: Father, you called us to be your children and we would not follow you. You sent Jesus, your only proper Son, to be our brother and our friend. He told us about you.

All: Father, you are good.

Cel: He was born on Christmas Day. His mother was Mary.

All: Father, you are good.

Cel: He taught the people. They listened to him.

All: Father, you are good.

Cel: Bad men nailed him to the cross and he died.

All: Father, you are good.

Cel: He rose up again alive. He made us all his brothers and sisters when we were baptised. We join together now and say:

All: Father, you are good. We are happy about that man Jesus, your only proper Son. Father, you are good. Come, Lord Jesus, come and be with us.

Cel: Father in heaven, you are truly good. You make us good in our hearts. Your Holy Spirit will come on these two presents that we hold up to you.

He holds them up.

Through your word, they will become for us the body and blood of your only proper Son, Jesus the Lord. A long time ago, in the night, Jesus and his friends eat together. Before he dies, Jesus takes bread. He holds it up to you, Father.

Celebrant holds the host up a little.

He calls you good, Father. He breaks the bread. And he says to his friends: 'Take this, all of you, and eat it: This is my body, which will be given up for you.'

Then he takes the wine in the cup. He holds it up to you, Father. *Celebrant holds the chalice up a little.*

He says to his friends: 'Take this, all of you, and drink from it. This is the cup of my blood, the blood of the new and everlasting covenant. It will be shed for you and for all men so that sins may be forgiven. Do this in memory of me.'

Let us say together:

All: The bread has become the body of the Lord. The wine has become the blood of the Lord. We cannot see this. By the word of the Lord Jesus, we believe it.

Cel: The Lord Jesus died for us.

All: We remember. It is good.

Cel: The Lord Jesus rose up again alive, and went to heaven.

All: We remember. It is good.

Cel: The Lord Jesus comes again.

All: We remember. It is good.

Cel: Father in heaven, we give you these two presents. This living bread—it is the body of the Lord Jesus. This living wine—it is the blood of the Lord Jesus. Your Holy Spirit will make us of one mind and one heart. You call us here. We are happy with you. We will follow what you say. Soon, we will eat that food, the body and blood of your Son. Then we will be of one mind and one heart. Father in heaven, remember Paul our Pope, and James our Bishop; remember all bishops and priests. Remember all the people of God, especially those who are here. Remember all your people who have died as your friends.

All: Father, you are good.

Cel: Now let us say a good word to the Father, to the Son, to the Holy Spirit, to God, to the Three in One, for ever and ever.

All: Amen.

D. From the Philippines

The following text comes from *Celebration: A Sourcebook for Christian Worship* (Quezon City, New Day Publishers, 1975). The book was compiled and written by Lydia N. Niguidula, of the United Church of Christ in the Philippines, under the joint sponsorship of the Research Center of Silliman University and the National Council of Churches in the Philippines.

Presentation of the offering of money and bread and wine

An offering hymn or doxology

This may be sung as the offerings are collected and brought forward. The congregation shall stand during the presentation.

Offertory prayer
Minister/Liturgist: Our loving Father, we offer these gifts from our labor. We bring this money, part of our earnings. May it help advance the work of your Church, not only within her walls, but also to the larger community.

We bring these elements for the common meal we are about to partake of: they represent the fruit of the land you have loaned us to use; they remind us of our common need to nourish our bodies and to share with those who lack these necessities. They also symbolize the sanctity of common things which you can transform into a sacrament, a visible sign of an inward grace. Purify these tokens, O Father, for our use now in the sharing of these bread/camote/banana and wine/juice in this sacred meal of remembrance of him who shared his life with us. Through Jesus Christ our Lord. Amen.

OR

What is seen, O Lord, are a few tokens—bread and some wine (juice). What we intend with these tokens is the offering of ourselves and all that we have. Whatever wisdom and learning we have, whatever talents and worldly goods, are yours from the beginning and are offered here for your blessing.

As you promised to be present in the common meal of bread and wine, so also hallow our lives and the things of this world by your presence, that our days may be refreshed with meaning and purpose. We ask this in the name of Jesus Christ our Lord.

Consecration of the Elements

Minister: Let us now in faith set aside this bread and this wine for the holy use as symbols of the body and blood of our Lord Jesus Christ. Let us pray:

Heavenly Father, may the Lord Jesus Christ, our great High Piest, be present with us as he was among his disciples, and make himself known to us in the breaking of the bread and the sharing of the cup. To you be praise and glory with your Son, our Savior and the Holy Spirit, now and forever.

People: Amen.

OR

Minister: God our Father, Maker of heaven and earth, pour out your glory on this our sacrifice of praise. Send now your Holy Spirit upon us and our celebration: consecrate this bread and this cup set aside as our offering of thanks to you for your love and mercy, that with the Holy Spirit these may be the means by which we recall with penitence and thanksgiving your sacrifice through your Son our Lord.

Grant us the sincerity to offer you ourselves as a living sacrifice, holy and acceptable to you. Blessed are you, O Lord, our God. Amen.

Thanksgiving or eucharistic prayer

Here may be included the great thanksgiving of God's people as well as the specific concerns of the local community. If a creed has not been offered earlier in the service, this Thanksgiving Prayer ought to contain some of the doctrines of the Church for which a worshipping community may give thanks. The following may be used. The congregation shall stand for this.

Minister: We give you thanks and praise, our Father, for all that you have done for the world. We must not take even our existence for granted: it is your love which has given us life.

Here particular thanksgiving may be inserted as appropriate.

We praise you and thank you, Almighty Father, because you are our God, our Creator, and our Sustainer.

Blessed are you, Father, that you have given us this day and this hour.

Blessed are you, Father, in all the things you have made: in plants and in animals and in men, the wonders of your hand.

Blessed are you, Father, for the food we eat, for bread, for wine, and for laughter in your presence. Blessed are you, Father, that you have given us eyes to see your goodness in the things you have made, ears to hear your word, hands that we may touch, and bless, and understand.

We give you thanks that, having made all things, you keep them and love them.

We praise you through our Lord Jesus Christ. Amen.

OR

Minister: Lift up your hearts.

People: We lift them up to the Lord.

Minister: Let us give thanks to the Lord our God.

People: It is right that we should.

Minister: We give you thanks, O God, through your Son, Jesus Christ, whom in this, the last of all periods of time, you sent to save and redeem us and to tell us what you wanted of us. He is your Word, inseparable from you. You made all things through him and you were well pleased with him.

People: You sent him from heaven to a virgin's womb; he lay in that womb and took flesh, and you were presented with a Son, born of the Holy Spirit and of the virgin. He did what you wanted him to do, and when he suffered, acquiring thereby a people for you, he stretched out his hands to free from suffering those who believed in you.

Minister: When he was handed over to undergo the suffering he himself had chosen, thereby to destroy death, to break the chains the devil held us in, to crush hell beneath his feet, to give light to the just, to make a covenant and manifest his resurrection, he took bread, gave thanks, and said to his apostles: Take this and eat it, this is my Body that is broken for you. In the same way he took the chalice, saying: This is my blood that is to be shed for you. When you do this, you will be commemorating me.

All: Calling then his death and resurrection to mind, we offer you bread and a chalice, and we thank you for enabling us to stand before you and serve you.

Minister: We ask you to send down your Holy Spirit on the offering Holy Church makes you, to unite all who receive holy communion and to fill them with the Holy Spirit, for the strengthening of their faith in the truth.

All: So may we give you praise and glory through your Son Jesus Christ. Amen.

The holy communion

The minister, taking the bread in his hands and breaking it, shall say:
The bread which we break is the communion of the body of Christ.

Then, the Minister shall lift the cup or pour the wine into a cup and say:
The cup of blessing which we bless is the communion of the blood of Christ.

OR

The Minister may recall the origin of the Lord's Supper through the reading of the Words of Institution, breaking the bread and lifting or pouring the cup at the appropriate moments in the reading. Any of the following texts may be used:

Matthew 26:26–29

Mark 14:22–25

Luke 22:19–20; 18

I Corinthians 11:23b–26

The sharing or the distribution of the bread and cup

Minister: And now, ministering in Christ's name, I give you this bread and this cup.

OR

Minister: Come, for all things are now ready.

OR

Minister: Holy things for the holy! One only is holy, One only is the Lord: Jesus Christ, to the glory of the Father. Come, and receive the Body and Blood of Christ.

The bread and cup are distributed in the manner to which the people are accustomed. This is an opportune time for quiet meditation, preferably without background music at times, especially for congregations used to it. On other occasions, contemporary songs of communion may be sung by the choir to be joined in by the congregation when they are ready.

Prayer of thanksgiving and dedication

Minister/Liturgist/Unison: Almighty and everlasting God, we give you thanks for feeding us with the spiritual food of the body and blood of our Saviour Jesus Christ. With the broken bread which we have partaken we have eaten an invisible loaf, given each day no larger than our need; the broken bread of your humiliation purging us of pride and pretense. With such broken bread we depart from the table of one whose life was broken that ours might be mended, to shine at last with his spirit at the doing of your will on earth where all things are incomplete until your blessings rest upon them.

OR

Father, we put back into your hand all that you have given us, rededicating to your service all the powers of our minds and bodies, all our worldly goods, all our influence with others. All these, O Father, are yours to use as you will. All these are yours, O Christ. All these are yours, O Holy Spirit. Speak in our words today, think in our thoughts, and work in all our deeds. And seeing that it is your gracious will to make use even of such weak human instruments as what we are in the fulfillment of your mighty purpose for the world, let our lives today be the channels through which some little portion of your divine love and pity may reach the lives around us. And to your name be all the glory and the praise, even unto the end. Amen.

Hymn of dedication or fellowship *(Congregation standing)*

Benediction *(Congregation standing)*

Minister: God sends you from the gathered church to be scattered and let loose in a world that is resistant to him. Into your varied occupations, may you make your world his world, a world that is "new in Christ." May God's spirit go and abide with you.

All: Amen.

OR

Minister: Go now, remembering what we have done here, responding and responsible wherever you are. You can never be the same again. Go to be his people wherever life takes you, and may the Lord be with you; and may peace and joy forever accompany you.

Ascription of glory (*Congregation standing*)
Minister: To him be glory, worship and praise.
All: Amen.
Minister: To God be the glory, honor, majesty and praise.
All: Amen.

E. The Zaïre Rite for the Mass

This text is reproduced from *Afer* 17 (1975), pp. 243–48, where it is preceded by the following introductory note:

In response to several requests, AFER is publishing an English translation of the 'Rite Zaïrois de la Célébration Eucharistique' offered for experimental use in Zaïre by the Liturgical Committee of the Episcopal Commission for Evangelisation. As a real attempt to modify the Roman Rite in accordance with African tradition and mentality, it may stimulate liturgical thinking in other parts of the continent, notably in East Africa, which shows little sign of life in this matter. Some of the prayers have been slightly shortened in this version.

1. Opening of the celebration

1. Invocation of the saints.
After bowing to the altar and greeting the people, the celebrant gives a brief introduction to the readings of the day. Then he invites the faithful to unite themselves to the entire communion of saints. He says:

Brothers and sisters, we who are living on earth are not the only followers of Christ; many have already left this world and are now with God. But together with them, we make up one great family. Let us join ourselves to them, and especially to the saints, so that this sacrifice may gather us all together into one body.

All stand, and the celebrant makes the following prayers:

C: Holy Mary, be with us; you who are the Mother of God, be with us. Here is our prayer: be with us, and be with all who celebrate mass at this time.

People: Be with us, be with us all.

C. Saint N. (the patron saint or saints), be with us: you who are the patron of our parish, be with us. Here is our prayer.... (as above)

People: Be with us, be with us all.

(This prayer is repeated using the name of the saint of the day, if desired).

C: Holy people of heaven, be with us: you who see God, be with us: here is our prayer...

People: Be with us, be with us all.

C: And you, our ancestors, be with us, you who have served God with a good conscience, be with us. Here is our prayer....

People: Be with us, be with us all.

2. *'Gloria in excelsis':* or other suitable song. This is sung joyfully. The faithful dance in their places, while the celebrant and the other ministers dance around the altar.

3. Opening Prayer.

C: Brothers and sisters, let us raise our hands in prayer.

All raise up their hands: this attitude is a sign of the oneness of the hearts of all as they pray together.

II. Liturgy of the Word

4. *Reading as usual,* with song. In solemn masses, the reader asks the celebrant for a blessing before the reading.

5. *Enthroning the Gospel:* Before proclaiming the Gospel, the celebrant shows the Gospel book to the people, and the following dialogue is made:

C: Brothers and sisters: the Word was made flesh

People: And he dwelt among us.

C: Let us listen to him.

All remain in silence for a few moments

6. Proclamation of the Gospel.

C: The Good News, as Saint N. has written it

People: Glory to you, Jesus Christ, glory to you.

(or) Announce it, announce it, we are listening.

The celebrant then proclaims the Gospel, after inviting the people to sit down. He concludes as follows:

C: He who has ears to hear

People: Let him hear!

C: He who has a heart to receive

People: Let him receive!

7. Homily

8. Profession of faith (Credo) if it is to be said.

9. Penitential rite.

C: Brothers and sisters, the word of God has enlightened us. We know that we have not always followed it. Let us ask the Lord to give us the strength we need to lead better lives.

Silent pause; and then, the people express their sorrow by taking up an attitude of repentance: head slightly bowed, arms crossed on the breast.

C: Lord our God, like the insect that sticks onto our skin and sucks our blood, evil has come upon us. Our living power is weakened. Who can save us? Is it not you, O Father? Lord, have mercy.

People: Lord, have mercy.

C: Before you, O Father, before the Virgin Mary, before all the saints, we confess that we have done wrong: Give us the strength we need to lead better lives. Christ, have mercy.

People: Christ, have mercy.

C: Before our brothers, before our sisters, we confess that we have done wrong: give us the strength to lead better lives, save us from falling back into the shadows. Lord, have mercy.

People: Lord, have mercy.

C: Most Holy Father, weaken in us whatever drives us to evil; forgive our faults, because of the sacrifice of your Son Jesus Christ; may your Spirit take possession of our hearts, and may our sins be drowned in the deep and silent waters of your mercy. Through Christ, our Lord.

People: Amen.

In a solemn mass, the celebrant sprinkles the people with holy water, and a song with a baptismal theme is sung, such as 'Asperges me' or 'Vidi aquam'. Then the sign of peace is exchanged.

10. Prayer of the Faithful can be said here.

III. Liturgy of the Eucharist

11. Preparation of the Offerings.

Offertory procession: *some members of the assembly bring the gifts to the altar, while a suitable song is sung. When the gift-bearers reach the sanctuary, where the celebrant is waiting, the singing stops. Firstly, the gifts intended for the needy of the community are offered while one of the bearers says:* Priest of God, here is our offering, May it be a true sign of our unity.

The priest makes a sign of gratitude: for example, a slight clapping of his hands. He then takes the gifts, and, with the help of his ministers, he places them in a suitable spot. Then the bread and wine are presented by two people, who say together:

O priest of God, here is bread, here is wine: gifts of God, fruits of the earth, they are also the work of man. May they become food and drink for the Kingdom of God.

The priest takes the bread and wine, places them on the altar, and, if necessary, silently washes his hands. If incense is used, he now blesses the incense.

12. The celebrant invites the people to pray:

C: Brothers and sisters, let us raise up our hands in prayer.

All stand and take up the attitude of prayer, and the priest says the prayer over the gifts, to which all reply: Amen.

13. The Eucharistic Prayer.

A minister rings the hand-bell, and says:

Brothers and sisters, let us take heed and make ready our hearts.

A silent pause of a few moments.

C: Let us praise the Lord.

People: Praise to you, our God.

C: Let us give thanks to the Lord our God.

People: Yes, to our God.

Theological part of the eucharistic prayer.

Lord our God, we thank you, we praise you, you, our God and our Father, you, 'sun too bright for our gaze', you the all-powerful, you the all-seer, you, the Master of men, the Master of life, the Master of all things, it is you we praise, it is to you that we give thanks, through your Son Jesus Christ the one who is our mediator with you.

People: Yes, he is our mediator!

Christological part of the prayer

C: Holy Father, we praise you through your Son Jesus, our mediator. He is your Word, the Word that gives life. Through him, you created heaven and earth; through him you created our river, the Zaïre. Through him, you created our forests, our rivers, our lakes. Through him you created the animals who live in our forests, and the fish who live in our rivers. Through him you created the things we see, and also the things we do not see.

People: Through him you have created all things!

C: You have made him Lord of all things; you have sent him among us to be our Redeemer and Saviour. He is our God made man. By the Holy Spirit, he took flesh of the Virgin Mary. This we believe.

People: Yes, this we believe!

C: You sent him, with the task of gathering all people together, of making all mankind one family: your family. He obeyed you: he died on the cross, he conquered death, he rose from the dead: death has no longer any power over him.

People: He rose again: he has overcome death!

C: This is why we sing, in union with all the angels and saints: You are holy!

People: Holy holy holy, Lord God of the universe. Heaven and earth are filled with your glory. May salvation come to us from heaven. Blessed is he who comes in the name of the Lord. May salvation come to us from heaven!

C: You are holy, Lord, our God. Your only Son our Lord, Jesus Christ, is holy. Your Spirit is holy. You are holy, almighty God. We beseech you: hear us.

Pre-consecratory epiclesis

The celebrant makes the following prayer with his arms stretched out, the palms of his hands turned upwards—the gesture of offering.

C: See this bread; see this wine: see them, and make them holy. May your Holy Spirit come down upon these gifts that we offer to you, so that they may become for us the body and blood+of Jesus Christ our Lord.

Before he was given up for us, as he freely accepted his suffering and death, Christ our Lord took bread, gave thanks, broke it, and gave it to his disciples, saying: Take this and eat it, all of you. This is my body which will be given up for you.

A drum or gong can be beaten gently until the end of the consecration

People: This is your Body: we believe.

C: At the end of the meal, he took the cup, he gave thanks once again and gave the cup to his disciples, saying:

Take this and drink from it, all of you; for this is the cup of my blood, the blood of the new and everlasting pact of brotherhood. It will be poured out for you and for all men, so that sins may be forgiven. Do this in memory of me.

People: This is your Blood; we believe.

C: How great is the mystery of faith!

People: Lord, you have died; Lord, you have risen; Lord, you will come again in glory: we believe, we believe!

Anamnesis

C: Lord, we remember that your Son, our Lord, has died and is risen. We offer you the bread of life, we offer you the cup of salvation; we give you thanks. For you have chosen us to stand before you as your people.

Post-consecratory epiclesis

C: Lord God almighty, have mercy on us. Send your Spirit upon us to gather us into unity; for we are about to eat the Body of Christ; we are about to drink the Blood of Christ.

People: Lord, may your Spirit gather us into unity.

Intercessions

C: Lord, remember your Church, scattered all over the world. May all Christians love one another, as you have loved us. Be mindful of Pope N. Be mindful of our Bishop N. Be mindful of all who keep faithfully the faith received from the Apostles. Be mindful also of the rulers of our country.

People: Be mindful of them all.

C: Be mindful, also, Lord, of our beloved ones who died in the hope that they would rise again. Be mindful of them. Be mindful of all men who have left this earth. Be mindful of them, and receive them into your holy light.

People: Lord, be mindful of them all.

C: Look on us also with your merciful love. Make us share in eternal life with Mary, the ever-virgin Mother of God, with the Apostles and with the saints of all ages—those who have loved you, and been loved by you. Grant that we may praise you for ever with them, through Christ our Lord.

May we glorify your name, your great and wonderful name, Father, Son, and Holy Spirit now and for all ages.

People: Praise to you, glory to you, today, tomorrow, and always, Amen.

IV. Holy Communion

14. The Lord's prayer and the 'Libera nos'. These continue as usual. During the 'Our Father', all have their arms raised in union with the celebrant.

15. The breaking of the bread. Also as usual, with some variations to the usual prayers given as alternatives.

16. Communion. As usual.

Each one says 'I believe' as he receives communion.

17. Concluding rite. As in Roman Missal.

Joy is the atmosphere of the final dismissal and exit. The people leave the Church singing and dancing for joy.

III

PASTORAL SETTING

Illustrative material is provided here from places as far apart as Latin America, Sri Lanka, West Germany and Zaīre. There are reflections by Catholics, Orthodox and Protestants.

Individuals and groups are invited to think out in their own situations the implications of liturgical and doctrinal convergences concerning the Lord's Supper.

1. WITNESS FROM THE ORTHODOX CHURCHES

Two documents are included from *Martyria/Mission: The Witness of the Orthodox Churches Today*, edited by Ion Bria (Geneva, WCC, 1980): "The liturgy after the Liturgy" and "Confessing Christ through the liturgical life".

THE LITURGY AFTER THE LITURGY

Ion Bria

In the discussion of the consultation organized by CWME Desk for Orthodox Studies and Relations in Etchmiadzine, Armenia, 16–21 September 1975,[1] on the topic "Confessing Christ through the Liturgical Life of the Church", the question was raised: What is the relationship between the "liturgical spirituality", the personal spiritual experience gained by a meaningful participation in the Liturgy, and the witness to the Gospel in the world, witness which belongs to the very nature of the Church and is rooted in the advent of the Spirit at Pentecost? The consultation spoke of "the indispensable continuation" of the liturgical celebration and stated very clearly that "the Liturgy must not be limited to the celebration in the Church but has to be continued in the life of the faithful in all dimensions of life".

The second part of the Etchmiadzine consultation dealt with several aspects of the organic unity between liturgical spirituality[2] and witness, indicating methods and approaches which could be used to accomplish that unity. However, that consultation did not go deeply into the question of the continuation of Liturgy in life; so the participants were asked to provide their comments based on the initial discussion. One comment which in fact summarizes the original debate was sent by Bishop Anastasios Yannoulatos, professor at the University of Athens, which follows in a revised form:

"The Liturgy is not an escape from life, but a continuous transformation of life according to the prototype Jesus Christ, through the power of the Spirit. If it is true that in the Liturgy we not only hear a message but we participate in

---

*This text was first published in *Internal Review of Mission*, Vol. LXVII. No. 265, January 1978.
[1] "The Etchmiadzine Report", *International Review of Mission*, Vol. 64, No. 256, 1975, pp. 417–421.
[2] Metropolitan Georges Khodre, "La spiritualité liturgique", *Contacts*, 23, 93, pp. 4–12.

the great event of liberation from sin and of *koinonia* (communion) with Christ through the real presence of the Holy Spirit, then this event of our personal incorporation into the Body of Christ, this transfiguration of our little being into a member of Christ, must be evident and be proclaimed in actual life.

"The Liturgy has to be continued in personal, everyday situations. Each of the faithful is called upon to continue a personal 'liturgy' on the secret altar of his own heart, to realize a living proclamation of the good news 'for the sake of the whole world'. Without this continuation the liturgy remains incomplete. Since the eucharistic event we are incorporated in Him who came to serve the world and to be sacrificed for it, we have to express in concrete *diakonia*, in community life, our new being in Christ, the Servant of all. The sacrifice of the Eucharist must be extended in personal sacrifices for the people in need, the brothers for whom Christ died. Since the Liturgy is the participation in the great event of liberation from the demonic powers, then the continuation of Liturgy in life means a continuous liberation from the powers of the evil that are working inside us, a continual reorientation and openness to insights and efforts aimed at liberating human persons from all demonic structures of injustice, exploitation, agony, loneliness, and at creating real communion of persons in love.

"This personal everyday attitude becomes 'liturgical' in the sense that (a) it draws power from the participation in the sacrament of the Holy Eucharist through which we receive the grace of the liberating and unifying Spirit, (b) it constitutes the best preparation for a new, more conscious and existential participation in the Eucharist, and (c) it is a living expression—in terms clear to everybody—of the real transformation of men and women in Christ."

What is the meaning of "the liturgy after the Liturgy"?

In recent years, there has been a strong emphasis in Orthodox ecclesiology on the eucharistic understanding of the Church.[3] Truly, the Eucharist Liturgy is the climax of the Church's life, the event in which the people of God are celebrating the incarnation, the death and the resurrection of Jesus Christ, sharing His glorified body and blood, tasting the Kingdom to come. The ecclesial *koinonia* is indeed constituted by the participation of the baptized in the eucharistic communion, the sacramental actualization of the economy of salvation, a living reality which belongs both to history and to eschatology. While this emphasis is deeply rooted in the biblical and patristic tradition and is of extreme importance today, it might easily lead to the conclusion that Orthodox limit the interpretation of the Church to an exclusive worshipping community, to protecting and to preserving the Good News for its members. Therefore a need was felt to affirm that the Liturgy is not a self-centred service and action, but is a service for the building up of the one Body of Christ within the economy of salvation which is for all people of all ages. The liturgical assembly is the Father's House, where the invitation to the banquet

---

[3] Stanley Harakas, "The Local Church: an Eastern Orthodox Perspective", *The Ecumenical Review*, Vol. 29, No. 2, April 1977, pp. 141–153.

of the heavenly bread is constantly voiced and addressed not only to the members of the Church, but also to the non-Christians and strangers.[4]

This liturgical concentration, "the liturgy within the Liturgy", is essential for the Church, but it has to be understood in all its dimensions. There is a double movement in the Liturgy: on the one hand, the assembling of the people of God to perform the memorial of the death and resurrection of our Lord "until He comes again". It also manifests and realizes the process by which "the *cosmos* is becoming *ecclesia*". Therefore the preparation for Liturgy takes place not only at the personal spiritual level, but also at the level of human historical and natural realities. In preparing for Liturgy, the Christian starts a spiritual journey which affects everything in his life: family, properties, authority, position, and social relations. It reorientates the direction of his entire human existence towards its sanctification by the Holy Spirit.

On the other hand, renewed by the Holy Communion and the Holy Spirit, the members of the Church are sent to be authentic testimony to Jesus Christ in the world. The mission of the Church rests upon the radiating and transforming power of the Liturgy. It is a stimulus in sending out the people of God to the world to confess the Gospel and to be involved in man's liberation.

Liturgically, this continual double movement of thanksgiving is expressed in the ministry of the deacon. On the one hand he brings and offers to the altar the gifts of the people; on the other, he shares and distributes the Holy Sacraments which nourish the life of Christians. Everything is linked with the central action of the Church, which is the Eucharist, and everybody has a diaconal function in reconciling the separated realities.

The Etchmiadzine consultation states that "the Church seeks to order the whole life of man by the sanctification of the time, by the liturgical cycles, the celebration of the year's festivals, the observance of fasts, the practices of ascesis, and regular visitation". It was therefore recommended that "an effort must be made to bring into everyday life the liturgical rhythm of consecration of the time (matins, hours, vespers, Saints' days, feast days)". The problem remains, however, for the Church today not only to keep its members in the traditional liturgical cycles, but to find ways to introduce new people into this rhythm.

How does the Church, through its liturgical life, invite the world into the Lord's House and seek the Kingdom to come? The actualization of this will be the great success of the Church's mission, not only because there is an urgent need for the Church to widen its vision of those outside its influence (Matt. 8:10), but also because the worshipping assembly cannot be a protected place any longer, a refuge for passivity and alienation.

In what sense does the worship constitute a permanent missionary impulse and determine the evangelistic witness of every Christian? How does the liturgical order pass into the order of human existence, personal and social, and shape the life style of Christians? In fact the witness of faith, which includes evangelism, mission and church life, has always taken place in the

---

[4]Ion Bria, "Concerns and Challenges in Orthodox Ecclesiology Today", *Lutheran World*, No. 3, 1976, pp. 188–191.

context of prayer, worship and communion. The missionary structures of the congregation were built upon the liturgy of the Word and Sacraments. There was a great variety of liturgies, confessions and creeds in the first centuries of Christianity, as there is today.

What does "the liturgy after the Liturgy" require?

"The liturgy after the Liturgy" which is an essential part of the witnessing life of the Church, requires:

1. An ongoing reaffirming of the true Christian identity, fullness and integrity which have to be constantly renewed by the eucharistic communion. A condition for discipleship and church membership is the existential personal commitment made to Jesus Christ the Lord (Col. 2:6). A lot of members of the Church are becoming "nominal Christians who attend the Church just as a routine". As the Bucharest consultation report[5] states: There are many who have been baptized, and yet have put off Christ, either deliberately or through indifference. Often such people still find it possible sociologically or culturally or ethnically to relate in some manner to the Christian community. The re-Christianization of Christians is an important task of the Church's evangelistic witness.

2. To enlarge the space for witness by creating a new Christian milieu, each in his own environment: family, society, office, factory, etc., is not a simple matter of converting the non-Christians in the vicinity of the parishes, but also a concern for finding room where the Christians live and work and where they can publicly exercise their witness and worship. The personal contact of the faithful with the non-believers in the public arena is particularly relevant today. Seeking for a new witnessing space means, of course, to adopt new styles of mission, new ecclesiastical structures, and especially to be able to face the irritations of the principalities and powers of this age.

There the missionary zeal of the saints and the courage of the confessors who run risks every hour and face death every day (1 Cor. 15:31) has a vital role. Since they are those who take the Kingdom of heaven by force (Matt. 11:12), the Church should identify and support the members who confess and defend the hope in Christ against persecutors (Matt. 5:10-12. John 15:20).

3. The liturgical life has to nourish the Christian life not only in its private sphere, but also in its public and political realm. One cannot separate the true Christian identity from the personal sanctification and love and service to man (1 Pet. 1:14-15). There is an increasing concern today about the ethical implications of the faith, in terms of life style, social, ethic and human behaviour. What is the *ethos* of the Church which claims to be the sign of the Kingdom? What is the "spirituality" which is proposed and determined in spreading the Gospel and celebrating the Liturgy today? How is the liturgical vision which is related to the Kingdom, as power of the age to come, as the beginning of the future life which is infused in the present life (John 3:5, 6:33), becoming a social reality? What does sanctification or *theosis* mean in terms of ecology and human rights?

Christian community can only proclaim the Gospel—and be heard—if it is a

---

[5]"The Bucharest Report", *International Review of Mission*, Vol. 54, No, 253, 1975, pp. 67-94.

living icon of Christ. The equality of the brothers and freedom in Spirit, experienced in the Liturgy, should be expressed and continued in economic sharing and liberation in the field of social oppression.[6] Therefore, the installation in history of a visible Christian fellowship which overcomes human barriers against justice, freedom and unity is a part of that liturgy after the Liturgy. The Church has to struggle for the fulfilment of that justice and freedom which was promised by God to all men and has constantly to give account of how the Kingdom of heaven is or is not within it. It has to ask itself if by the conservatism of its worship it may appear to support the violation of human rights inside and outside the Christian community.

4. Liturgy *means* public and collective action and therefore there is a sense in which the Christian is a creator of community: this particular charisma has crucial importance today with the increasing lack of human fellowship in the society. The Christian has to be a continual builder of a true koinonia of love and peace even if he is politically marginal and lives in a hostile surrounding. At the ideological and political level that koinonia may appear almost impossible.

However, there is an "open gate", namely the readiness of the human heart to hear the voice of the beloved (John 3:29) and to receive the power of God's Word (Matt. 8:8). Therefore more importance has to be given to the presentation of the Good News as a calling addressed to a person, as an invitation to the wedding house and feast (Luke 14:13). God himself is inviting people to his house and banquet. We should not forget the personal aspect of the invitation. In fact the Christian should exercise his personal witnessing as he practises his family life.

It is very interesting to mention in this respect that St John Chrysostom, who shaped the order of the eucharistic Liturgy ordinarily celebrated by Orthodox, strongly underlined "the sacrament of the brother", namely the spiritual sacrifice, the philanthropy and service which Christians have to offer outside the worship, in public places, on the altar of their neighbour's heart. For him there is a basic coincidence between faith, worship, life and service, therefore the offering on "the second altar" is complementary to the worship at the Holy Table.

There are many evidences that Orthodoxy is recapturing today that inner unity between the Liturgy, mission, witness and social diakonia, which gave it this popular character and historical vitality. The New Valamo Consultation (24-30 September 1977) confirmed once more the importance of the missionary concern for "liturgy after the Liturgy" within the total ecumenical witness of Orthodoxy. The consultation declared: "In each culture the eucharistic dynamics lead into a 'liturgy after the Liturgy' i.e. a liturgical use of the material world, a transformation of human association in society into koinonia, of consumerism into an ascetic attitude towards creation and the restoration of human dignity."[7]

Thus, through "liturgy after the Liturgy", the Church, witnessing to the

---

[6]George Munduvel, "La mission, incarnation et proclamation liturgique", *Journal des missions évangéliques*, Nos. 1-2-3, 1977 pp. 30-38.
[7]*Report of the New Valamo Consultation*, WCC, Geneva, 1978, p. 20.

CONFESSING CHRIST THROUGH THE LITURGICAL LIFE

I. Witness and worship

1. Throughout history, the worship of the Church has been the expression and guardian of divine revelation. Not only did it express and represent the saving events of Christ's life, death, resurrection and ascension to heaven but it also was for the members of the Church, the living anticipation of the kingdom to come. In worship, the Church, being the Body of Christ enlivened by the Holy Spirit, unites the faithful, as the adopted sons and daughters of God, the Father.

2. Liturgical worship is an action of the Church and is centred around the Eucharist. Although the sacrament of the Eucharist, since the very origin of the Church, was a celebration closed to the outsiders, and full participation in the Eucharist remains reserved for the members of the Church, liturgical worship as a whole is an obvious form of witness and mission.

3. The human person, through membership in the worshipping community, in spiritual poetry, in church music, in iconography, with body and soul (1 Cor. 6:20), actively participates in the gifts of grace. This involvement of the entire human nature—and not only of reason—in glorifying God, is an essential factor of Orthodox worship. It must be preserved and developed as a powerful means of Christian witness.

4. The involvement of the whole of man in the liturgical action presupposes that sanctification reaches not only man as an individual but his entire environment. The reverse is also true; one should take account of the fact that each Christian who actively participates in worship may bring into it his cultural heritage and personal creativity. This process presupposes a selection, based on Christian and moral values. Not everything in all cultural forms, known in the unredeemed world, is qualified to serve as meaningful liturgical expression. However, at all times, in the culture of the various nations, the Church has succeeded in finding and adopting cultural forms, which, through their richness and variety, were able to communicate the Gospel to these peoples in a manner akin to their mentality and their historical traditions.

5. The fact that Orthodoxy readily embraced the various national cultures and used them as powerful tools of mission does not mean that the unity of the Church—a God-established mark of the Body of Christ (Rom. 12:5)—can be sacrificed to values belonging to ethnic cultures (Col. 3:10–11; Gal. 3:28).

---

*This paper is the text of Report No. 1 from the Orthodox Consultation on "Confessing Christ through the Liturgical Life of the Church Today", held in Etchmiadzin, Armenia, 16–21 September 1975, reprinted from *International Review of Mission*, Vol. LXIV, No. 256, 1975, pp. 417–421.

6. Worship is the centre of the life of the Church, but it should also determine the whole life of every Christian. "Every tree that does not bear good fruit is cut down and thrown into the fire. Thus you will know them by their fruits. Not every one who says to me 'Lord, Lord' shall enter the Kingdom of heaven, but he who does the will of my Father who is in heaven" (Matt. 7:20–23). The realization of these words of Christ has a great significance for the success of the Christian mission.

7. Christ said: "Go ye therefore and make disciples of all nations, baptizing them in the name of the Father, and of the Son, and of the Holy Spirit" (Matt. 28:19). This means that together with worship other forms of Christian activity have great importance for mission, such as preaching, publications, personal contacts, welfare, religious education, youth movements, renewal of monastic life, etc. Each church should take advantage of these forms of mission if they are available to it.

8. In order to become a really powerful expression of the Church's mission in the world, worship must be meaningfully understood by its participants (1 Cor. 14:6–15). We have discussed those aspects of the Orthodox Liturgy which may make it appear as frozen and thus irrelevant. We are convinced of the necessity of making the liturgical language used in some countries more accessible to the average faithful, and we have considered the desirability to take initiatives (with the blessing of ecclesiastical authorities) which would make our forms of worship more comprehensible to young people (for example, catechetical explanations could precede the services). We agreed that preaching, being an essential part of worship, should never be omitted, whatever the number of those present at every occasion.

9. Among the means of achieving the participation of a greater number of faithful in the liturgical life of the Church, we have considered particularly, wherever possible, a greater involvement of the laity, including women, in those forms of worship which are allowed to them by the Church, especially in congregational singing, and also, wherever that is possible, the establishment of new worshipping communities outside the existing parishes and temples.

II. Proclamation of the Gospel in worship

A clarification of the word "liturgy" is necessary. In the vocabulary of the Orthodox churches the word liturgy refers to the central action of the corporate worship, which is the Divine Liturgy, the Eucharist. Traditionally, the sacraments were linked with the Divine Liturgy. The practice is still the same with the ordination of the deacon, the priest, and the bishop. However, the sacraments of baptism and chrismation, as well as of matrimony, are occasionally linked with the Divine Liturgy.

1. Proclamation should not be taken only in the narrow sense of an informative preaching of the Truth but above all of incorporating man into the mystical union with God. At every step of the Liturgy we encounter the Word of God.

The saving events of the divine economy although chronologically belonging to the past, through the Holy Spirit's action transcend time's limitation, become really present, and the faithful in the here and now live that which historically belongs to the past, and to the eschaton. In the Liturgy we do not have simply a memorial, but a living reality. It is an epicletic contemporization and consecration. A continuous *parousia*, a real presence of Christ emerges liturgically.

Bible and Liturgy must not be isolated as self-contained, autonomous entities. They were established to remain together, united foreover:

To whom to proclaim?

2. The Incarnation was for the whole people of all ages and redemption of the whole cosmos. The Holy Eucharist was instituted, among other things, to proclaim he death and the resurrection of our Lord "until He comes again". Thus, the following categories of people should directly or indirectly hear the message of the Holy Eucharist:

a) the members of the Church who try sincerely to practice the faith should be made true evangelists by the Gospel proclaimed to them; St John Chrysostom said: "I do not believe in the salvation of any one who does not try to save others";

b) the nominal Christians who attend the church just as a routine;

c) the mobile population, migrant workers, refugees, etc., some of whom have no permanent roots anywhere under the sun;

d) people of the diaspora of our modern age;

e) the non-Christians in the vicinity of our congregations and churches who are still to a large extent strangers to the healing and radiating power of the Gospel;

f) the fields where no one ever preached the Gospel.

How to proclaim the Gospel?

3. We have to state that during the Liturgy the readings from the Bible are done not as self-centred service and action, but in the service of the liturgical life of the Church. To accomplish the mission of the Church in proclaiming the Gospel, a variety of methods and approaches must be used, according to the possibilities and the needs of the local church:

a) the faithful should have continual education in understanding the meaning of the Liturgy and the message of the Gospel;

b) meaningful literature should be published, such as informative pamphlets, pictorial and illustrated publications, volumes of new homilies and sermons, etc.;

c) new forms of worship on the pattern of the old ones should be developed, having in mind the special needs of contemporary society (i.e. of travellers, youth, children, men in industry);

d) an effort must be made to bring into everyday life the liturgical rhythm of consecration of the time (matins, hours, vespers, saints days, feast days);

e) the mass media of television, radio, newspapers and others must be used;

f) a personal contact of the faithful should be established with the non-believers in order to transmit the personal spiritual experiences gained by a meaningful participation in the Liturgy;

g) as in the days following the Pentecost, a sharing "community" must be created to make the whole Church a practising "community of the saints and a holy nation";

h) a revision should be considered of the theological training of the priests, by emphasizing the importance of making them aware of the needs for pastoral care, missionary zeal and the proclamation of the Word;

i) the Orthodox Church should seriously study the renewing of the old tradition of having the order of the deaconess, as this is mentioned in early Ecumenical Councils.

The Liturgy must not be limited to the celebration in the church but has to be continued in the life of the faithful in all dimensions of life.

2. THE MASS IN LATIN AMERICA

Here Gustavo Gutiérrez speaks of the problems and the possibilities connected with the mass in Latin America. The extracts are taken from *A Theology of Liberation* (Maryknoll, Orbis Books, 1973). A brief passage from page 137 is followed by a longer section from pp. 262–65:

The Latin American Church is sharply *divided* with regard to the process of liberation. Living in a capitalist society in which one class confronts another, the Church, in the measure that its presence increases, cannot escape—nor try to ignore any longer—the profound division among its members. Active participation in the liberation process is far from being a . uniform position of the Latin American Christian community. The majority of the Church continues to be linked in many different ways to the established order. And what is worse, among Latin American Christians there are not only different political options within a framework of free interplay of ideas; the polarization of these options and the extreme seriousness of the situation have even placed some Christians among the oppressed and persecuted and others among the oppressors and persecutors, some among the tortured and others among the torturers or those who condone torture. This gives rise to a serious and radical confrontation between Christians who suffer from injustice and exploitation and those who benefit from the established order. Under such circumstances, life in the contemporary Christian community becomes particularly difficult and conflictual. Participation in the Eucharist, for example, as it is celebrated today, appears to many to be an action which, for want of the support of an authentic community, becomes an exercise in make-believe.

Eucharist and human brotherhood

The place of the mission of the Church is where the celebration of the Lord's supper and the creation of human brotherhood are indissolubly joined. This is what it means in an active and concrete way to be the sacrament of the salvation of the world.

"In memory of me"

The first task of the Church is to celebrate with joy the gift of the salvific action of God in humanity, accomplished through the death and resurrection of Christ. This is the Eucharist: a memorial and a thanksgiving. It is a memorial of Christ which presupposes an ever-renewed acceptance of the meaning of his life—a total giving to others. It is a thanksgiving for the love of God which is revealed in these events. The Eucharist is a feast, a celebration of the joy that the Church desires and seeks to share. The Eucharist is done within the Church, and simultaneously the Church is built up by the Eucharist. In the Church "we celebrate," writes Schillebeeckx, "that which is achieved outside the Church edifice, in human history." This work, which creates a profound human brotherhood, gives the Church its reason for being.

In the Eucharist we celebrate the cross and the resurrection of Christ, his Passover from death to life, and our passing from sin to grace. In the Gospel the Last Supper is presented against the background of the Jewish Passover, which celebrated the liberation from Egypt and the Sinai Covenant. The Christian Passover takes on and reveals the full meaning of the Jewish Passover. Liberation from sin is at the very root of political liberation. The former reveals what is really involved in the latter. But on the other hand, communion with God and others presupposes the abolition of all injustice and exploitation. This is expressed by the very fact that the Eucharist was instituted during a meal. For the Jews a meal in common was a sign of brotherhood. It united the diners in a kind of sacred pact. Moreover, the bread and the wine are signs of brotherhood which at the same time suggest the gift of creation. The objects used in the Eucharist themselves recall that brotherhood is rooted in God's will to give the goods of this earth to all people so that they might build a more human world. The Gospel of John, which does not contain the story of the Eucharistic institution, reinforces this idea, for it substitutes the episode of the washing of the feet—a gesture of service, love, and brotherhood. This substitution is significant: John seems to see in this episode the profound meaning of the Eucharistic celebration, the institution of which he does not relate. Thus the Eucharist appears inseparably united to creation and to the building up of a real human brotherhood. "The reference to community," writes Tillard, "does not therefore represent a simple consequence, an accidental dimension, a second level of a rite that is in the first place and above all individual—as the simple act of eating is. From the beginning it is seen in the human context of the meal as it was conceived in Israel. The Eucharistic rite in its essential elements is communitarian and orientated toward the constitution of human brotherhood."

A text in Matthew is very clear regarding the relationship between worship and human brotherhood: "If, when you are bringing your gift to the altar, you suddenly remember that your brother has a grievance against you, leave your gift where it is before the altar. First go and make your peace with your brother, and only then come back and offer your gift" (Matt. 5:23–24). This is not a question of a scrupulous conscience, but rather of living according to the demands placed on us by the other: "If...you suddenly remember that your brother has a grievance against you." To be the cause of a fracture of brotherhood disqualifies one from participation in that worship which celebrates the action of the Lord which establishes a profound community among men. "The Christian community," said Camilo Torres, "cannot offer the sacrifice in an authentic form if it has not first fulfilled in an effective manner the precept of 'love of thy neighbor.'" The separation of sacrifice from the love of neighbor is the reason for the harsh criticism which Jesus—speaking from a strong prophetic tradition—addressed to all purely external worship. For if "our relationship of service to our neighbor in the world (a relationship profoundly expressed in prayer and the liturgy) were in fact absent, then in this case the prayer and the whole liturgy, as well as our speaking of God...would fall into a vacuum and degenerate into a false and useless superstructure." This is how Paul understood it. Before recounting the institution of the Eucharist he indicated the necessary precondition for participation in it when he reproached the Corinthians for their lack of fraternal charity in their gatherings to celebrate the Lord's Supper (1 Cor. 11:17–34; cf. James 2:1–4).

The profound unity among the different meanings of the term *koinonia* in the New Testament both expresses and summarizes these ideas. Congar has pointed out that *koinonia* simultaneously designates three realities. First it signifies the common ownership of the goods necessary for earthly existence: "Never forget to show kindness and to share what you have with others, for such are the sacrifices which God approves" (Heb. 13:16; cf. Acts 2:44; 4:32). *Koinonia* is a concrete gesture of fraternal charity. Thus Paul uses this word to designate the collection organized on behalf of the Christians in Jerusalem; the Corinthians glorify God because of their "liberal contribution to their need and to the general good" (2 Cor. 9:13; cf. 2 Cor. 8:3–4; Rom. 15:26–27). Second, *koinonia* designates the union of the faithful with Christ through the Eucharist: "When we bless 'the cup of blessing,' is it not a means of sharing in the blood of Christ? When we break the bread, is it not a means of sharing in the body of Christ?" (1 Cor. 10:16). And third, *koinonia* means the union of Christians with the Father—"If we claim to be sharing in his life while we walk in the dark, our words and our lives are a lie" (1 John 1:6; cf. 1:3)— with the Son—"It is God himself who calls you to share in the life of his Son"(1 Cor. 1:9; cf. 1 John 1:3)— and with the Spirit—"The grace of the Lord Jesus Christ, and the love of God, and fellowship in the Holy Spirit, be with you all" (2 Cor. 13:14; cf. Phil. 2:1).

The basis for brotherhood is full communion with the persons of the Trinity. The bond which unites God and man is celebrated—that is, effectively recalled and proclaimed—in the Eucharist. Without a real commitment against exploitation and alienation and for a society of solidarity and justice, the Eucharistic celebration is an empty action, lacking any genuine endorsement by those who participate in it. This is something that many Latin American Christians are feeling more and more deeply, and they are thus more demanding both with themselves and with the whole Church. "To make a remembrance" of Christ is more than the performance of an act of worship; it is to accept living under the sign of the cross and in the hope of the resurrection. It is to accept the meaning of a life that was given over to death—at the hands of the powerful of this world—for love of others.

3. THE PAST AND FUTURE OF THE EUCHARIST VIEWED FROM SRI LANKA

The following passages are taken from *The Eucharist and Human Liberation* (Maryknoll, Orbis Books, 1979), by the Catholic priest Tissa Balasuriya. They occur on pages 58f, 36–39, 62f, 141–45.

The Eucharist and oppressed peoples

The history of the Eucharist is one of very close association with oppression. After Christianity became the religion of the Roman Empire, the celebration of the Eucharist was absorbed by the social establishment as a special expression of its triumph. It gave divine legitimation to power. Prior to that, catacombs and private houses were the meeting places of the eucharistic community. The Christians lived a rather underground existence, especially during times of persecution. With the conversion of Christianity and the Roman Empire to each other, the big imperial basilicas were made available to the churches. Thus during feudal times the lords of the manors had their own churches. The ecclesiastical and civil lords were closely linked in relationships of power and wealth.

There were naturally occasional conflicts between the secular and religious powers; but the millennium of feudalism was one in which by and large the power elite of the church was on the side of the feudal nobles and kings. It is important that this be remembered and reflected on when we try to understand this tradition of the Eucharist as subservient to power. It is only a few centuries ago that Europe left feudalism behind. And what are a few centuries for those who think of "eternal Rome" and its mission to rule the Christian world? Medieval Christianity tried to evolve some social norms concerning the just ruler, just price, and fair wages. These were good and useful. But there was no idea of changing the relationships of domination and dependence that feudalism implied. Today we should not blame the past. But neither can we afford to ignore it; for it lives with us as a permanent legacy. We have to ask ourselves how the church was able to integrate itself and the Eucharist within feudalism. This implied a fundamental acceptance of the social system with its good and bad. Further, it meant in practice that the powerful in the church were able to benefit from the operation of the system. They found a sacral niche within the feudal hierarchy of power and privilege. A reflection on this can be a lesson for us concerning alliances between power and the eucharistic celebration in our times.

We referred earlier to the intimate connection between the Eucharist and the colonial expansion of Europe. Here too it is enlightening to ask ourselves how and why it was possible for the Christian conscience to be so conditioned that the celebration of the Eucharist could go hand in hand with history's worst plunder and genocide. It is the peoples who have suffered such oppression who are able to understand the heinousness of these crimes. Whereas Jesus gave his life for others, and the Eucharist is a memorial of that self-sacrifice, in the colonial expansion the roles were reversed. The "Christians" were the robbers and plunderers. They murdered in the name of the expansion of western civilization and of the religion of Christ. Entire populations and civilizations were wiped out from the face of the earth. The pope in Rome, who is considered the guardian of the eucharistic message and mystique, presided over this division of the then known world between the two major Catholic powers of the day: Spain and Portugal.

The Eucharist, capitalism, and colonialism

Over the centuries the spirituality of the Eucharist—of giving and not of grabbing—was obliterated. The Eucharist went side by side with the worst and largest-scale exploitation that the world has ever seen. The tragedy of the subordination of Christianity to European power politics was also the tragedy of the Eucharist. As the priests and monks went hand in hand with the colonialists, the Eucharist was desecrated in the service of empire. The Eucharist was (one hopes unconsciously) perverted in the close alliance between imperialism and the church. Gold grabbed from the native people of South America was used to adorn Christian monasteries and churches, as in Lima, Peru. The gold used to decorate the ceiling of the Basilica of Saint Mary Major in Rome is claimed to have been brought from the new territories conquered for the Christian rulers and religion. These are symbols of the low level to which religion had sunk in the Europe of the colonial period. Hence we must not be so naive as to accept as "faith" whatever beliefs or practices prevail at any given time concerning the Eucharist. We must not think that the so-called simple faith of the people is innocent in itself. It has been evolved alongside the world's worst exploitation and did not contest it or, rather, it tended to justify the status quo.

At the beginning of the twentieth century Pope Pius X popularized the reception of the Eucharist. Children were admitted to Communion at the age of reason, that is, seven years. Frequent Communion was encouraged. But there was no emphasis on the social dimension of the Eucharist. This was still largely the individualistic phase of the Mass and the sacraments. The vast popularization of the reception of Communion may have spread individual devotion, but it did not make the sacrament a greater sign and cause of real unity in the Christian community or the world at large.

In the nineteenth and twentieth centuries the growth and development of the technologically superior countries went hand in hand with the large-scale exploitation of the proletariat in the rich countries and all of the people in the poor countries. The eucharistic ceremony did not disturb the peace of conscience of the exploiting capitalists; it tended to legitimize their nefarious activities. The prayers offered by the faithful were conducive to internalizing the relationships that were being built up within the emerging societies.

It is therefore understandable that increasingly the working classes in the European countries began to keep away from the Sunday Eucharist, for they did not see in the ceremony anything they were hoping for in their struggles against the human exploitation by their Christian overlords. For the Eucharist had become a means of helping the affluent people of the world.

It is not surprising that the working classes in Western Europe were "dechristianized" during the course of the past few centuries. Being Christian was judged by attendance at Sunday Mass: this was the concept of a "practising" Catholic. The Mass was unrelated to the struggles of the exploited working classes. It even helped in their exploitation; it contributed to their mental subjugation. It was a sort of opium of the exploited. Workers and their exploiters attended Mass side by side. Yet there was no unity; no communion. The exploitation continued. The priests generally preached obedience and submission on the part of the workers, and charity and paternalism by the capitalists. Gradually many workers dropped away from the Sunday Mass. Later on, they did not care to have their children baptized. For the Christian group had lost its real meaning as a community of loving sharing.

If the Eucharist is the center of Christian living, its evacuation of meaning was a cause and effect of the irrelevance of Christianity to people's central concerns as person and social being. When the Eucharist ceases to relate to integral human liberation, it ceases to be connected with Christ's life sacrifice; it does not then build human community; it does not, therefore, help constitute the kingdom of God on earth; it does not even honor God objectively. It becomes a ritual without life, like the type of sacrifices condemned by God in the Old Testament.

On the other hand, as Christianity gets revitalized, the Eucharist, its chief act of worship and sacrifice, acquires meaning and relevance. It is thus that we have in the contemporary Christian renewal a revaluation of the Eucharist.

Vatican Council II helped very much toward the updating of the eucharistic liturgy. It made possible alterations in the language of the liturgy, in its choice of more suitable Gospel texts. It simplified the ceremonial and made it less rigid. The council invited a greater participation of the faithful in the Eucharist. It encouraged the adaptation of the liturgy to the customs and culture of the peoples.

At the same time, the council left all control over the liturgy and its changes in the hands of the authorities in Rome and the local bishops. During the past twelve years the official church has gradually embarked on effecting these changes, but usually with a certain reluctance and caution.

However, today the main trends in the evolution of the eucharistic theology and devotion take place outside the official circles concerned with the control of the Eucharist, that is, the Roman curia and the local diocesan authorities. It is groups that are engaged as Christians in the active search for personal and societal liberation that are spearheading new approaches toward the Eucharist. These insist on the celebration being truthful, authentic, forming community, leading to action, and increasing genuine sharing among persons and groups. In participating in the sacrifice of Christ, they find inspiration and strength in their efforts to be more authentic persons committed to the integral liberation of persons.

The Eucharist is in captivity. It is dominated by persons who do not experience oppression in their own selves. Even within the poor countries, the church leaders generally belong to and side with the affluent elite. The Eucharist will not be liberated to be true to its mission so long as the churches are captive within the world's power establishments. The eucharist has to be liberative; it should lead to sharing and genuine love. But in its social impact it fails to do so. It has been interpreted conservatively, rigidly, and formally. If, on the other hand, it were to become the ferment of contemporary Christianity, the churches would change radically. It is when Christians make a fundamental option against oppression, and struggle against it, that the Eucharist itself will be liberated. Already this is happening among certain groups committed to integral human liberation in the perspective of Jesus Christ.

Even with reference to interchurch ecumenism this is an important consideration. The Christian churches have differed and divided over their eucharistic teaching and practices also. But the more important point for the future getting together of the churches is not the exact doctrinal resolution of their divergences concerning the Eucharist or other issues of dogma. It is the option of the churches concerning the present struggle against oppression all over the world that will be the dividing line. Perhaps the churches as a whole will not make such options. They have not been able to express themselves unequivocally even about the Vietnam war or apartheid. Those who opt to struggle with the oppressed, the weak, the excluded, and the marginalized will be on one side, whatever their church denomination. Today the major division among Christians cuts across the frontiers of churches. Communion in the liberation struggle is increasingly becoming a more uniting factor than affiliation to ecclesiastical groups. When these issues are taken seriously communion within the same church becomes difficult unless it involves at least a desire for human liberation from oppression. Interclass communion is likely to be increasingly under question.

These are issues which Christians and the churches have to face in the coming years. Ecumenism in the sense of exchange of pulpits, visits by church leaders to each other, and beating of breasts for the evils of the Reformation will soon achieve its limited objectives. Repentence by Christians together for their whole historical complicity in the exploitation of the oppressed nations, classes, and sex is a more urgent and deeper requirement. As it takes place the Eucharist will be progressively liberated. The Eucharist, well celebrated, can also help raise this new consciousness and sensitivity among followers of Jesus Christ of all denominations.

The Eucharist and a new world order

The existing world order, or disorder, is quite contrary to the values of the Eucharist. Whereas the Eucharist is the sacrament of loving sharing, the world system is greedily exploitative. The Eucharist should build community; but world relations are destroying persons and peoples. The Eucharist is universalist; the world is racist. The power of the Eucharist tends toward an egalitarian society; but the world powers are hegemonistic. Whereas the Eucharist motivates humble service, arrogant domination prevails on the international scene. The eucharistic bread is a common meal for all; but bread in the world is a commodity for trade. In the eucharistic ideal, land is for common use: in the present system of nation-states, land is for the successful conquerors. The Eucharist gives a priority to persons; in international relations, power and profit prevail.

There is much injustice within countries. But the injustice at the world level is much more tragic. What is worse is that it is precisely those who profess to be Christians who are the main exploiting powers. Those who celebrate the Eucharist are also the chief agents of arms production, selfish profit maximization, ostentatious waste, and land-grabbing. We can thus see the terrible crimes with which the Eucharist has been and is associated historically and today.

Since the Christian churches are quasi-universal in their presence, they have a very grave responsibility toward the correction of these disorders at the world level. They must have effective strategies for bringing about the needed mental and structural changes at the world level. This is particularly urgent because there is as yet no world governmental agency capable of controlling the greed of nation-states. The churches are linked throughout the world. Earlier, they generally had an influence for domesticating peoples within capitalism and imperialism. Now, they can be powerful agents of human liberation—if they really want to be so.

The theology of the Eucharist must become planetary. *We need a global spirituality*. This is not an abstract or distant ideal. The bread used for the Eucharist in Sri Lanka is sometimes from Australia, Canada, or the United States. The wine may be from southern Europe. In a similar vein, when the British people go to Mass on a Sunday they meet persons from several countries. At the same Mass there will be directors and workers from companies like Unilever, Shell, and Nestlé that have bases in about two-thirds of the world. Our daily life is related to different parts of the world. Our meals, our clothes, our transport, all link several peoples of the world. Many of us eat daily bread produced by the sweat of exploited peoples' labor. Since the Eucharist is the sacrament of unity, it must also be the sacrament of world justice.

The meaning of the church as *one, universal,* and *Catholic* must be rethought in terms of the planetary oneness of the human family today. The churches can be most significant alliances for liberation if the eucharistic groups across the world are linked to each other. This can take place around issues and action programs. This happens somewhat when there is a natural calamity such as a major earthquake. But there is no similar consciousness of the worldwide continuing calamity of tens of millions dying of hunger. Conscience has not been awakened to these. Where the news media bring us the tales of woe, we have built up our defences. Patchwork charity is often the furthest we are prepared to go.

The tragedy of the human race is being so rapidly aggravated that eucharistic groups cannot neglect their global responsibility for long without being guilty of reducing religious ceremony to hypocrisy. The opposition to the Vietnam war by the more sensitive United States groups showed the potential of the reflecting eucharistic group to be a catalyst of desirable action even in a big country like the United States. The internationalization of the concern for sharing bread should be one of the directions in which the Eucharist can and must evolve during the coming decades. This in turn will help give meaning to personal life and to community. Christian ecumenism would then be more related to inter-people justice. The prayer of Jesus at the Last Supper "that they may all be one" will then have a more profound significance for our times and problems.

The churches must have a conscious policy for bringing about international sharing on a basis of justice and not charity. The wealth, resources, and land of the world must be for all, and especially for those in need. The sharing of technology cannot be merely on the principle of further profit accumulation for the powerful. The Christian approach to the transfer of technology has to be much more egalitarian than anything that the United Nations Conference on Trade and Development (UNCTAD) or the United Nations itself has so far proposed. The eucharistic relationship to the Jewish Jubilee Year, when lands were returned and debts written off, can be a powerful motivation for a just reconsideration of the growing debt among nations. The common table of the Eucharist, where the same Lord is received all over the world, can be a very strong motivation for approaches like the UNCTAD Common Fund for ensuring a fair deal for the producers of primary commodities.

In its planetary dimension, the theology of the Eucharist is still in its infancy. The churches have to think together collectively, creatively, and relevantly. They can come into this world-wide struggle as a committed ally of the weak. The religious orders and congregations which are international, and which have dedicated persons in many countries at the grassroots level, can be the conveyor belts of such thinking and action. The minimum they could do would be to support the reformist policies of such world bodies as UNCTAD, the International Labour Organisation, the Food and Agriculture Organization, and the World Health Organization. But we need to go much further if we are to respond to the revolutionary demands of the Gospel of Jesus Christ:

The churches must evolve a planetary catechesis to communicate the message of human unity in justice. The pastorate needs strategies of action, transforming the eucharistic groups into a people on the march toward integral liberation. In this, intense struggle and active contestation are inevitable. Risk-bearing would return to the eucharistic table. The cross would be the lot of many believers then. Along with all others who are in the same struggle, Christians then would be crusaders for a more holy cause of making human life worthwhile for all on earth. Today we have the means to do so, but we lack the determination and the political will to live the Gospel in the real world.

Eucharistic gatherings would then be among the vanguard of the building of the new world in hard work, real sharing, and justice. As the churches begin to relate to these issues, they will forget their petty concerns with rubrics and ritualism and enter the heart of the human search today. They will then be among the foremost harbingers of the real new international economic order, which has to be a foretaste of the ultimate kingdom of peace and justice promised by God in Jesus Christ:

"To the poor man God dare not appear except in the form of bread and the promise of work. Grinding pauperism cannot lead to anything else than moral degradation. Every human being has a right to live and therefore to find the wherewithal to feed himself." Mahatma Gandhi

4. THE LORD'S SUPPER IN AN AFRICAN INDEPENDENT CHURCH

The Church of Jesus Christ on Earth by the Prophet Simon Kimbangu came into being as a result of the work of Simon Kimbangu in 1921. Throughout the period of Belgian colonial rule in Zaïre, the Kimbanguists lived a clandestine existence, with their prophet spending thirty years in prison. Now probably the largest independent church in Africa, the Kimbanguists were received into membership of the WCC in 1969.

The following passages are extracted from Marie-Louise Martin, *Kimbangu: An African Prophet and his Church* (Oxford, Blackwell, 1975). An introduction from page 161 is followed by a description of the first celebration of the Lord's Supper by the Kimbanguists in 1971 (pp. 179–182):

The introduction of the celebration of the Lord's Supper was being seriously considered, and when I arrived in April 1968 in Kinshasa this was one of the very first questions which I was asked in the ministerial council. It had been hoped to introduce the Lord's Supper in December 1966 on the occasion of the consecration of the large church in Matete-Kinshasa, but people were not yet ready for this. Why? 'The Lord's Supper, the real presence of Christ, means so much to us that we are still seeking the proper form in which to express it,' one of the ministers told me. Prior to 1959 many of the Kimbanguists were given the Communion in the Catholic or one of the Protestant churches, of which they were nominal members. Others (relatively many) were members of the Salvation Army, in which no sacraments are administered, neither baptism nor Communion. Still others became members of the Kimbanguist Church from traditional African religion or—in the towns—from an indefinable religiosity. Hence, an appropriate form of sacrament was difficult to find. Should it be the Catholic rite, some form of Protestant practice, or perhaps the Orthodox rite? (For some years Kimbanguists have had connections with the Greek Orthodox Church.) What are the elements which should be used—manioc or banana bread, or bread made from imported wheat? What should be used to represent the blood of Christ? What meaning does the Lord's Supper convey?

Long and serious considerations had to be made concerning the form appropriate to its content and the African mode of expression. Serious and patient study preceded the introduction of the Last Supper's celebration. The Lord's Supper was celebrated for the first time on the fiftieth anniversary of the Kimbanguist Church, on 6 April 1971.

***

From 2 to 7 April 1971, the great jubilee celebrations of the church took place. They began on 2 April in Matadi-Mayo near Kinshasa in remembrance of the day when, in 1960, the coffin with the mortal remains of Simon Kimbangu was taken from Lubumbashi to N'Kamba and was laid there for a night. On 6 April, exactly fifty years after Kimbangu had performed his first healing in answer to prayer, the first celebration of Holy Communion was held. It was at this time that Joseph Diangienda announced that his father had already administered the Communion on one occasion before his arrest in 1921. 350,000 pilgrims went in the middle of the rainy season to N'Kamba and camped there in the open, despite the rain and the alternating heat and cold, in order to take part in the celebrations. They had reached the 'holy city', in lorries and on foot, on the terrible road going through the bush from Mbanza-Ngungu to N'Kamba. During the special service, Joseph Diangienda announced the nature of the elements to be used in the Communion, namely bread baked from a mixture of potatoes, maize and bananas (in which the latter served as 'yeast') and 'wine' made of honey and water.

L. Luntadila wrote an explanation of this, which was given to the press under the title *Réflexions sur la Sainte-Cène* ('Thoughts on the Lord's Supper'). In it he says that 'The foods used to make the elements are found in Zaïre and the neighbouring countries. In order to be obedient to the spirit of the Gospel our church has chosen African foods, just as Christ in His day used bread and wine, the daily foods of Palestine.' Thus the Kimbanguist Church (in exactly the same way as, for instance, in its attitude towards the place of women in the work of the church) has freed itself from pure dogmatism. 'Honey is praised in the Bible as a noble food.' Luntadila reminds us that the Old Testament manna tasted 'like wafers made with honey' (Ex. 16:31). In Psalm 81:16 Luntadila found a parallel between honey and blood, and quoted, 'I would feed you with the finest of the wheat, and with honey from the rock I would satisfy you.' Behind this, unconsciously, there may possibly be the ancient Catholic doctrine of 'concomitance', according to which in the body of Christ, represented by the bread, the blood is already present as well. He may have also been thinking of the water from the rock, however. A rational explanation followed this biblical explanation: 'Honey is a food which contains the vitamins and minerals which the body needs and which enter the blood directly. That is why honey was the food of John the Baptist (Matt. 3:4), the food which encouraged meditation, prayer, and purity. Hence, honey still continues to be the food of the contemplative monks in Ethiopia.' He referred at this point to parallels between the prayer-life of the Ethiopian Church and that of the Kimbanguists. Then followed a further reference to the Bible, to Luke 24:42, where we read that the risen Christ ate 'a piece of broiled fish' and—according to some ancient textual sources (the author)—'a honeycomb' in order to reveal Himself to the disciples as the living Christ. There then followed a spiritual exhortation: 'Just as pollen is transformed by bees into honey, so we too should be inwardly transformed by the Holy Spirit so that we can be witnesses to the risen Christ.' Finally, it is said that the bee was a symbol in ancient Egypt and therefore in Africa.

After speaking about the honey (there is no mention of the lifegiving water!) Luntadila went on to consider the bread:

> Just as the body which was given for us saves us, so maize and potatoes have saved millions in the world. Just as the ingredients maize, potatoes,

and bananas are mixed, so the body of Christ is formed of men and women of all races and lands. Just as potatoes were formerly introduced from America and have now spread over almost the whole earth, so it is our task as the light of the world to proclaim to all peoples the Good News from Palestine.

Then there followed a quotation from the Didache prayer (from the post-apostolic period): 'Just as this bread, broken and once scattered on the hills, was gathered and made into a whole, so may Thy church be gathered from the ends of the earth into Thy Kingdom.' 'The white clothes of those who distribute the Lord's Supper remind us that our sins are washed away and forgiven through the death of Christ. They anticipate the glory and purity of those who will be partakers, as the ransomed, of the Kingdom of Heaven when Christ returns.' This was followed by a reference to Revelation 7:14 and presumably indirectly to the sealing which preceded the Communion. So much for the reflections of Luntadila, which give a picture of the kind of Bible exposition which is found not only in the Kimbanguist Church, but in many churches of Africa.

The elements were consecrated by the sons of Kimbangu in the mausoleum of their father and then borne in solemn procession (after the sermon) to the enormous congregation gathered in the open air. Joseph Diangienda led the way, followed by the *sacrificateurs*, then the highest dignitaries of the church, the members of what is called the *Collège* or *Conseil des Sages* ('Council of the Wise'), which is made up of Kimbangu's fellow-workers from the period of persecution, and which was called into being in 1963 in Mbanza Ngungu. Behind them came the leaders of the church of the People's Republic of the Congo and Zambia and the regional delegates (the highest church officials in the various regions of Zaïre). All were dressed in white. The elements were borne before the assembled congregation on simple wooden platters, the honey-water already in tiny glasses, by the dignitaries appointed to distribute them. The words of institution were read out, the elements blessed, and then the great moment had come. Joseph Diangienda handed the Lord's Supper first to his two brothers and the aged assistants of his father. Then Pierre Ndangi handed it to him. The dignitaries of the church came next. Then it was taken to the believers, who were grouped in local congregations, whilst the flute orchestra played quietly in the background. A hundred thousand people knelt on the grass under palm roofs to receive the symbols of the body and blood of Christ. The distribution had to continue on 7 April until all were 'satisfied'. The joy was, despite all the composure and calmness, unmistakable. The Kimbanguists were in the 'new Jerusalem' and living in the 'last times'.

On 11 April the Lord's Supper was celebrated in Kinshasa-Matete for all those who were unable to go to N'Kamba, and a fortnight later in Brazzaville. Since then Joseph Diangienda has undertaken journeys throughout the country, for he wants to be personally present wherever the Lord's Supper is distributed for the first time.

The Communion is to be celebrated three times a year—at Christmas, at Easter, and on the anniversary of the death of the prophet (12 October). 'Why so infrequently?' we asked Joseph Diangienda. 'So that it does not become a mere habit', he replied.

I would like to draw a parallel between the celebration of the Lord's Supper, as I experienced it in N'Kamba, Kinshasa-Matete, and Brazzaville, and the feeding of the Five Thousand in the gospels, which can indeed be seen exegetically as an anticipation of the Communion. We may ask whether it is theologically admissible to modify the elements used by Christ. I think, however, that passages like John 21:9–13, the feeding of the Five Thousand, and also Luke 24:30 (the meal with the Emmaus disciples) leave this possibility open. Just as the Lord of the church chose a humble and little-educated African as His ambassador, so He is also free to bless African elements through which to be one with believers and to bind them together as the body of Christ.

This first Communion was, contrary to what we had expected, not an open Communion. It was surely not intended as a rebuff to Christians of other churches. It may have been a sign of humility that there was as yet no wish to press this innovation on Christians of other denominations.

5. PROPOSALS FROM A WEST GERMAN KIRCHENTAG

A forum meeting at the Church of St Lawrence, Nuremberg, in connexion with the Kirchentag of 1979 made the following proposals, called the *Lorenzer Ratschläge*. Eucharistic celebrations became a prominent feature of the Kirchentag that year, thanks to the initiative of Pastor Georg Kugler of Rummelsberg, who also chaired the group which produced these "St Lawrence Proposals".

Incitement to hope

We are called to hope. Our words and deeds should give courage to the world. And the manner of our celebration lets people know the content of our hope.

At this Kirchentag in Nuremberg we have had a new experience of the Lord's Supper as a meal of hope. But we have also spoken about the scarcely inviting or encouraging form which the celebration of this meal often takes among us. Many Christians find our celebrations gloomy and impersonal; they are even frightened by them; they feel no relief. Others see no connexion with the questions they face in their own lives or in the life of society. Many of us suffer under the fact that the Lord's Supper has become a sign of separation. Yet we find many people turning to this meal. Therefore those of us responsible for this forum on the Lord's Supper would like to incite Christians, congregations and Church leaders in a hopeful direction.

Living differently

The bread and wine we bring to the altar are a reminder that God has made us and all creatures. Every celebration of the Lord's Supper is therefore a harvest festival. We cannot praise the Creator and at the same time exploit and destroy his creation. Our eucharist must be matched by steps towards a new way of life from day to day as persons and as a society. We must learn how to proceed more carefully with the gifts of this earth.

The following can be the first signs of this at the celebrations of the Lord's Supper:

—Bringing to the table bread and wine, signs of God's goodness, becomes an action in its own right.

—We use real bread as a basic sign of our daily sustenance.

—We express our care for creation in prayers of thanksgiving and hymns.

—We look for visible expressions of our creaturely joy.

—We take seriously periods of fasting as initiation into a simpler life.

—We frame concrete intercessions and also confess the sins of our own prosperity.

Acting in solidarity

The bread and wine we receive at Jesus' table make us hunger and thirst for the coming of God's justice. We cannot be the guests of the Crucified, without living the solidarity he practised. So the Church is celebrating the meal unworthily, if it does not live in solidarity; it is belying the hope offered to the hungry and the oppressed.

The following are the first signs of that solidarity in our celebrations of the Lord's Supper:

—We give space, as we have done at this Kirchentag, to remembering hunger and oppression.

—We express in concrete intercessions our hope for God's justice.

—We look for forms of a credible thank-offering and bring to the meal what we want to share.

—We invite strangers and aliens to the meal and take account of their presence in the forms of our celebration.

—We go to the sick and the lonely and celebrate the meal with them.

—We also use grape-juice for the sake of alcoholics.

Thinking universally

Jesus invites everybody. There is room at his table for people who are otherwise enemies. This is the place of reconciliation. The world is left without hope if the one table becomes a place of separation. If you sit at Jesus' table, you can no longer pursue your private interests. You learn to think universally. Christians of all churches have come closer to one another. Many have shared so much together that they can no longer accept inherited divisions. We feel this separation particularly at the table of Jesus.

—We remind our church leaders that our common faith and experiences reach further than current regulations permit.

—We ask Christians in the different churches to stop looking at the others in terms of past positions and instead to examine how the Lord's Supper is understood in the other churches today.

—For all our impatience we try also to understand people's fears and to recognize our different spiritual ties.

—We call for each to visit the others at worship.

—We expect a lot from concrete mutual intercession at the eucharistic celebration.

—We pray for the leaders and members of other churches.

—We encourage the Protestant churches to celebrate the Supper more often.

—On behalf of Catholic Christians we ask Protestants to deal more carefully with the elements that remain from the Supper.

—We suggest the use of items from the liturgy of other churches.

Children not to be excluded

Jesus welcomed the children who were brought to him. At his table they can recognize him along with all who partake; and they can grow in fellowship with him and with all participants. There is no substantial reason for excluding them from the Supper any longer.

—Therefore we encourage all congregations to include the Lord's meal in family services or to hold celebrations with and for children.

—We especially call on parents to allow their children to join in.

—We ask worship leaders to give services a form more suitable for family participation.

A human celebration

The Lord's Supper is worship "with hearts and hands and voices". The whole person should experience that God is good. Many signs of joy and fellowship express this. We have found some to be particularly important:

—We are looking for spontaneous elements of praise and thanks.

—We should like more communal singing and music-making.

—We are discovering festive decorations and ornaments.

—We are looking for eucharistic prayers in which many can take part.

—We are shaping the church space so we can feel comfortable.

—We are also celebrating in homes.

—We keep a seat for the unexpected guest even at the smallest celebrations.

—We are creating possibilities for communicating to one another our experiences, fears and hopes.

—We gather in a circle round the altar.

—We pass the bread and wine round with suitable words.

—We shake hands at the kiss of peace.

We, too, are aware that these proposals are only a start. That is specially true for the signs we can give of a changed future. Our hope is that we shall discover such signs in the process of rediscovering the Lord's meal—the centrepoint of the assembled Church and the paradigm of our shared life together.

6. THE WORSHIP OF THE CONGREGATION

In April 1979, the WCC sub-unit on Renewal and Congregational Life held a workshop on "The Worship of the Congregation" at the Orthodox Academy, Gonia/Chania, Crete. Some paragraphs of its report are here reproduced.

Worship and culture

10. The Gospel is both universal and particular. It preaches Jesus of one time and place to people of every age and nation. In principle, there need be no conflict between the universal character of the Gospel and its particular character. In fact, however, the preaching of the message raises delicate problems of translation as the attempt is made to find an expression which is both faithful to the original and yet intelligible in a different culture than that of Jesus. Such efforts risk presenting the Gospel in forms that other Christians cannot regard as true expressions of the faith. There is need therefore to discern a universal norm and to respect legitimate variety of expression.

11. Stated most simply, the *universal norm* of Christianity is Jesus Christ. As far as worship is concerned, Christian liturgy is taking place when it is possible to discern Jesus Christ in the reading and exposition of the scriptures, which bear earliest witness to him; when prayers are being made "in his name"; when his sacramental presence is experienced; and when he is seen in the quality of life displayed by the worshippers also beyond the special moments of the cult. The discernment of Jesus Christ under these aspects is not without its problems: scriptural exegesis and interpretation is involved, with the danger of error on the part of scholar and preacher; prayer which is truly "in the name of Christ" demands the schooling of discipleship; the sacramental presence of Jesus Christ has been the subject of dispute among Christians; attempts to "follow Christ" in ethical behaviour always take place within the limits of particular circumstances.

12. Diverse *particular forms* are shaped by many factors. Culture changes with time. There is also at any one time a great mixture of different peoples with different cultures, and these interact with one another. This variety and interaction take place within the context of a common humanity. As a witness to God who is both the beginning and end of humanity, the Church of Jesus Christ will guard and affirm all that is positive in a culture; it will challenge and criticize all that runs counter to God's design.

13. The particular elements and peculiar expressions of liturgy are a necessary consideration in the quest for liturgical renewal. The New Testament itself translated Semitic forms into Hellenistic expressions as Christianity was spread to the Greeks. The means adopted by Peter and Paul to present Christ to Jews and Gentiles showed variety and cultural

adaptations (e.g. Acts 17). Furthermore, modern scholars have detected hymns of the early Church's liturgical celebrations which stem from Hellenistic congregations (e.g. Col. 1:15–20; Phil. 2:5–11).

14. Thus cultural adaptation is canonized by its presence in Scripture. The biblical model sets such translation as a permanent task for every generation in every culture. There is also the accepted truth that God is universal Creator, and created people of differing cultures are meant to have multiple characteristics. Furthermore, the Incarnation of Jesus Christ is the supreme expression of the need to become incarnational in our respective settings.

15. *Symbols* provide an illustration of the importance of cultural diversity for liturgical renewal. There are universally accepted archetypes—e.g. eating together, greetings, motherhood, light—which are related to everyday life. They are living aids that speak profoundly to men and women in their own situations. When used in liturgy, these symbols normally serve the sense of the divine presence. These archetypes are manifested in various symbolic forms in various cultures, for human beings are symbol-making creatures. Liturgy cannot exist without symbols, and a rediscovery of the place and use of symbols is a necessary ingredient in liturgical renewal.

16. Symbols generally involve the whole person with *all* his/her senses. Churches which shape their worship solely for the ear or even for the intellect alone need to recover an appreciation of all the aesthetic senses. For example:

(a) The recurrent tendency to portray Christ and the biblical scenes in terms of the artist's own culture should be encouraged.

(b) For many centuries some churches have known the value of the icon as a visible means of contact with the hidden reality it represents, and other churches could well learn from this.

(c) With music, men and women express themselves in ways which people of other cultures also can appreciate—consider, for example, the widespread use of spirituals that originated with blacks in North America. Moreover, music is never purely a matter for the ear alone; it engages by its rhythm the whole person.

(d) In liturgy, processions, gestures and other bodily postures are viewed as vivid symbols conveying spiritual meanings. For example, forms of salutation vary from country to country, yet they carry with them the meaning of mutual acceptance, peace and blessing.

(e) Dress has always been a way in which people of a particular time and place express their identity. Individuals fulfilling liturgical functions have usually been distinguished by special vestments, and churches should reflect carefully on the meaning conveyed by such symbols.

Recommendations

30. Current developments concerning the eucharist lead us to propose that the World Council take further steps to help the churches give *liturgical expression to their emerging doctrinal agreement*. Specifically, we recommend the preparation of one or more liturgical structures that accord with the consensus already achieved, to be offered to the churches as contributions to

their own efforts at liturgical revision and for possible use as "approved alternatives" to existing denominational forms. Further, in view of the work now being done in several places to prepare alternative ecumenical texts for the eucharistic canon, it is proposed that the WCC seek to make such texts as well as other material for worship more widely available for use as desired by the churches.

7. THE EUCHARISTIC LITURGY OF LIMA

Introduction

This liturgy was prepared for the plenary session of the Faith and Order Commission in Lima and was used for the first time there on 15 January 1982. It was also used in the Ecumenical Centre Chapel in Geneva on 28 July 1982 during the meeting of the Central Committee of the World Council of Churches, with Dr Philip Potter, the General Secretary, as the presiding minister. It was again used at the Sixth Assembly of the World Council of Churches in Vancouver with the Archbishop of Canterbury as the presiding celebrant.

In composing this liturgy for the Lima Conference, my aim was to illustrate the solid theological achievements of the Faith and Order document, *Baptism, Eucharist and Ministry* (cited henceforth as BEM). The Lima liturgy is not the only possibility: the convergences registered in BEM could be expressed in other liturgical forms, according to other traditions, spiritualities or cultures. No "authority" attaches to this particular liturgy, save that accruing to it from the fact of its having been used on certain significant ecumenical occasions.

Celebration and celebrants

The Lima liturgy is characterized by its fullness and is perhaps more suitable for a particularly solemn celebration. It has already been used in a simplified form by a number of groups. Some examples of possible simplification will be given at the end of this introduction.

According to the indications given in the BEM document, the Christian liturgy should be regularly celebrated, at least every Lord's Day and on feast days. This eucharistic celebration will include the proclamation of the Word of God and the communion of the members of the Body of Christ in the power of the Holy Spirit (E31). The eucharistic liturgy thus consists of three parts. The introductory part unites the people of God in confession, supplication and praise (confession of sins, litany of the *Kyrie*, and the *Gloria*). The second part, the liturgy of the Word, begins with a prayer of preparation. It includes the three proclamations: of a prophet (first lesson), an apostle (second lesson), and Christ (the Gospel). Then the voice of the Church is heard in the sermon, making the eternal word contemporary and living. The sermon is followed by silent meditation. The faith of the Church is then summarized in the Creed and all human needs presented to God in the intercession. The third part, the liturgy of the eucharist, consists essentially of the great eucharistic prayer, preceded by a short preparation and followed by the Lord's Prayer, the sign of peace, and communion. We shall return to these elements in more detail. (They are listed in E27.)

The liturgy is an act of the community. This is even indicated in the etymology of the term "liturgy"—*leitourgia*—service of the people. It is not a clerical solo performance but a *concert* of the whole Christian community, in which certain of its members play a special part, in accordance with their different charisms and mandates. At ecumenical meetings, the liturgy of the Word will be shared by worship leaders (officiants) of several traditions, while the liturgy of the eucharist will associate as assistants of the principal celebrant those authorized by their own church to concelebrate on such occasions.

Normally the *presiding pastor* at the liturgy (bishop or presbyter, M29–30) gives the salutation, the absolution and the prayer; the pastor leads the liturgy of the Eucharist by praying the great eucharistic prayer: the preface, the *epiclesis* (I and II), the institution, the *anamnesis* and the conclusion; the pastor also offers the prayer of thanksgiving and gives the benediction. The *congregation* sings or says all the responses and the Amens; it recites together the confession, the Gloria (or it alternates with an officiant, unless it is sung), the Creed (said or sung) and the Lord's Prayer (said or sung). The biddings in the litany of the Kyrie and in the intercessions, the verses of the Gloria, the preparation and the mementos, the introduction to the Lord's Prayer and the prayer of peace, may be shared among *other officiants*. Three *readers* are assigned to read the lessons (the Gospel is read or sung by a deacon in the Orthodox, Roman Catholic and Anglican traditions); a *preacher* is assigned to deliver the sermon.

Sources and meanings

The entry hymn which accompanies the procession of the officiants, or even of the entire community, should preferably be a psalm, appropriate to the liturgical season or the festival being celebrated, punctuated by a suitable antiphon, simple enough for all to join in between the verses sung by the choir. On the first Sunday in Advent, for example, the entry hymn is Psalm 25, with the antiphon:

To you, Lord, I lift my heart;
Those whose hope is in you will not be disappointed.

The psalm may, however, be replaced by a chorale or a hymn whose liturgical use is well-attested. In the Lutheran tradition, for example, the chorales mark certain Sundays. When the procession ends, the Gloria is sung ("Glory be to the Father and to the Son and to the Holy Spirit...") and the antiphon is repeated a last time.

The principal celebrant then gives the salutation, a custom which probably goes back to primitive liturgical usage, and the text for which is provided for us by St Paul (2 Cor. 13:13). It was restored to favour in the revised post-conciliar Roman Catholic liturgy, and it often forms part of Reformed and Lutheran celebrations.

The confession, said by the whole congregation, is followed by the absolution pronounced by the principal celebrant. Both have been taken from the *Lutheran Book of Worship* published by the Joint Lutheran Liturgical Commission for the churches in the United States and Canada.[1]

Slight alterations have been made in the English text to employ more inclusive language.

The litany of the Kyrie is a brief initial supplication. This litany derives traditionally from the Byzantine Liturgy which always begins with it. Here, however, it is shorter, containing only three petitions on the themes of baptism, eucharist and ministry, which take their cue from three New Testament passages: Eph. 4:3-5, 1 Cor. 10:16-17 and 2 Cor. 5:18-20. These petitions may be altered to suit the circumstances. Provision could also be made for penitential petitions in place of the confession, and these would then come immediately after the salutation.

The form used in the revised Roman Catholic liturgy is familiar:

Lord Jesus, sent by the Father to heal and save us all, have mercy on us.
—*Kyrie eleison.*

O Christ, who came into the world to call all sinners, have mercy on us.
—*Kyrie eleison.*

Lord, lifted up into the glory of the Father where Thou dost intercede for us, have mercy on us. —*Kyrie eleision.*

May the almighty God have mercy on us all; may He pardon our sins and bring us to eternal life. —*Amen.*

The opening litany of the Orthodox Liturgy of St John Chrysostom could also be used.

This litany of supplication is followed by the hymn of praise: "Glory to God in the highest..." From the beginning of the liturgy, therefore, place is provided for the three fundamental attitudes of Christian prayer: penitence, supplication and praise.

The liturgy of the Word opens with prayer. In contemplation, preparation is made for hearing the Word of God. This prayer varies according to seasons, festivals and circumstances. Here it is based on the themes of the BEM document. It evokes Jesus' baptism in the River Jordan, the messianic *anointing* of Christ who is consecrated prophet, priest and king. It asks for a fresh outpouring of the Spirit upon the *baptized,* the deepening of desire for communion with Christ in the *eucharist,* and consecration to the *service* of the poor and those in special need of Christian love.

The first reading is taken either from the Old Testament, or from the Acts of the Apostles or the Book of Revelation. At Lima, the passage chosen was Ezekiel 47:1-9, on the water flowing from the source in the Temple, recalling the baptismal immersion which purifies, cleanses and gives life. The meditative hymn which follows is usually the fragment of a psalm, sung responsively. Appropriate verses to follow this Ezekiel passage about the life-giving water would be Psalm 42:2-3, 8-9, with the antiphon taken from Ezekiel 36:25:

I will sprinkle clean water upon you and will cleanse you from all your uncleannesses.

The second reading is a short passage from one of the Epistles. At Lima it was 1 Peter 5:1-11, on the theme of ministry. The Alleluia then sounds out as an acclamation of welcome to the Gospel. For example:

Alleluia! Alleluia! The disciples of Emmaus recognized the Risen Lord in the breaking of the bread. Alleluia!

The Gospel is then read by a deacon or a third reader. At Lima the Emmaus passage from Lk. 24:25-32 was read, on the theme of the eucharistic meal preceded by Christ's exposition of the Scriptures.

The sermon applies the message of the Word of God to our life today. It is the voice of the Church, echoing that of the prophets, apostles and Christ. A moment of silent recollection gives time for each to meditate on the Word received.

The Creed is then said or sung as a résumé of the history of salvation. Either the Nicaeno-Constantinopolitan (Nicene) Creed or the Apostles' Creed may be used. In an ecumenical spirit of fidelity to the original text of the Nicene Creed, we use here that form approved at the Council of Constantinople in 381, as was done at the Lima Conference and at the WCC Central Committee meeting in Geneva. The 1600th anniversary of this Council in 1981 by and large restored this primitive text to its rightful place of honour, reconciling East and West in the expression of fundamental faith.

The prayer of intercession unites the believing community, now nourished by the Word of God, in prayer for the needs of the Church and the world. The pattern and style adopted here are those of the litany of Pope Gelasius (+496) which reflects the Kyrie in use in Rome at the end of the fifth century.[2] The themes of the six intentions include the outpouring of the Spirit on the Church; the leaders of the nations, justice and peace; the oppressed and all the victims of violence; then (following the BEM themes) the unity of the churches in baptism; the communion of the churches around the one table; the mutual recognition of ministries by the churches.

The liturgy of the Eucharist begins with the presentation of the bread and wine, accompanied by two benedictions from the Jewish liturgy (also used in the revised Roman Catholic liturgy), and by a prayer inspired by the *Didache*. This preparation is completed by the very ancient eucharistic acclamation "*Maranatha*" ("Come, Lord!" or "The Lord is coming", 1 Cor. 16:22).

The great eucharistic prayer begins with a composite preface, which also takes its themes from the BEM document. First of all, thanksgiving for creation is focused on the life-giving Word, giving life in particular to the human being who reflects the glory of God. In the fullness of time Christ was given as the way, the truth and the life. In the account of Jesus' life, the preface recalls the consecration of the Servant by baptism, the last supper of the eucharist, the memorial of the death and resurrection, and the presence of the Risen Saviour in the breaking of the bread. Finally, the preface refers to the gift of the royal priesthood to all Christians, from among whom God chooses ministers who are charged to feed the Church by the Word and sacraments and thereby to give it life.

In conformity with the Alexandrian and Roman traditions, the invocation of the Holy Spirit (the *epiclesis*) precedes the words of the institution of the Holy Supper.[3] The reminder of the work of the Holy Spirit in the history of our salvation is inspired by the liturgy of St James (4th century). This is also used in the liturgy of the Evangelical Lutheran Church of France (1977, alternative VIII). The *epiclesis* asks for the Holy Spirit to be poured out, as on Moses and the prophets, on the Virgin Mary, on Jesus at the River Jordan, and on the apostles at Pentecost, to transfigure the thanksgiving meal, so that the bread and the wine become for us the Body and the Blood of Christ. The idea of transfiguration by the Spirit of life and fire is intended to point to the consecration of the bread and wine in a sacramental and mystical manner transcending all our understanding and all our explanation (E14–15). The congregation punctuates this *epiclesis* with the sung response: "Veni Creator Spiritus—Come, Creator Spirit!"

Just as the beginning of the *epiclesis* took up the themes of the preceding *Sanctus* (O God, Lord of the *universe*, you are *holy* and your *glory* is beyond measure), so too the beginning of the institution links up with the *epiclesis* and to its response, by referring to the Holy Spirit. This indicates the unity of the action of the Spirit and of Christ in the eucharistic mystery. The Holy Spirit accomplishes the words of the Son who, "on the night in which he was betrayed, took bread..." By the Holy Spirit, these historical words of Jesus become alive and contemporary: bread and wine become the Body and the Blood of Christ. "The Holy Spirit makes the crucified and risen Christ really present to us in the eucharistic meal, fulfilling the promise contained in the words of institution" (E14). The Holy Spirit "makes the historical words of Jesus present and alive" (E14). The blessing of the bread and the cup is accompanied, as in the Jewish liturgy, the passover meal in particular, by thanksgiving. The rendering of "Do this for the remembrance of me" is preferred in order to avoid the subjective idea of a mere souvenir. The eucharist is a memorial, an *anamnesis*, i.e. making present and alive the saving event of the cross and the presentation of Christ's unique sacrifice to the Father as an urgent prayer of the Church. The acclamation which concludes the institution has been adopted in many recent liturgical revisions: Roman Catholic, Anglican, Swedish, American Lutheran. It associates the congregation with the proclamation of the memorial. The *anamnesis* is the celebration of the "memorial of our redemption". The sacrifice of the cross and resurrection, made present and active for us today in the eucharist, is central in the *anamnesis*. But, as the BEM document says, what is recalled in thanksgiving in the eucharist is the whole existence of Christ (E6).

In the present liturgy, certain events are emphasized because they correspond to the BEM themes: the baptism of Jesus, his last meal with the apostles, his ministry as High Priest who makes intercession for us all. In the eucharist the whole people of God are united with Christ's unique priesthood, each member in accordance with the charism and ministry received. We present the memorial of Christ, i.e. we show forth to the Father the unique sacrifice of the Son as the urgent supplication of the Church and we say to God: "Do you remember the sacrifice of the cross and, in virtue of this unique sacrifice, source of all blessings, grant us and all human beings the abundance of blessings obtained for us in the work of salvation and liberation accomplished by Jesus Christ." This is the *anamnesis* or memorial, the making of the unique sacrifice livingly present and the intercession that the Father may remember Christ's work on our behalf. The eschatological acclamation is uttered as an act of faith affirming the coming of the Lord: *"Maranatha"*!

The eucharist, given in the Spirit to the church as a precious gift, is received by the Father as an intercession and a thanksgiving, one with the very offering of the Son which reestablishes us in the covenant with God.

In a very beautiful text of 1520, Luther showed how the intercession of Christ and the offering of the Church are intimately united in the eucharist:

It is not we who offer Christ, but Christ who offers us (to the Father). In this way, it is permissible, indeed helpful, to call the ceremony a sacrifice; not in itself, but because in it we offer ourselves in sacrifice with Christ. In other words, we lean on Christ with a firm faith in his covenant, and we present ourselves before God with our prayer, thanksgiving and sacrifice, only in the name of Christ and by his mediation...without doubting that He is our Priest in heaven before the face of God. Christ welcomes us, he presents us, ourselves, our prayers and our praise (to God); he also offers himself in heaven for us...He offers himself for us in heaven and with himself, he offers us.[4]

A second *epiclesis* then invokes the Holy Spirit on the congregation, a fresh outpouring consequent on communion in the Body and Blood of Christ. This effusion of the Spirit rallies together the Body of Christ, the Church, and inspires it to spiritual unity; it makes the congregation a living offering to the glory of God; it anticipates the coming Kingdom. Here, once again, the eucharistic prayer is punctuated by an acclamation: either the response "Veni Creator Spiritus", echoing the second *epiclesis,* or, once again, the eschatological *"Maranatha".*

According to the Western tradition, this is where we mention all those for whom we wish especially to pray, remember those who preceded us in the faith, and all the cloud of witnesses by whom we are compassed about. These *mementos* make explicit our concern for the whole Christian community on which the Holy Spirit has just been invoked, which explains their location here after the second *epiclesis.* In a shorter liturgy they could be omitted and their content transferred to the moment of intercession (No 16). The wording of the *mementos* is inspired by the Eucharistic Prayer III in the draft text "Word, Bread and Cup".[5] After a final *"Maranatha",* the eucharistic prayer is rounded off by a trinitarian conclusion, traditional in Western liturgies.

The introduction to the Lord's Prayer recalls the unity of all Christians in baptism, which incorporates them into the Body of Christ and gives them life by the one Spirit. This unity of Christians permits them to say together the prayer of the children of God, the Lord's Prayer. It also permits them to renew among themselves the peace of Christ and they give each other a sign of reconciliation and friendship.

The breaking of the bread during the *Agnus Dei* hymn is announced in the manner of the Reformed tradition: "The bread which we break is the communion in the body of Christ..." (1 Cor. 10:16).

In the prayer of thanksgiving we give thanks to God for the unity of baptism and the joy of the eucharist; we pray for full visible unity and for recognition of the signs of reconciliation already given; finally, we pray in hope that those who have already tasted of the meal of the Kingdom may also share the heritage of the saints in light (Col. 1:12). After the final hymn before the benediction, the presiding minister may give a brief message of dispatch on mission, for example, by repeating the central biblical text on which the sermon was preached.

Possible simplifications

This eucharistc liturgy may also be shortened in order to adapt it to different circumstances.

The introductory part may consist only of the hymn, the salutation, the litany of the Kyrie and the Gloria (1–2, 5–6), omitting the confession. It may even consist simply of a hymn—a psalm or Gloria—and then go straight into the prayer (1 or 6, then 7).

The liturgy of the Word always begins with a prayer, suited to the season, the festival or circumstances. There may be only two lessons instead of three: the first lesson or the Epistle, and always the Gospel. Between the two readings a psalm and alleluia, or simply the alleluia, may be sung. The sermon should always focus on some aspect of the message of the Word of God. The Creed has not always formed part of the eucharistic liturgy and it may be reserved for Sundays and feast days. A choice may be made between the intercession (16) and the *mementos* (25), using only one or the other. This would then give the simplified pattern: sermon, silence, preparation for the eucharist (13, 14, 17).

The liturgy of the Eucharist always begins with preparation (17). It necessarily includes the following elements: the preface (19) adapted to the season, festival or circumstances, and permissibly in a shorter version; the first and second *epiclesis* (21 and 24); the institution (22); the *anamnesis* (23) and the conclusion (26). The *mementos* may be omitted if already integrated in the intercession (16). The prayer of peace after the Lord's Prayer can be omitted, retaining only the announcement: "The peace of the Lord be with you always..." (28).

The prayer of thanksgiving may be a free prayer, provided it is always brief and well-structured. The liturgy ends with a final hymn, if possible, by a brief word of dispatch on mission, according to the occasion, and by the benediction.

The Eucharist at the centre of the community and its mission

The life of the first Christian community is described in the Acts of the Apostles as follows: "And they devoted themselves to the apostles' teaching and fellowship, to the breaking of the bread and prayers... And day by day, attending the temple together and breaking the bread in their homes, they partook of food with glad and generous hearts, praising God and having favour with all the people. And the Lord added to their number day by day those who were being saved" (2:42–47).

These verses epitomize the whole life of the Church through the ages. The Church will assume different faces through the centuries but only if these fundamental elements are found within it will it truly be the Church of Christ. We have here the model by which it will be able to measure this fidelity in the course of history. All periods of renewal in the Church will be due to the return to these original springs.

In this description of the primitive Christian community, seven elements may be discerned which must always be respected by the Church if it is to remain faithful to its origins and keep within the succession of Christ's purpose and of the apostolic foundation: the hearing of the Word of God, the celebration of the breaking of the bread, the offering of prayers, concern for communion as brothers and sisters, the sharing of material blessings, the unity of praising God and witnessing in the world, and the mission accomplished by the Lord who builds the church and increases it.

The Christian community is born of the hearing of the Word of God: the reading of the Bible and the preaching of the Word. Thanks to the meditation on this living Word, it is gradually built up and strengthened. The Holy Scriptures, read, preached and meditated on, distinguish the Christian community radically from every other human society or religious group. The increasing assimilation of the main themes of the Word transforms the community; it becomes a place of liberation, peace, joy, celebration, friendship, influence and hope... The Church cannot live unless it constantly returns to this life-giving source, the Word of God. This is why its worship is focused on the reading of the prophets and apostles, on the proclamation of the Gospel of Christ, on the preaching of and reverent reflection on the Truth in the Spirit. This Word of God feeds the Christian community and makes it grow; it makes it a centre of attraction and it sends it out into the world to announce the glad tidings.

On Easter evening, the Risen Lord, joining his disciples on their way to Emmaus, interpreted to them the things concerning himself in all the scriptures. His Word prepared their hearts to recognize him. But it was when he sat at table with them, when he took the bread, blessed it and gave thanks, that their eyes were opened and their hearts, set on fire by his Word, recognized him in the breaking of the bread (Lk. 24:27-32).

This is why, when the Church celebrates the presence of the Risen Lord in its midst, chiefly on the Lord's Day, it proclaims his Word and is fed in the thanksgiving Meal: it recognizes him in the Scriptures and in the Breaking of the bread. Thus the complete Christian liturgy includes the proclamation of the Word of God and the celebration of the Eucharist.

This proclamation and this celebration are surrounded by the prayers of the Church. The first Christians "devoted themselves to... the prayers" and "they attended the temple day by day". The primitive Church continued the discipline of Jewish prayers. It wished to observe day by day, with regularity, "the prayers of the hours", in the Temple in Jerusalem, which would be at the origin of the liturgy of the daily office. This liturgy included the singing of psalms, the reading of the Word, and intercessions. This regular offering of prayers by the Christian community seals the communion of the Church and constitutes a sacrifice of praise and intercession in which its communion with God is constantly renewed.

Brotherly and sisterly communion and concord are the consequences of this relationship between the community and its Lord by means of the Word, Eucharist, and Prayer. They are the marks of an authentic ecclesial life. They are expressed concretely in such actions as the *agape* meals when Christians take food together and share their material possessions with those in need. Joy and simplicity are the distinctive marks of this communion of solidarity among brothers and sisters. There is no contradiction between the praise of God and presence in the world; the one does not detach us from the other. The community whose primary work is the celebration of the praise of God is welcomed by the people around it, because it is one of brotherhood and sisterhood, simple and joyous.

The Eucharist is at the very heart of the Church's life. With the Word and the prayers, it creates the communion of brothers and sisters, their sharing with one another, and makes the community present for the world and radiant with Christ. The eucharist builds up the Church, in unity and for the world, and makes it the missionary Church.

MAX THURIAN

NOTES

[1] *Lutheran Book of Worship*, Minneapolis, Augsburg Publishing House. Minister's Edition, 1978, p. 195.
[2] B. Capelle, "Le Kyrie de la messe et le pape Gélase", *Revue Bénédictine*, 1934, pp. 136–138. A. Hamman, *Prières des premiers chrétiens*, Paris, Fayard, 1952. pp. 349–352.
[3] *Fragment of Der-Balyzeh* (sixth century), attesting the liturgy of St Mark; *Quam oblationem* of the Roman Canon and *epiclesis* of the new liturgical prayers. See my book, *Le mystère eucharistique*, Paris, Centurion-Taizé, 1981, pp. 89–99, to be published by Mowbray, Oxford, 1983.
[4] WA VI, 369.
[5] Consultation on Church Union, USA.

THE EUCHARIST

Liturgy of entrance

1 ENTRANCE PSALM (with antiphon and Gloria Patri; or hymn)

2 GREETING*

P: The grace of our Lord Jesus Christ, the love of God, and the communion of the Holy Spirit be with you all.

C: And also with you.

3 CONFESSION

C: Most merciful God, we confess that we are in bondage to sin and cannot free ourselves. We have sinned against you in thought, word and deed, by what we have done and by what we have left undone. We have not loved you with our whole heart; we have not loved our neighbours as ourselves. For the sake of your Son, Jesus Christ, have mercy on us. Forgive us, renew us, and lead us, so that we may delight in your will and walk in your ways, to the glory of your holy name. Amen.

4 ABSOLUTION

P: Almighty God gave Jesus Christ to die for us and for the sake of Christ forgives us all our sins. As a called and ordained minister of the Church and by the authority of Jesus Christ, I therefore declare to you the entire forgiveness of all your sins, in the name of the Father, and of the Son, and of the Holy Spirit.

C: Amen.

5 KYRIE LITANY

O: That we may be enabled to maintain the unity of the Spirit in the bond of

---

*P = Presiding Minister
C = Congregation
O = Another Celebrant

peace and together confess that there is only one Body and one Spirit, only one Lord, one faith, one baptism, let us pray to the Lord.

(Eph. 4:3–5)

C: Kyrie eleison.

O: That we may soon attain to visible communion in the Body of Christ, by breaking the bread and blessing the cup around the same table, let us pray to the Lord.

(1 Cor. 10:16–17)

C: Kyrie eleision.

O: That, reconciled to God through Christ, we may be enabled to recognize each other's ministries and be united in the ministry of reconciliation, let us pray to the Lord.

(2 Cor. 5:18–20)

C: Kyrie eleison.

6 GLORIA

Glory to God in the Highest,
—And peace to God's people on earth.

Lord God, heavenly King, almighty God and Father,
—We worship you, we give you thanks.

We praise you for your glory,
—Lord Jesus Christ, only Son of the Father,

Lord God, Lamb of God,
—You take away the sin of the world: have mercy on us;

You take away the sin of the world: receive our prayer;
—You are seated at the right hand of the Father: have mercy on us.

For you alone are the Holy One,
—You alone are the Lord,

You alone are the Most High: Jesus Christ, with the Holy Spirit,
—In the glory of God the Father,
Amen.

Liturgy of the Word

7 COLLECT

P: Let us pray: Lord God, gracious and merciful, you anointed your beloved Son with the Holy Spirit at his baptism in the Jordan, and you consecrated him prophet, priest and king: pour out your Spirit on us again that we may be faithful to our baptismal calling, ardently desire the communion of Christ's body and blood, and serve the poor of your people and all who need our love, through Jesus Christ, your Son, our Lord, who lives and reigns with you, in the unity of the Holy Spirit, ever one God, world without end.

C: Amen.

8 FIRST LESSON (Old Testament, Acts or Revelation)

9 PSALM OF MEDITATION

The Eucharistic Liturgy of Lima

10 EPISTLE

11 ALLELUIA

12 GOSPEL

13 HOMILY

14 SILENCE

15 NICENE—CONSTANTINOPOLITAN CREED (text of 381)

We believe in one God, the Father, the Almighty, maker of heaven and earth, of all that is, seen and unseen.

We believe in one Lord, Jesus Christ, the only Son of God, eternally begotten of the Father, Light from Light, true God from true God, begotten, not made, of one Being with the Father; through him all things were made. For us and for our salvation he came down from heaven; by the power of the Holy Spirit he became incarnate from the Virgin Mary and was made man. For our sake he was crucified under Pontius Pilate; he suffered death and was buried; on the third day he rose again in accordance with the Scriptures; he ascended into heaven. He is seated at the right hand of the Father, he will come again in glory to judge the living and the dead, and his kingdom will have no end.

We believe in the Holy Spirit, the Lord, the giver of life, who proceeds from the Father; with the Father and the Son he is worshiped and glorified; he has spoken through the Prophets. We believe in one holy catholic and apostolic Church. We acknowledge one baptism for the forgiveness of sins. We look for the resurrection of the dead, and the life of the world to come. Amen.

16 INTERCESSION

O: In faith let us pray to God our Father, his Son Jesus Christ and the Holy Spirit.

C: Kyrie eleison.

O: For the Church of God throughout all the world, let us invoke the Spirit.

C: Kyrie eleison.

O: For the leaders of the nations, that they may establish and defend justice and peace, let us pray for the wisdom of God.

C: Kyrie eleison.

O: For those who suffer oppression or violence, let us invoke the power of the Deliverer.

C: Kyrie eleison.

O: That the churches may discover again their visible unity in the one baptism which incorporates them in Christ, let us pray for the love of Christ.

C: Kyrie eleison.

O: That the churches may attain communion in the eucharist around one table, let us pray for the strength of Christ.

C: Kyrie eleison.

O: That the churches may recognize each other's ministries in the service of their one Lord, let us pray for the peace of Christ.

C: *Kyrie eleison.*

(Spontaneous prayers of the congregation)

O: Into your hands, O Lord, we commend all for whom we pray, trusting in your mercy; through your Son, Jesus Christ, our Lord.

C: *Amen.*

Liturgy of the Eucharist

17 PREPARATION

O: Blessed are you, Lord God of the universe, you are the giver of this bread, fruit of the earth and of human labour, let it become the bread of Life.

C: *Blessed be God, now and for ever!*

O: Blessed are you, Lord God of the universe, you are the giver of this wine, fruit of the vine and of human labour, let it become the wine of the eternal Kingdom.

C: *Blessed be God, now and for ever!*

O: As the grain once scattered in the fields and the grapes once dispersed on the hillside are now reunited on this table in bread and wine, so, Lord, may your whole Church soon be gathered together from the corners of the earth into your Kingdom.

C: *Maranatha! Come Lord Jesus!*

18 DIALOGUE

P: The Lord be with you

C: *And also with you.*

P: Lift up your hearts.

C: *We lift them to the Lord.*

P: Let us give thanks to the Lord our God.

C: *It is right to give him thanks and praise.*

19 PREFACE

P: Truly it is right and good to glorify you, at all times and in all places, to offer you our thanksgiving O Lord, Holy Father, Almighty and Everlasting God. Through your living Word you created all things, and pronounced them good. You made human beings in your own image, to share your life and reflect your glory. When the time had fully come, you gave Christ to us as the Way, the Truth and the Life. He accepted baptism and consecration as your Servant to announce the good news to the poor. At the last supper Christ bequeathed to us the eucharist, that we should celebrate the memorial of the cross and resurrection, and receive his presence as food. To all the redeemed Christ gave the royal priesthood and, in loving his brothers and sisters, chooses those who share in the ministry, that they may feed the Church with your Word and enable it to live by your Sacraments. Wherefore, Lord, with the angels and all the saints, we proclaim and sing your glory:

20 SANCTUS

C: *Holy, Holy, Holy....*

21 EPICLESIS I

P: O God, Lord of the universe, you are holy and your glory is beyond measure. Upon your eucharist send the life-giving Spirit, who spoke by Moses and the Prophets, who overshadowed the Virgin Mary with grace, who descended upon Jesus in the river Jordan and upon the Apostles on the day of Pentecost. May the outpouring of this Spirit of Fire transfigure this thanksgiving meal that this bread and wine may become for us the body and blood of Christ.

C: Veni Creator Spiritus!

22 INSTITUTION

P: May this Creator Spirit accomplish the words of your beloved Son, who, in the night in which he was betrayed, took bread, and when he had given thanks to you, broke it and gave it to his disciples, saying: Take, eat: this is my body, which is given for you. Do this for the remembrance of me. After supper he took the cup and when he had given thanks, he gave it to them and said: Drink this, all of you: this is my blood of the new covenant, which is shed for you and for many for the forgiveness of sins. Do this for the remembrance of me. Great is the mystery of faith.

C: Your death, Lord Jesus, we proclaim! Your resurrection we celebrate! Your coming in glory we await!

23 ANAMNESIS

P: Wherefore, Lord, we celebrate today the memorial of our redemption: we recall the birth and life of your Son among us, his baptism by John, his last meal with the apostles, his death and descent to the abode of the dead; we proclaim Christ's resurrection and ascension in glory, where as our Great High Priest he ever intercedes for all people; and we look for his coming at the last. United in Christ's priesthood, we present to you this memorial: Remember the sacrifice of your Son and grant to people everywhere the benefits of Christ's redemptive work.

C: Maranatha, the Lord comes!

24 EPICLESIS II

P: Behold, Lord, this eucharist which you yourself gave to the Church and graciously receive it, as you accept the offering of your Son whereby we are reinstated in your Covenant. As we partake of Christ's body and blood, fill us with the Holy Spirit that we may be one single body and one single spirit in Christ, a living sacrifice to the praise of your glory.

C: Veni Creator Spiritus!

25 COMMEMORATIONS

O: Remember, Lord, your one, holy, catholic and apostolic Church, redeemed by the blood of Christ. Reveal its unity, guard its faith, and preserve it in peace. Remember, Lord, all the servants of your Church: bishops, presbyters, deacons, and all to whom you have given special gifts of ministry. (Remember especially....)

Remember also all our sisters and brothers who have died in the peace of Christ, and those whose faith is known to you alone: guide them to the joyful feast prepared for all peoples in your presence, with the blessed Virgin Mary, with the patriarchs and prophets, the apostles and martyrs.... and all the saints for whom your friendship was life. With all these we sing your praise and await the happiness of your Kingdom where with the whole creation, finally delivered from sin and death, we shall be enabled to glorify you through Christ our Lord;

C: *Maranatha, the Lord comes!*

26 CONCLUSION

P: Through Christ, with Christ, in Christ, all honour and glory is yours, Almighty God and Father, in the unity of the Holy Spirit, now and for ever.

C: *Amen.*

27 THE LORD'S PRAYER

O: United by one baptism in the same Holy Spirit and the same Body of Christ, we pray as God's sons and daughters:

C: *Our Father,....*

28 THE PEACE

O: Lord Jesus Christ, you told your apostles: Peace I leave with you, my peace I give to you. Look not on our sins but on the faith of your Church. In order that your will be done, grant us always this peace and guide us towards the perfect unity of your Kingdom for ever

C: *Amen.*

P: The peace of the Lord be with you always

C: *And also with you.*

O: Let us give one another a sign of reconciliation and peace.

29 THE BREAKING OF THE BREAD

P: The bread which we break is the communion of the Body of Christ, the cup of blessing for which we give thanks is the communion in the Blood of Christ.

30 LAMB OF GOD

C: *Lamb of God, you take away the sins of the world, have mercy on us.*
Lamb of God, you take away the sins of the world, have mercy on us.
Lamb of God, you take away the sins of the world, grant us peace.

31 COMMUNION

32 THANKSGIVING PRAYER

In peace let us pray to the Lord: O Lord our God, we give you thanks for uniting us by baptism in the Body of Christ and for filling us with joy in the eucharist. Lead us towards the full visible unity of your Church and help us to treasure all the signs of reconciliation you have granted us. Now that we have tasted of the banquet you have prepared for us in the world to come, may we all one day share together the inheritance of the saints in the life of your heavenly city, through Jesus Christ, your Son, our Lord, who lives and reigns with you in the unity of the Holy Spirit, ever one God, world without end.

C: *Amen.*

33 FINAL HYMN

34 WORD OF MISSION

35 BLESSING

P: The Lord bless you and keep you. The Lord make his face to shine on you and be gracious to you. The Lord look upon you with favour and give you peace. Almighty God, Father, Son and Holy Spirit, bless you now and forever.

C: Amen.

SELECT LIST OF BOOKS ON THE EUCHARIST AND ITS THEOLOGY

Allmen, J.J. von, Essai sur le Repas du Seigneur (Neuchâtel: Delachaux & Niestlé, 1966) = The Lord's Supper (London: Lutterworth, and Richmond: John Knox, 1969).

Baciocchi, J. de, L'eucharistie (Paris: Desclée, 1964).

Bobrinskoi, B., Heitz, J.J., & Lebeau, P., Intercommunion (Paris: Mame, 1969).

Bouyer, L., Eucharistie: théologie et spiritualité de la prière eucharistique (Paris: Desclée, 1966).

Brilioth, Y., Nattvarden i evangeliskt gudstjänstliv (Stockholm: Svenska Kyrkans Diakonistyrelses Bokförlag, second edition 1951) = Eucharistic Faith and Practice: Evangelical and Catholic (London: SPCK, 1930).

Buxton, R.F., Eucharist and Institution Narrative: A study in the Roman and Anglican traditions of the consecration of the eucharist from the eighth to the twentieth centuries (Great Wakering: Mayhew McCrimmon, 1976).

Clark, F., Eucharistic Sacrifice and the Reformation (Westminster, Maryland: Newman Press, 1960; second edition Oxford: Blackwell, 1967).

Clark, N., An Approach to the Theology of the Sacraments (London: SCM, 1956).

Cochrane, A.C., Eating and Drinking with Jesus (Philadelphia: Westminster, 1974).

de Jong, J.P., De eucharistie, symbolische werkelijkheid (Hilversum: Gooi & Sticht, 1966).

Delorme, J., and others, The Eucharist in the New Testament (London: Chapman, and Baltimore: Helicon, 1964).

Dix, G., The Shape of the Liturgy (Westminster: Dacre, 1945; new edition with an updating appendix by P. Marshall, New York: Seabury, 1982).

Durrwell, F.X., L'eucharistie, présence du Christ (Paris: Editions ouvrières, 1971).

Dussaut, L., L'eucharistie, pâques de toute la vie (Paris: Cerf, 1972).

Eisenbach, F., Die Gegenwart Jesu Christi im Gottesdienst (Mainz: Grünewald, 1982).

Espinel, J.L., La Eucaristía del Nuevo Testamento (Salamanca: San Esteban, 1980).

Forte, B., La chiesa nell'eucaristia (Naples: D'Auria, 1975).

Giraudo, C., La struttura letteraria della preghiera eucaristica (Rome: Biblical Institute, 1981).

Jeremias, J., Die Abendmahlsworte Jesu (Göttingen: Vandenhoeck & Ruprecht, third edition 1960) = The Eucharistic Words of Jesus (London: SCM, and New York: Scribner, 1966).

Kilmartin, E.J., The Eucharist in the Primitive Church (Englewood Cliffs: Prentice-Hall, 1965).

Lash, N., His Presence in the World (London: Sheed & Ward, and Dayton, Ohio: Pflaum, 1968).

Lebeau, P., Le vin nouveau du royaume (Paris: Desclée de Brouwer, 1966).

Lécuyer, J., Le sacrifice de la nouvelle alliance (Le Puy: Mappus, 1962).

Leenhardt, F.J., Le sacrement de la sainte cène (Neuchâtel: Delachaux & Niestlé, 1948).

Leenhardt, F.J., Ceci est mon corps (Neuchâtel: Delachaux & Niestlé, 1955) = "This is my body" in O. Cullmann and F.J. Leenhardt, Essays on the Lord's Supper (London: Lutterworth, and Richmond: John Knox, 1958).

Maldonado, L., La Plegaria eucaristica (Madrid: BAC, 1967).

Martelet, G., Résurrection, eucharistie et genèse de l'homme (Paris: Desclée, 1972) = The Risen Christ and the Eucharistic World (London: Collins, 1976).

McCormick, S., The Lord's Supper: a Biblical Interpretation (Philadelphia: Westminster, 1966).

McKenna, J.H., Eucharist and Holy Spirit (Great Wakering: Mayhew-McCrimmon, 1975).

Neuenzeit, P., Das Herrenmahl: Studien zur paulinischen Eucharistieauffassung (Munich: Kösel, 1960).

Powers, J.M., Eucharistic Theology (New York: Herder, 1967).

Ramsey, I.T., and others, Thinking about the Eucharist: Papers by members of the Church of England Doctrine Commission (London: SCM, 1972).

Rattenbury, J.E., The Eucharistic Hymns of John and Charles Wesley (London: Epworth, 1948).

Schillebeeckx, E., Christus, sacrament van de Godsontmoeting (Bilthoven: Nelissen, 1960) = Christ the Sacrament (London and New York: Sheed & Ward, 1963).

Schillebeeckx, E., Christus tegenwoordigheid in de eucharistie (Bilthoven: Nelissen, 1967) = The Eucharist (London and New York: Sheed & Ward, 1968).

Schmemann, A., Sacraments and Orthodoxy (New York: Herder, 1965) = The World as Sacrament (London: Darton Longman & Todd, 1966).

Schmidt-Lauber, H.C., Die Eucharistie als Entfaltung der Verba Testamenti (Kassel: Stauda, 1957).

Schulz, H.J., Die Byzantinische Liturgie: Vom Werden ihrer Symbolgestalt (Freiburg: Lambertus, 1964).

Schulz, H. J., Ökumenische Glaubenseinheit aus eucharistischer Überlieferung (Paderborn: Bonifacius, 1976).

Smolarski, D.C., Eucharistia: a Study of the Eucharistic Prayer (Ramsey: Paulist, 1982).

Süss, Th., La communion au corps du Christ (Neuchâtel: Delachaux & Niestlé, 1968).

Thurian, M., L'eucharistie: mémorial du Seigneur, sacrifice d'action de grâce et d'intercession (Neuchâtel: Delachaux & Niestlé, 1959) = The Eucharistic Memorial (London: Lutterworth, and Richmond: John Knox, 1960-61).

Thurian, M., Le mystère eucharistique (Paris: Centurion-Taizé, 1981) (English translation to be published by Mowbray, Oxford).

Thurian, M., Klinger, J., and Baciocchi, J.de, Vers l'intercommunion (Paris: Mame, 1970).

Tillard, J.M.R., L'eucharistie, pâques de l'Eglise (Paris: Cerf, 1964).

Wainwright, G., Eucharist and Eschatology (London: Epworth, 1971; updated edition New York: Oxford University Press, 1981).

Zizioulas, J., Tillard, J.M.R., and Allmen, J.J. von, L'eucharistie (Paris: Mame, 1970).